From Here to There

Leslie Hills

This is a work of fiction and that all characters, organizations and events portrayed in this novel are either products of the author's imagination or are used fictitiously.

ISBN: 1482051893

ISBN 13: 9781482051896

Library of Congress Control Number: 2013901407

CreateSpace Independent Publishing Platform, North Charleston, South Carolina

Prologue

"Who are you?" said the caterpillar.
Alice replied rather shyly, "I hardly
know sir, just at present---at least I
knew who I was when I got up this
morning, but I think I must have
been changed several times since
then."

Lewis Carroll

"To Mother," I said, raising my champagne glass high in the air."

"Yes, to Mother," repeated Barbara, putting her arm around my waist. "The woman who only wanted the best for us." We held our glasses up as we waited and stared at the figure lying on the other side of the roof. Finally, Natalie rolled over on her side, looked over at us, and said, "Define best."

"Oh, Natalie," Barbara said as she carefully shuffled across the roof to get closer to Natalie.

"You promised you wouldn't spoil this. You know she always wanted the best for us."

Natalie sniffed her champagne, stuck her finger in the glass, then licked it. "How can you be so sure?" she asked.

It took Barbara a few minutes to answer, but she finally said, "Didn't she say you always looked best in blue?"

"Blue? No. She thought I looked best in red. But I thought you were talking about something a little more important than colors. I thought—"

"I was," Barbara snapped as she waved her glass around in the air. "When Sara suggested this idea, you promised to behave. Can't we just sit up here and remember her the way she was?"

Natalie sat up, looked at me, and raised her glass.

Barbara tried again. "To Mother," she said.

"To Mother," I repeated.

"À notre Mère," Natalie said and winked at me.

We all raised our glasses and took a sip, but as Natalie lowered her lips to the rim of her glass she mumbled, "Red."

"Blue," Barbara shot back.

"Red."

"Blue."

The three of us were drinking champagne on the lower edge of Reverend Dobb's roof. It was an appropriate place to pay tribute to our mother because we had spent a lot of time and energy one afternoon trying to coax her down from this very spot. In the middle of trying to get her down, I had asked her, "Mother, just why do you like being on the roof so much?" She had tap danced across the roof to where I was standing, and without missing a beat had answered, "Well, for goodness' sake, girl! Where else can I get this bird's-eye view?" It was as logical an explanation as any from an eighty-three-year-old woman who suffered from Alzheimer's.

From our perch atop the brown-shingled rectory that had been our childhood home, I watched as three young girls whizzed by on purple mountain bikes, pumping their legs like pistons as they inched up the steep incline at the end of our road, propelling themselves up and over the top of the hill, and finally squealing in delight as they flew effortlessly down the hill on the opposite side. I remembered how my legs would ache as I pushed as hard as I could to get to the pinnacle of that very same hill. How I'd fly over the top and plunge downward, going faster and faster, as the wind blew my hair straight back from my face and the red and white plastic streamers on my handlebars whipped the knuckles of my clenched hands. And after I had coasted to a stop at the bottom of the hill, I'd pause only long enough to catch my breath, turn my bike around, and head back up that hill again.

"Red."

"Blue."

"Red."

I stood up and pointed my glass over the rooftops. "Look, you can see the hospital from here." Barbara and Natalie stopped arguing and turned to look at the horizon. The cupola of Johns Hopkins Hospital, the hospital where we had all been born, rose above the treetops and reflected the sunlight off its golden dome. Natalie slipped her arm into the crook of Barbara's, and Barbara leaned over and whispered something into Natalie's ear. They laughed. And I was suddenly overcome by a feeling of thankfulness for Mother's illness—a thought so unsettling I shook my head to get rid of it. How could I think such a thing? Alzheimer's had stolen Mother from us and had replaced her with someone we didn't know. We had all dealt with that loss in different ways. Barbara had fought hard to get back the mother from our childhood. Natalie had watched Mother's slide into dementia with detachment. And while I had tried to help Barbara, I had also found myself fascinated with the stranger who wore Mother's face—a stranger who turned out to be the catalyst in helping me discover who my mother had been; a stranger who helped me see who my sisters were; and ultimately, a stranger who helped me uncover who I had become.

Chapter One

"An intelligent servant will rule over a worthless son."

Proberbs

I was born in February in the fifties, during one of the worst blizzards Baltimore had ever seen. The headlines from the newspaper that day screamed, "Baltimore is Stuck!" I know because Malqueen, our cook, saved the paper for me. According to the lead story that day, the National Weather Service reported that a record twenty inches of snow fell in a twenty-four-hour period over the Baltimore metropolitan area, paralyzing the city and knocking out power for three days. Malqueen, who years later told me she had tried to stop my parents from going out in "that terrible storm," said she just knew Mother and Father would never make it to the hospital. She had told Father, "Don't you go out in this mess, Reverend. You'll just get stuck. Call Doc Bennett down the street. Smarter to just have that baby here."

It was the wrong thing to say to Mother. For as long as I can remember, if Malqueen said, "The sky is blue," Mother would snap back, "Nonsense, Malqueen. That sky is teal." So, naturally when Malqueen told Father not to go, Mother heaved up her swollen body from her favorite chair, put on her coat, and told Father, "Get your coat, William. If we start now, we'll have plenty of time. I'm not about to start delivering babies at home at this stage of the game."

What Mother didn't count on was the usual ten-minute ride to the hospital taking two hours. Malqueen said she and Barbara watched from the warmth of the sitting room window as Father slowly and carefully backed the car out of the driveway, only to send it into a spin in the middle of Roland Avenue when he tried to go forward. "There they was," Malqueen said, "sittin' in the middle of the road facing oncoming traffic. The Lawd sure was looking out for 'em. Yessir. He seen to it that they was the only fools out on the road that day."

Barbara said that the snow was coming down so fast and thick that Father had to stick his head out the window to see, and even after he managed to get the car turned around the right way, he still couldn't negotiate the snow-packed street that well.

Malqueen added, "That old black Chevy of your father's looked just like one of them little bouncin' steel balls in a pinball machine. It bounced from the curb to the median strip and back over to the curb again...all the way up the street."

After two hours of bouncing off curbs and getting stuck in drifts, Mother went into serious labor. But Malqueen's prediction didn't pan out because they did get to the hospital in time. Father said the emergency room nurse took one look at Mother, put her in a wheelchair, and ran her onto the elevator and up to delivery. I was born minutes later much to the relief of Father and Mother. Of course, that wasn't the whole story. I didn't hear the uncut version until I was five and my sister Natalie felt it was her duty to enlighten me on the real events of my birth.

Unlike my sisters, I apparently never made it to the delivery room. According to Natalie, I was born in the elevator just as the door opened to the seventh floor. Natalie told me that Father said it was by the grace of God that a janitor happened to be in front of the elevator crawling around on his hands and knees looking for a pack of matches he had just dropped. When the doors opened, I popped out of Mother, and the janitor, who must have had the reflexes of a wide receiver, caught me in midair. If he hadn't, I might have landed on my head and done serious damage to myself. Natalie said Mother had been mortified by my flying Wallenda act and had forbidden Father from telling anyone in the family about it. But Father, who could never keep a good story to himself, had told Mother's sister, Florence, and she had blabbed to the rest of the clan. When Mother found out Aunt Flo had spilled the beans, she was furious and she refused to speak to her. But Aunt Flo was also Mother's favorite sister, and Father was convinced they'd be, "yakking to each other again in no time. You just wait and see." Unfortunately, Mother never did get to talk to Aunt Florence again. Aunt Flo, who was visiting Mother's other sister, Rebecca, went hiking in Glacier National Park by herself one day and met up with a mountain lion. Natalie liked to scare me with how the mountain lion had "chewed on Aunt Flo until the only thing left was a pile of bones that had been licked clean." But Barbara said that wasn't true at all. She told me that Aunt Flo had bravely fought off the mountain lion with a stick and her bare hands, but in the struggle she had fallen off a cliff and broken her neck. I'm still not sure which version frightened me more. Years later when I asked Mother just what had killed Aunt Flo, she had shaken her head and said, "Stubbornness. That's what killed her. I told her never to go hiking without her Colt 45…especially in Montana. But she just wouldn't listen. She'd say, 'Oh Caroline, it's not like when we were children. It's a modern world.' Well, I guess somebody forgot to tell the mountain lion that."

According to Barbara, the alienation and subsequent death of Aunt Florence hurt Father as much as it did Mother. Father adored Aunt Flo, partly because she was so outspoken, and partly because she was not at all impressed with the fact that Father was an Episcopal priest. Mother's family had been Quakers. Their idea of a worship service was to sit on tree stumps in a clearing in the woods on their farm in Montana and quietly commune with the Lord. Grandfather would read from the Bible, and Aunt Flo said he would often stop mid-verse, lean over and tap Grandmother on the knee, and say, "Elizabeth, is that a meadowlark I hear?" And Grandmother would smile up at him and say, "Yes, dear, I believe it is." Then my grandparents would spend the next hour or so discussing birds instead of religion.

On several occasions, small bands from the Flathead Indian tribe would hunker down on the perimeter of the clearing and listen to Grandfather read from the Bible. Grandfather would acknowledge them with a curt nod, but he never spoke to them. And Aunt Flo said they never really knew for sure if the Indians understood any of the scriptures. But as soon as Grandfather said, "Amen," the Flathead Indians would quietly get up and disappear back into the darkness of the woods. As a child, I loved to hear about the Indians. But my favorite story was the one about the grizzly bear.

Aunt Florence told Father that the huge bear just ambled out of the woods one day, casually walked over to Mother, sniffed her hair, and sat down next to her like she was his long lost friend. Grandfather, who had one hand on his shotgun and one hand on his Bible, never stopped reading. The bear eventually tired of Ephesians or just decided Mother didn't smell as good as he first thought because Aunt Florence said he took one last whiff of Mother, rolled on his back a few times, and then got up and left. Father said Aunt Flo was convinced that it was the bear incident that made Mother "turn Episcopalian," although Mother didn't become an Episcopalian until after she married Father.

But Mother couldn't change Aunt Flo's mind. Aunt Florence would say to Mother, and anyone else who happened to be in the vicinity, "I just can't come up with any other logical reason, Caroline, for you to give up a solid religion like Quakerism for all that ceremonial mumbo jumbo." Episcopalians "were just too showy for her taste," and she "worried about the values of people who sat on mahogany pews in soaring cathedrals and squinted through stained glass windows in order to catch a glimpse of God."

I was named after Aunt Florence, but no one in the family ever called me that. I have always been called Sara, which is my middle name. I was eight when I finally got around to asking Mother why they never called me Florence. She was in Father's study at the time and we were putting together a pamphlet for her Ladies Luncheon Group. I was collating and she was stapling. She had looked up at me from the desk and said, "Because it just never suited you."

"Well, why did you name me that then?"

"I didn't," Mother said, taking her fist and pounding down on the stapler. "It was all your father's idea."

Since I hated the name Florence anyway, I never brought up the subject to Father. I was afraid he would feel obligated to start calling me Florence, or Flo, or even worse, Flossy. I was grateful that the name "didn't suit me" and thankful that I had a halfway decent middle name like Sara.

I guess I had always suspected there was something else going on the day I was born besides a blizzard. I had overheard Mother moan about how big Barbara's head had been and how she had been in labor for thirty-six hours with her. I had also heard her tell Frances Lymington that when the nurse handed her Natalie in the hospital she had screamed because she thought she had given birth to an albino. But I never heard Mother talk about my big head, or how long she had been in labor with me, or even if I had any hair when I was born. Every time someone mentioned my birth, Mother changed the subject.

Natalie told me that she felt it was her duty to tell me the real truth "so I wouldn't be surprised by it later in life." She also felt obligated to tell me that "everybody in the family was afraid that I would be born odd in the head" because Mother was forty-four when she found out she was pregnant with me. When I asked Natalie what "odd in the head" meant, she had knocked on my forehead and said, "You know...no brains...goofy...weird." And then she had widened her eyes and said, "Wow...like you really are!" I had burst into tears and run out of the room. And it was Barbara who found me sobbing on my bed.

"Sara, what's wrong?" she said, sitting down beside me. I had buried my head into my pillow and I mumbled, "Natalie says I was born in an elevator and that I'm odd in the head." I heard Barbara sigh. She pulled me up next to her and said, "You're not odd in the head. Why do you let Natalie get to you like that? She's teasing you."

"I wish she'd leave me alone."

"You have to learn to ignore her, Sara. The more you react to her, the more she'll tease you." It was good advice. But I was oversensitive and shy, the perfect prey for Natalie.

Barbara pulled me up from the bed. "Come on. Let's go get some of Malqueen's cookies. That'll make you feel better." She nudged me along the hallway to the kitchen, but halfway there I stopped dead in my tracks. "The story's true isn't it?" I asked.

"What story?" Barbara said, pushing me on. "That I was born as the elevator doors opened?" Barbara folded her arms and looked down at me. "Yes," she said, "but so what? You had an exciting birth...that's all. Nothing else has changed. You're still you and," she added, picking me up and twirling me around as I screamed in delight, "we still love you."

And so I learned two important things at the ripe old age of five: I could always count on Barbara for support and love; and I could always count on Natalie for the truth—even when I didn't want to hear it.

Natalie told me the second truth when I was six years old. I was concentrating on the toe of my Oxfords as I jumped from white square to white square in our checkerboard-tiled foyer, and I was halfway across the hall when a voice from behind stopped me.

"Must be nice to be able to hop around all day. Don't you have something to do? Like practice the alphabet?"

I lost my balance and dropped my leg.

"Cat got your tongue? But then what do you have to talk about? Guess they don't discuss the Berlin airlift in kindergarten, do they?"

I stared at my big sister and said nothing.

5

"Wait until you get to 'real' school. That's when the trouble begins. Homework every night about stuff you can't possibly understand and will never ever use in your lifetime…like algebra. Who gives a bee's nest about $x + y = z$?" Natalie twirled a blond curl around her finger.

I continued to stare at her.

"Would you close your mouth and stop staring at me? God, it's bad enough strangers stare at me. Now my own sister's doing it."

I closed my mouth. But I continued to stare at Natalie because it was hard not to. Like most families, ours was a blend of nationalities: a lot of Scotch, a little Irish, some English, and even some mysterious Mediterranean mix that no one wanted to admit to. The women in our family were an average-looking brood of brown hair and brown eyes. But somewhere in our genetic makeup, a Viking had invaded, leaving Nordic genes that had lain dormant for generations. They finally asserted themselves in Mother's womb, where they mutated in the form of Natalie. At fourteen, Natalie was five feet ten inches tall with legs that seemed to go on forever (a term I didn't know at five but learned later in life from my cousin Bruce.) She had a figure that rivaled my Barbie's and eyes the color of aquamarines. And, even more maddening, her hair was naturally platinum. Our phone had started ringing for her when she was just thirteen, which had horrified Father.

"Caroline," he had sputtered. "She's only thirteen! She can't accept dates at thirteen."

Mother had agreed with him. "Of course she can't go out on dates. She's much too young." But after that, Mother treated Nat differently. "Natalie, go change your sweater. Wear the blue one. It matches your eyes." Or, "Natalie a little curl to your hair wouldn't hurt." And, "Wear the red dress, Natalie; with your height you'll be stunning."

Natalie sat down on the bottom step of the spiral staircase and studied me.

"Kid," Natalie rarely called me Sara, "what are you doing hopping around the foyer on a beautiful day like today? Don't you have any friends? You really ought to make an effort to get out of this mausoleum once in a while. After all, who knows how long we'll be here."

This was news to me. Why wouldn't we be here forever?

"Don't look so dopey. You do understand that this isn't our house."

My face must have betrayed me.

"Oh God, nobody's told you that yet? Listen, this house belongs to the Diocese. Do you know what that word means?"

I didn't, although I had heard Father say the word.

"The house belongs to the church. Father works for the church, and if Father loses his job or gets transferred to somewhere else, say Dunkirk..." Natalie made a gruesome face to indicate how horrible Dunkirk was. "...then we have to move. Bye-bye happy home. Hello to gray, grimy steel-town Dunkirk."

Bye-bye? What was Natalie saying? I loved our house. I felt safe here. Leave? To go to Dunkirk? Where was Dunkirk? And why was it so awful? I looked down and traced a white square with the toe of my Oxford.

"Listen, I'm just telling you this stuff for your own good. Nobody ever told me anything. I don't want you to hear any of this from some rich brat at BrownWood...some rich brat telling you that the only reason you're at BrownWood in the first place is because you got to go for free because your father is an Episcopal priest...that your family is really poor and doesn't even own their own home or..." My eyes were locked with Natalie's, but I began to step backward slowly in the direction of the kitchen. "...stuck in class with girls who get a weekly allowance that's bigger than what I get in a year. Girls who talk about 'coming out' and Hunt Cup and...Hey! Where are you going?"

The phone rang and Barbara's voice interrupted from upstairs. "Natalie, it's for you...again." Natalie just sat there staring into space.

"Natalie! Did you hear me? I said the phone!"

Natalie jumped up and yelled, "OK, OK, OK. I'm coming!" I watched her white ponytail bounce up the stairs and heard the door to her room slam shut. I looked around at the empty black-and-white tiled foyer that I now knew didn't belong to us and took off for the kitchen. I whizzed past Malqueen, made a beeline for the cabinet table, and crawled inside. I heard Malqueen's voice above me.

"What you doin' under there?"

"Nothin'."

"You know how your Mama feels bout you bein' under there."

I opened the backside of the bottom cupboard and pulled out my drawing paper and crayons.

"Shouldn't let you keep that stuff in the cupboard. Ain't right a six-year-old hidin' under a table drawin' pixtures and readin' books," Malqueen mumbled. "Should be outside, playin' with other six-year-olds." Malqueen's rolling pin whacked the pie dough on the table above me. "Stayin' in this here big old house, nobody to talk to except a bunch of old people and one teenager who thinks she knows it all. Ain't right, ain't right at all." The rolling pin whacked the dough again, and then I heard a door squeak open as Malqueen pulled what smelled like chocolate chip cookies from the oven. "Mister and Missus too busy to pay much attention, sisters too old and wrapped in themselves, just ain't right." I heard a knock behind me, and I automatically opened the door, reached up from under the table, and took the cookie that Malqueen handed me. I rolled hot chocolate chip cookie dough around in my mouth while Malqueen resumed her battle with the dough above me. "'Telligent people live in this house. I just wonder 'bout the ways of the Lawd sometime...not that I question His word, mind you, His word is good Amen. Jus that I question why He arrange some of the things the way He do."

"Malqueen, who are you talking to?" I heard Father's deep voice ask.

"Talkin' to my maker, Reverend Gorman. Askin' Him why He do what He do."

"Ah, Malqueen, trust in the Lord. Remember that The Lord is my light and my salvation; whom should I fear? The Lord is my life's refuge; of whom should I be afraid? When evildoers come at me to devour my flesh, My foes and my enemies themselves stumble and fall. Though an army encamp against me, my heart will not fear; though war be waged upon me, even then will I trust." Father stopped talking and waited patiently.

Finally, Malqueen said, "Psalm 27 verses one through three." I heard Father sigh happily and continue on down the hall to his study. Malqueen waited until she heard his door close.

"'Telligent people live in this house. Reverend 'bout the most 'telligent one I know, but even he don't see the forest for the trees sometime. All that scripture in his head that he think so special. That ain't special, that just memory. Don't mean much less you use it. Common sense now that special." I heard the knock again and reached up for another cookie. "But he a good man. Not a mean bone in his body. Now her...hmmph. She a different story. Piece a work she is. Well maybe that what he need. The Lawd provides, Amen to that.

See him wearing them bishop robes someday. Not that it matters to him. But, Lawd, it matter to her. Amen to that again."

Malqueen's low rhythmic voice and the warmth from the oven made me sleepy. I leaned my head against the cabinet and slowly drifted off, feeling safe and secure from an unknown place called Dunkirk. And just when I couldn't keep my eyes open any longer a horrible thought came to me: if we had to leave, would Malqueen go with us?

Malqueen came into our family the summer before I was born. Father loved to tell how he had "discovered" her on the front porch the day after he and Mother had moved into the old rectory on Roland Avenue. He had gone outside to bring in the newspaper when he had almost collided with a smiling caramel-colored woman barely five feet tall.

"Excuse me," Father said to her. "May I help you?"

"The Lawd helps those that helps themselves." "Yes, He does. 'Entrust your works to the Lord, and your plans will succeed.'"

"Proverbs, chapter 16 verse 3. Always have...always will."

"Good gracious! You know your scripture. What brings you here?" Father repeated.

"I'm here for the housekeeper job."

"I'm very sorry, but there is no housekeeping job."

"Who then is the faithful and prudent servant whom the master has put in charge of his household to distribute them their food at the proper time?" Malqueen leaned forward and raised her eyebrows at Father. Father admitted that he had to think for a moment or two before he came up with, "Mathew 24, verse 46."

"Verse 45, I really need the job."

"Are you sure it's verse 45?"

"Sure as I'm standing here. You hire somebody else?"

"No, it's just that there isn't any money in the budget for a housekeeper."

"Ain't you the Reverend?"

"Well, yes, I am. But there's still no money for a housekeeper."

Malqueen leaned over, picked a rose off the trellis, and sniffed it.

"I mean, I know my wife would love to have help, especially with a new baby on the way and just moving in and all...but I can't—"

"William! Are you still outside?" Mother called from the hallway. "I just received the most amazing call. Do you remember Edward Sayer? The board member? He had the most exciting news. Seems the Diocese has allotted us money for a housekeeper. Can you believe that? I'm so excited. Now I can really help you. I can host luncheons, volunteer..."

Father looked at Malqueen sniffing the rose, and Malqueen returned his gaze and said, "Looks like you might need a housekeeper after all."

"Yes, it does," Father said. "The Lord works in mysterious ways."

"He do appear to sometimes," laughed Malqueen as she followed Father into the house to meet Mother. But of course, that meeting didn't go as well as the meeting with Father.

"Caroline," Father announced, "I've found you a housekeeper. Meet... oh dear...I'm terribly sorry, what did you say your name was?"

"Name's Malqueen Dixon. Pleased to meet you."

"How do you do, Mrs. Dixon. But I'm afraid we don't require your..."

"Malqueen. Just call me Malqueen. I don't have no references, but I helped raise sixteen brothers and sisters in Snow Hill. I cook real good."

"How admirable. Sixteen brothers and sisters? Excuse us...er... Malqueen. William, could I see you in the study for a few minutes?"

Mother and Father left Malqueen in the sitting room staring up at a huge oil painting of Mother's father. The painting showed my very formidable grandfather smoking a peace pipe with Sitting Bull. It had been painted back in 1889 when Grandfather was governor of Montana. At least once a month, for as long as I can remember, Mother would question Father's decision to hang that particular picture in the sitting room.

"William, do you really think that picture is appropriate?"

"Caroline, it's a marvelous piece of history. Of course it's appropriate."

"You don't think the Indians look a little too...you know...naked?"

"Oh, don't be ridiculous, Caroline. They aren't naked. They're in full headdress and they have loincloths on. That's what Indians wore back then."

"Well, dear, if you say so. They just look so...hmmmmmmmm."

The fact that Mother didn't want to hire Malqueen didn't seem to bother Malqueen at all. Father said that when Mother dragged him off to the study for their "discussion," Malqueen stepped closer to the painting, squinted up at the Paxton original, and grinned. Later on, Mother denied being so dead set against hiring Malqueen, saying that Father was "just exaggerating, and that first meeting hadn't happened like that at all." But every time she said that, Malqueen would roll her eyes up in her head and leave the room. Father would turn away and smile, and Mother would turn beet red. But Father was always diplomatic, and he'd wait for Mother to leave the room before he would continue the story.

"William, we can't just hire anybody off the street. We know nothing of this woman. Who is she?"

"She says her name's Malqueen Dixon and she's from Snow Hill."

"I've never heard of Snow Hill, have you?"

"Somewhere on the Eastern Shore, I think."

"Do you want to entrust your children and home to a person with no references? We don't even know if she can cook!"

"She said she helped raise sixteen brothers and sisters. Of course she can cook. I say we hire her for a trial period. How about two weeks? Then if it doesn't work out, we'll let her go. Besides, she seems to know her scripture."

"Knowing one's scripture does not qualify one for the job of maintaining a household. William, she has no references."

"Caroline, trust in the Lord."

Father later said that he had made up his mind to hire Malqueen when she was able to quote chapter and verse back to him that first meeting on the front porch. He just had to convince Mother she was right for the job.

As Father predicted, Malqueen could cook. My earliest memories are of a house filled with the aroma of fresh-baked bread, apple pies, and sugar cookies. Our neighbors would stop at the end of our driveway, sniff the air, and sigh wishfully.

"Roast beef..."

"Turkey with gravy..."

"Ham and cabbage..."

"Hmmm...apple pie."

And it was fortunate for Malqueen that she was such a good cook because Mother thought she was a terrible housekeeper.

"Malqueen, this table hasn't been dusted in two weeks."

"It hasn't? I'll get to it today," Malqueen would promise. But she wouldn't. The only thing Malqueen liked to dust was the painting of Grandfather and Sitting Bull.

"Malqueen, don't forget the tables over there," Mother would remind her.

"Get to 'em right after this."

Mother would return a half hour later to find Malqueen still occupied with the painting.

"Malqueen, I really don't think you need to spend quite so much time on that painting. There are other things to dust."

"Fine paintin' this is. Fine paintin'. Needs good care."

Father, who happened to be passing by the sitting room, overheard their conversation.

"Well," Mother said proudly, "it is quite an amazing painting, isn't it? Not many people can say they actually knew Sitting Bull, let alone smoked a peace pipe with him. Father told me this was painted after the massacre at Little Big Horn and Sitting Bull had been hiding out in Canada for five years. Look how brave and handsome he looks." Mother, of course, was talking about her father.

"He 'bout the handsomest man I ever seen."

"Why thank you, Malqueen."

Malqueen turned around and looked at Mother. "Didn't know you was related to Mr. Bull. Yessir, fine lookin' man that Sittin' Bull."

This exchange sent Mother right back into Father's study. "William, she doesn't clean."

"The place looks fine to me," Father would say as he sneezed and dust bunnies swirled out from under his desk.

"There's dust all over Rebecca's sideboard, William. When my sister gave us this furniture I promised I'd take good care of it. Her antiques must be treated with respect. Besides, I can't entertain in a filthy house. You have to talk to her."

But Father didn't. What he ended up doing was making a deal with Malqueen. She became the cook, and Father told Mother to hire a cleaning lady.

"William, I do not have enough money in my household budget to hire a cleaning lady."

"Don't worry about the money. Hire someone and I'll give you the money."

"From where? You won't even buy yourself a new suit. Just where do you—" "Caroline, trust in the Lord."

Mother did just that the next day. In fact, she trusted Him so much she hired two cleaning ladies.

"Two cleaning ladies, Caroline? Do we really need two?" Father asked patiently.

"You said to hire someone. It's a big house, and I couldn't get one without the other."

"Oh?"

"They're two sisters from Locust Point—you know, the Polish section of town—and their husbands won't let them take the bus unless they travel together. They really are reasonable, and they come highly recommended. Missy Norwich's sister-in-law, Millicent Fenmore—you remember her husband Buzzy, the one with the drinking problem—had them for five years until they moved too far out in the Valley last September and—"

"Caroline?"

"Yes?"

"Just hire them."

Mother kept her two cleaning ladies, and Father got to keep Malqueen. And even though Mother resented Malqueen's encyclopedic knowledge of the Bible and the easy banter she and Father exchanged during the day, Mother also realized that Malqueen allowed her the freedom she needed to chair committees and attend luncheons. Malqueen and Mother established a cool truce.

According to Barbara, Malqueen was also responsible for the table I so loved to hide under. We had inherited the table with the house, and Mother was ready to donate it to Goodwill when Malqueen intervened.

"'Scuse me, Missus Gorman," Malqueen interrupted as Mother and Father discussed how to get the massive wooden table out of the kitchen. "I think this one here will do just fine."

"Malqueen, I'm sure you do. But Reverend Gorman and I have decided on more of a modern look, a chrome and aluminum set with matching chairs."

"Shame to spend good money on somethin' you don't need. This here table is sturdy, top must be six inches thick. Fine top for rollin' out pastry dough. I can just smell them apple pies bakin' in the oven."

Father must have smelled them too because suddenly he had doubts about a new kitchen set. "Caroline, are you certain we need a new table?"

"William, we've discussed this! We decided on a chrome set."

"Don't think dough roll out so good on chrome and 'luminum," Malqueen said as she rubbed the top of the old wooden table.

"Malqueen, I don't think it matters one way or the other."

"Caroline, that chrome set was rather expensive."

"I want the chrome and aluminum set."

"Shame spending the church's money on chrome and 'luminum, 'specially when the family be eatin' in the dining room anyways."

"I'm sure there will be times when we'll want to have an informal meal in the kitchen, Malqueen," Mother said.

"I don't think that proper. Do you Miz Gorman? The Reverend's family should eat in the dining room. Kitchen for the help. Dining room for the family." Malqueen continued to run her hand over the pitted and scarred butcher block table top and smiled.

"Well, Caroline, she does have a point...about the money, I mean."

"Excuse us, Malqueen. William? The study?"

Barbara said she didn't know what was said in the study that day but the table stayed. In fact, Malqueen even got Father to move it.

Father and Barbara were cleaning out the basement of the rectory one morning. As they were lugging boxes up the stairs and through the kitchen to the car, Malqueen stopped Father and asked, "Reverend Gorman? You gotta few minutes for me?"

Barbara said Father dropped the box of books he had been carrying, threw his hands up in the air, and recited, "Let me know, O Lord, my end and what is the number of my days, that I may learn how frail I am. A short span you have made my days, And my life is as nought before you; only a breath is any human existence."

Malqueen was washing the breakfast dishes and she didn't even look up when she answered, "Psalms 39 verse five and six, Reverend. But I just needs five minutes, not the rest of your life. If you just move this table against the windows, I'd be most grateful."

"Give us grateful hearts, our Father, for all thy mercies, and make us... Uh! This table weighs a ton!" Father said as he tried to lift one end of the table and couldn't. "How far do you want to move this thing?"

"Right here," Malqueen said, drying her hands and moving over to stand in front of the floor-to-ceiling windows. "Don't lift it, Reverend. Push it. That's it." Malqueen and Barbara watched as Father pushed the table slowly back against the window. When the table was where Malqueen wanted it, she smiled and looked up at Father and said, "Thank you very much, Reverend. And that verse you was spouting off ain't in my Bible. Must be one of them 'Piscopal prayers."

Father wiped his brow with his handkerchief and said, "It is. Why do you want the table in front of the window? Won't it block out all the light?"

"Doesn't block out the light. Besides, I want to be able to look out at the garden and see the seasons change when I roll out my dough." Malqueen winked at Father and then said, "Ecclesiastes 3."

"But I didn't say anything, Malqueen!"

"I know. But you were thinkin' it."

I don't remember when I discovered I could hide under that huge wooden table that Malqueen so loved. Malqueen told me I was three.

"Malqueen! Have you seen the baby?" Mother asked, dashing through the kitchen in a mad search for me.

"You lose that child again?"

"I didn't lose her. She just crawled away. I was only on the phone for a few seconds. She was right at my feet and then she was gone. Where is that little rascal?" Mother dashed out and down the hallway.

"Always losin' that baby," Malqueen said to herself as she snapped the ends off a string bean. "Never seen a mother so busy. Busy on the phone. Busy with meetins. Busy with luncheons. BusyBusyBusy. So busy she lose her own baby. Just don't understand that woman. Gets a perfectly good baby, and at her age that something,' and what do she do? She keep losin' it!"

I giggled from under the table.

"Lawd! Now I hearin' voices from under the table. I best stop talking 'bout people."

I giggled again.

"Now I knows I heard that!" Malqueen said as she bent down and opened one of the cabinet doors that ran along the front of the wooden table.

"BOO!" I yelled.

Malqueen jumped back and shrieked, "Lawda mercy! Child, child, child, we got to get you out from under there. If your mama finds you in here, she'll rip me up one side and down the other." I crawled out. Malqueen scooped me up, ran down the hall, and dumped me on the rug in Father's study. "Now, you stay there like a good baby till your mama gets you," she whispered. "Miz Gorman!" Malqueen yelled up the stairs, "you check the Reverend's study? I think I hear somethin' in there."

Mother ran back down the stairs. "How could she get in there? I told William to keep that door closed."

Malqueen said she stood out in the hallway and made sure Mother "found" me before she went back to the kitchen and her string beans. But after that incident, she couldn't keep me out of the kitchen or from under the table. I started dragging dolls and books in there with me, and eventually Malqueen let me stay. Malqueen would hear my mother's footsteps in the hallway and yell, "It's OK, Miz Gorman, the baby with me."

Mother would stick her head in the kitchen and I would wave a cookie at her from the stool beside the table. "Are you sure you don't mind, Malqueen?"

"No, I don't mind."

Mother would blow me a kiss and hurry off to make yet another phone call. As soon as she was gone, I'd crawl under the table.

"How can I mind?" Malqueen would mumble to herself. "If I don't watch the baby, the baby will get lost again. Better to have the baby with me than chasin' all over the house lookin' for the baby. Probably find the baby drowned in the toilet or something. What do that woman think? And such a quiet baby too. Never cries. Most babies wah, wah, wah. But not this baby. All this baby want to do is eat and draw pixtures."

Which is exactly what I was doing when I heard the kitchen door swing open. I was drawing a picture of our house, the one Natalie had just informed me didn't belong to us, when I heard Barbara's voice.

"I smelled those cookies from upstairs. I have to have one before I die," Barbara said, plucking one off the cookie sheet. "You know, Malqueen, if I continue to eat your cookies I'll never fit in my wedding dress."

"Might not be a bad idea."

"Malqueen!"

"Just sayin' might be better to wait. You're only twenty. What's the big rush?"

"Mother says he's too good a catch to let slip away. He's not only one of the best looking boys in Baltimore, he's also one of the richest."

"He may be rich, but he ain't no catch."

I heard Barbara pull one of the kitchen stools over to the table. "And just what's wrong with him?"

"Bad case of swivel-neck."

"Swivel-neck?"

"That's when you put a man in a room full of pretty girls and he loses control over his neck muscles."

"Oh pooh. Is that all? So he likes to look at pretty girls. All men look at pretty girls."

"Maybe. But most men don't do it in front of their intended."

"So you think he should be sneaky about it?"

"Not sneaky, discreet. A man should have some control over his own neck muscles."

"Malqueen, you sure have some funny ideas. It really doesn't bother me."

"Well, it should."

"Why on earth should it?"

"'Cause if a man can't control somethin' easy like a neck muscle, he gonna have a real hard time controlling the muscle he think with."

"Now you've really lost me. Why would a guy who appreciates pretty women have trouble controlling his mind?"

"Never said nothin' 'bout no brain," said Malqueen as she rolled the dough into a log. "Muscle I'm talking about ain't located in his head."

I heard Barbara choke on her cookie and laugh. "Malqueen! If Mother heard you—"

"Your mama only hear what she want to hear. She wants you to marry that rich swivel-head when you was already dating that nice Cover boy. What ever happened to him anyway?"

"Tommy? Oh, I don't know. It just kinda fizzled out. Actually, he never seemed all that interested."

"He was plenty interested. His neck only swiveled in your direction. I thinks the one who wasn't interested was your mama...wasn't interested in his bank account."

There was silence above me for a few minutes and finally Barbara said, "Do you really think Randall flirts too much?"

"Let's talk about this later. I forgot little ears was under the table."

"Oh no, is she under there again?" Barbara opened the cabinet door and stuck her head inside. "Sara, get out from under there. If Mother sees you we'll never hear the end of it."

"Amen to that. I also think little ears is upset about somethin' somebody said to her. And you know who that somebody might be."

"Sara, did Natalie say something to upset you?"

"No."

"Sara, tell me the truth. What did Natalie say?"

"Nothin'."

Barbara sighed. "Listen, pumpkin, don't believe everything Natalie tells you. Natalie has a bad habit of embellishing the truth. You know what that means? Like making stuff seem better or worse than it really is. You know how dramatic Natalie is."

I heard Malqueen snort. "Dramatic? Just sounds like lyin' to me."

"Come on, get out of there before Mother comes back in the kitchen."

"Oh, we're probably safe. The Missus don't stop by the kitchen much no more."

"Really? When did that happen?" Barbara asked.

"You know how your mama likes to pester me while I'm tryin' to get dinner ready? Well, one night she blows into my kitchen, all fired up she is, and she starts in with the same old question: 'Malqueen, what is the menu for this evening?' I tell her I'm makin' roast beef, mashed taters and gravy with green beans, and apple pie for dessert. Out the door she goes, leavin' a trail of that Che-nelle No.5 behind her, to tell the Reverend over them double gin martinis they drinks too many of every night what I'm serving for dinner." Malqueen stops, frowns, and then continues. "So I do start fixin' the taters, but right in the middle of peeling 'em, I changed my mind. I fixed rice instead of potatoes and peas instead of beans." Malqueen looked up and smiled at the memory.

"And?" Barbara said as I leaned out from under the cabinet to hear the rest of the story.

"After dinner, your mama comes roaring through the kitchen and starts in with, 'Malqueen, why did you tell me we were having potatoes when we were having rice? And what happened to the string beans?' I looked her straight in the eye and told her, 'Missus Gorman, them potatoes gone to seed. And when I got the beans out I found them ugly rust marks on 'em. I figure I can't be servin' the Reverend's family bad potatoes and diseased beans, now can I?' The Reverend comes in right behind your mama, sees her red face, and says, 'Malqueen, what a magnificent meal. The rice was perfect, and you fixed my favorite, peas. Caroline, did I tell you the Bishop sent us some brandy? Let's go to the study and have a sip. Shall we? Your mama's eyes almost fell out of her head when she heard the word 'Bishop.' She took your Daddy's arm and disappeared outta my kitchen and ain't been back since."

I heard Barbara laugh and say, "For a while at least."

"I hope it's longer than a while," Malqueen sighed.

"Did you see what arrived today?" Barbara said, changing the subject.

"Your bridesmaids' dresses?"

"Oh, you saw the boxes in the hallway. I can't wait to see how the girls look in then. And I also got a certain flower girl's dress."

I flew out from under the table and climbed onto Barbara's lap. "Show me, show me, show me!" Barbara hugged me and laughed.

"You two look like two peas from the same pod," Malqueen said, smiling as she brushed flour from her hands. "Look here," she said as she held up a silver serving tray and our faces stared back at us. We could have been mother and daughter; instead, we were sisters fifteen years apart.Barbara squeezed me tighter and said, "Malqueen, watch over the little one while I'm on my honeymoon. Make sure she doesn't spend all her time under the kitchen table."

"Already do that. Trouble is sometimes I think it's better for her if she's under the table instead of wandering round this house gettin' information from Miss Blond Ponytail Know-it-All Drama Queen."

"Natalie means well. She just speaks before she thinks."

"Oh, she thinks all right. Only it's always 'bout herself."

"She's just going through a difficult age. Thirteen is no picnic."

"Neither was eleven or twelve. Why you defend her all the time?"

"Because she's my sister. And I'm older and wiser—or so Father keeps telling me. You ought to understand family loyalty and responsibility. You come from a family of sixteen!"

"Don't mean a dang thing. Six of 'em dead. Rest of 'em might as well be. Worthless bunch of nothins."

"Whatever happened to blood is thicker than water?"

"Person said that musta been an only child."

It wasn't until years later that I discovered that Barbara, Natalie, and I really were considered only children. Barbara was eight years older than Natalie, and Natalie was seven years older than me. I was sitting in the office of my best friend's husband, Oscar, a well-respected psychiatrist at Johns Hopkins Hospital, and he was explaining the scientific study of birth order to me.

"You see, Sara, when siblings are seven or more years apart in age, psychiatrists consider each sibling an 'only.'"

I stared at Oscar and wondered what he was getting at.

"Say you have three kids and they're three years apart. Our studies show that the oldest child is smart, somewhat of a perfectionist, and the one driven to do 'the right thing.' The middle child is the adventurer, or the 'free spirit' of the family. They leave home as soon as possible and are known 'for doing their own thing.' The youngest child, or the baby, is considered 'the cherished one.' She's the comedian, the happy-go-lucky child, the one the rest of the family wants to protect."

I started to disagree with him, but Oscar held up his hand to stop me.

"However," he continued, "when siblings are spaced as far apart as you, Natalie, and Barbara are, then standard sibling behavior gets tossed out the window." He stopped, folded his hands, and stared out into the hallway.

"And what does any of this have to do with my sister's suicide attempt?" I had asked him.

"Sara, I know you don't feel comfortable making medical decisions for her right now. You don't think you're responsible enough do you?" It was my turn to look out into the hallway.

"Sara?" Oscar said, leaning forward. "Don't you see? It doesn't really matter what you think. What matters is what she thinks. She respects what you've done with your life. She trusts you."

I remember thinking at the time that Oscar was just trying to make me feel better. How could I do this? How could I be responsible for another human being's sanity? It didn't make sense, and I didn't want the responsibility. And yet at the same time, I knew I had to make a decision. I took Oscar's advice and institutionalized my sister.

Chapter Two

——————— • ———————

"Honor your father and your
mother."

Exodus

I spent a great deal of time with Father. I would sit in his worn black leather chair, listening to him practice his sermons and speeches, and invariably going off the subject to discuss sports.

"For only in the kingdom of God can we all find true happiness, he would preach, raising his unruly thick white eyebrows and looking toward heaven. The kingdom is yours, said the Lord; do not fall prey to seeking out the darkness in life. Do you believe Irsay just packed up the Colts and snuck out in the middle of the night?"

"Can we sue?" I'd asked at the time.

"I don't know. I mean, what recourse do we have? The team belonged to him, and if the owners let him get away with it, then we're sunk."

"I can't imagine Baltimore without a football team."

"Neither can I."

"And what happens to our seats?" I asked. Father had owned season tickets to the Colts since 1956.

"Good question. I'm calling the mayor in the morning. Must be something he can do." We both shook our heads. "Where was I?"

"Out the darkness in life..."

"Right. Out the darkness of life."

I adored Father and sought out his company whenever I could. And I never really thought too much about why I preferred Father's company to Mother's until I met Lettie.

Mother took me to school that first day of first grade and abandoned me, or so it seemed at the time. She had walked me through the big double oak doors of BrownWood's main entrance and had stood me in front of room 125. The door opened, Mother pushed me in, and when I turned around for her, she was gone. I found myself face-to-face with fifteen girls I had never met before. I knew I was supposed to take a seat, but all I could see was a roomful of blurred navy plaid uniforms. Lettie saved me.

"Here's an empty desk," she waved from the back of the room, "over here, over here." I gratefully fixed on her waving arm and sat down next to her.

"Hi! My name is Letitia Larue Wittridge," she said, hanging over her desk, "but everybody calls me Lettie cause Letitia is too hard to say, and I'm five and a half, which is very young to be in first grade, but the school said it was OK for me to come because I'm smart and so I did, and I live on Roland Avenue, what's your name?"

Before I could say anything, Lettie continued.

"I'm very excited to be in school because I don't have any brothers or sisters I'm an only child, and I don't have anybody to play with 'cept my dog Winkie and my two cats Maude and Winston, and they're fun, 'cept Winkie hates it when I dress him up in my father's clothes and put hats on his head, but they can't talk so I need 'tellectual stimulation, or so Mummy says."

I started to giggle.

"Why are you laughing?"

"You talk so fast."

"What's your name?"

"Sara."

"Sara, that's a nice name, but it's too plain for you, I think you need another name, how about Saralee like the cakes 'cause your hair is the color of that chocolate cake and I just adore chocolate cake, don't you? Do you want to come over and play sometime, Saralee?"

I did. And Lettie came over and played at my house as well. It turned out I had accomplished quite a coup in befriending Letitia Larue Wittridge. Lettie was right out of Baltimore's Blue Book, that unassuming little book that dictated to Baltimore Society who was worth associating with, and by omission, who was not. Her father owned Wittridge Investments, and her mother chaired every major charity and social event in Baltimore. And, of course, Mother was thrilled beyond belief.

"Sara, do you mean to tell me Grace Wittridge's daughter is coming over to play with you after school tomorrow?"

"Lettie Wittridge, yes."

"William, do you know who Grace Wittridge is?"

"Yes, Caroline, I know who Grace Wittridge is."

"The Wittridges are in the society pages every week. They're 'old money,' William. This is just grand. I wonder if I can get her to our Ladies Luncheon next month. However did our little Sara manage that?"

I didn't tell them "our little Sara" hadn't managed anything. It was all Lettie's doing. Left to my own devices, I'd still be under the kitchen table. But meeting Lettie changed all that.

Our house was not as grand as the Wittridges'. But Lettie didn't seem to notice. She especially liked the kitchen and, of course, the company of Malqueen.

"Malqueen, this is my new friend Letitia Larue Wittridge."

Malqueen wiped her hands on a tea towel, reached out, and shook Lettie's hand. "Pleased to meet you, Miss Wittridge."

"Pleased to meet you, Miss Malqueen, but nobody calls me Miss Wittridge or even Letitia, everybody just calls me Lettie cause it's easier to say, and I'm real happy to be here and smell those cookies, what are they? Chocolate chips? I love chocolate chips and I love peanut butter too and so does my dog Winkie even when it gets stuck on his teeth and he tries to wipe it off on the furniture."

I had never seen Malqueen speechless before, but she was that day. Lettie rambled on and on, and Malqueen shook her head up and down and smiled. And after Lettie left, Malqueen patted me on the head and said, "Glad you found Miss Lettie."

Which is not to say Lettie didn't get on Malqueen's nerves.

"Malqueen, tell us that story about picking crabs in the packing plant in Snow Hill and how you used to let the crabs go when you had to go to the bathroom."

"Child, that is the story. Ain't nothin' left to tell. How 'bout some quiet for jus' a few minutes whiles I get the meat ready for dinner? Ain't you got some homework to do?"

Since Lettie and I both couldn't fit under the table, Malqueen let us sit at the far end of her wooden table and "help" her make dinner.

"Now get me the pepper."

I ran over to the cupboard and got it.

"Malqueen, how come sometimes you use lots of pepper and other times you don't. Like when you made that meat loaf the other day you didn't use pepper at all, but today with the chicken you're just pouring it on."

"Different spice for different food. Get me some of that honey."

I ran for the honey.

"Do you put honey on the chicken? I bet that tastes wonderful, Malqueen. Can I taste it when you're finished 'cause I love honey."

"Get me the duct tape."

I stopped in the middle of the kitchen and looked back at Malqueen.

"Tape? Whatcha gonna tape, Malqueen? Can't tape the chicken, can you? I never heard of taping food."

"Ain't gonna tape the food. Gonna tape somethin' else shut if I don't get some quiet 'round here."

"What? Oh I get it! I guess I do talk a lot, don't I, Malqueen? Sometimes I talk so much I give Mummy a headache and she has to go lie down for a while, and then I have to whisper everything to her until her headache is gone."

"Spects you give her lots of them headaches. Ever turn them 'talkers' off?"

"Talkers? That's funny, Malqueen…talkers. I'll have to remember to tell Mummy about that. I tell her everything."

When I finally did meet Lettie's mother, Grace Wittridge, it was in her closet. Lettie and I were in her parents' bedroom dressed in her mother's silk dresses, wobbling around in satin pumps, and trying to get Mr. Wittridges's white dress shirt on Winkie, the Wittridge's dog. The dog, whose official title was Mr. Wink the Third of Roland Park, was a prize-winning boxer who only tolerated this humiliation because he knew we had dog biscuits in our purses. I thought it amazing that Lettie was allowed to play in her parents' bedroom. I was never allowed in my parents' bedroom unless I was invited. And I was never invited. We had just gotten the shirt buttoned up over Winkie's broad white chest, and I had started to attach Mr. Wittridge's navy and white polka-dot tie to the dog's collar, when a voice behind us said, "Hello, darlings."

I turned around and found myself eye-to-eye with Lettie's "Mummy." Grace Wittridge couldn't have been more than four feet eleven inches tall. With auburn hair, blue eyes, and an elfin smile, Mrs. Wittridge looked more like one of my dolls than the mother of my best friend.

"Mummy!" Lettie screamed and ran to her.

"Shhh, darling. Remember quiet tones…quiet tones. Is this who I think it is?" Mrs. Wittridge said, looking at me.

"Mummy, this is Sara Gorman my best friend in the whole world, and we're playing dress-up like you said we could with Winkie. Where did that dog go?" Lettie said, looking around the closet as I caught sight of Winkie slinking down the hallway with a black patent leather purse in his mouth.

"Oh no! Mummy, he's got one of your purses!"

"Never mind, Winkie," Mrs. Wittridge sighed as snorts and banging could be heard out in the hall. "I'll deal with Winkie later. Let me say hello to Sara."

Mrs. Wittridge, still holding onto Lettie, turned to me and extended her hand. I reached out for hers and saw that mine was bigger.

"How do you do, Mrs. Wittridge," I mumbled.

"I do very well. I'm so pleased that you and Lettie have been spending so much time together. I must call your mother and father and invite them to dinner one evening. Lettie, dear, what do you have on?"

"Your jade dress. The one you wore to the Hendersons' Ball."

"I remember the ball, Lettie, but you've got it on backward. Here, let me turn it around. And Sara, those pearls should be wrapped this way. See? It gives the dress a smarter look. How lovely you both look. Lettie, go get the blue dress I wore to Mrs. Winston's tea for Sara. I do believe blue is her color. That's right, that's the one. Now, let's see if we can find the blue suede shoes that match," Mrs. Wittridge said, crawling on her hands and knees in the back of the closet.

"Lettie, look over in that box. I think—" A knock on the door caused us all to turn. Cerise, the Wittridges' Jamaican housekeeper, stood at the door.

"Excuse me, Miz Wittridge. But Mr. Alexander Benedict is on the telephone. He says it is most important. Something about the hospital fund. And this bad dog," Cerise had Winkie by the collar and dragged him into the bedroom, "has torn your good patent leather purse to pieces, just all to pieces in the hallway. Do you wish me to put this bad, bad, bad dog in the backyard?" With each emphatic "bad" Cerise pulled the choke chain tighter around the dog's neck.

"Thank you, Cerise. Just tell Mr. Benedict I'm indisposed. I'll call him back later. Oh, and you can let Winkie go. I'm sure he won't tear up anything else."

Cerise gave the choke chain another hard tug before she reluctantly released Winkie. The dog nose-dived back into the closet and leaned against Mrs. Wittridge, who grabbed his snout and gave him a kiss on the nose. Cerise shook her head in disgust and left the room. But as she walked back down the hall we could all hear her mumble, "Hmmph. Let the bad dog go. Hmmph. Tell Mr. Benedict she in-dis-posed. Hmmph. Should beat that bad dog. Rips everything to shreds—purses, dresses, shoes—can't leave a thing in that bad dog's path. Kisses the bad dog on the lips. Somebody should just put that dog in the yard and leave the gate open."

"Cerise, we can still hear you," Grace Wittridge sang out after her.

"Sorry, Miz Wittridge." Cerise did lower her voice but we still heard, "Hmmph. Should yank the bad dog's teeth out. Then the dog be in-dis-posed."

"Now," said Mrs. Wittridge, "where were we? Oh, I know, the blue shoes for Sara. Here they are!" Grace Wittridge pulled them out of the box. "Lettie, do I still have the matching purse to that dress?"

"No, Mummy. I think that's one of the purses 'the bad dog' ate."

"Well, in that case, find the silver one; it's very chic, and I don't think Winkie likes sequins." We all laughed as Winkie grabbed a blue suede shoe and ran out of the room.

Grace Wittridge was one of those rare people who seemed to be able to do everything well. She was smart, successful, and everybody loved her. I'm sure she had her faults. I look back and try to remember a single time when she didn't seem genuinely overjoyed to see us; a single time when she became angry and raised her voice to us; a single time when she made us wait in order to conduct business or talk on the telephone. But I can't. And even after she knew she was dying, Lettie and I always came first.

Chapter Three

•

"She is clothed with strength and dignity."

Proverbs

Grace Wittridge was diagnosed with breast cancer the summer Lettie and I turned eleven. She insisted she was fine and continued to chair her committees and raise money for her charities. But after surgery and four weeks of chemotherapy, the tumor returned. She began having trouble breathing, and she spent more and more time in bed. Lettie and I began spending our afternoons with her. Every day after school, we would run to the Wittridges' house, jump on her mother's white lace-covered bed, and do our homework.

"Darlings, what do we have to do today?" Mrs. Wittridge would ask us.

"We have to write an essay," I said.

"What about?" she asked me.

"Rime of the Ancient Mariner."

"Goodness. That brings back memories. I still remember how that starts."

"Well, it's just plain spooky if you ask me," Lettie said.

"Oh, I don't know. It's really quite 'spellbinding.'" Grace Wittridge leaned back into her down pillows and almost disappeared. Her illness had reduced her already small frame to seventy pounds. The doll-like hands that had once twirled pearls around our necks and zipped up the backs of our play dresses shook when she tried to hold a teacup. An oxygen tank rested discreetly under the nightstand next to her bed, and dozens of pill bottles were lined up on the same table. Mrs. Wittridge had a private nurse; but it was Lettie who kept track of her mother's medicine and learned how and when to administer the oxygen.

Lettie looked at her mother, then at me, and made a decision. "THEATER," she yelled. I jumped up and grabbed a blanket off the bed. Lettie ran for the closet and got one of her father's walking sticks, a hat, and a sport coat. "Who do you want to be?" she asked.

"The Mariner," I said.

"You always want to be the star. But OK, I'll be the guest."

Grace Wittridge smiled and settled back to watch the show.

I put the blanket around me, messed up my hair, and leaned on the stick. Lettie plopped the hat on her head and put one of her father's coats on.

"You need a beard," Mrs. Wittridge said. "Go into the bathroom for gauze."

I ran into the bathroom, grabbed a box of cotton gauze, and wrapped it around my ears so it hung down on my chin. Lettie positioned herself at the end of her mother's bed. I slowly staggered toward Lettie as Grace Wittridge began the poem. "It is an ancient Mariner and he stoppeth one of three."

"By thy long gray beard and glittering eye," Lettie asked, "Now wherefore stoppst thou me? The bridegroom's doors are opened, wide, And I am next of kin; The guests are met, the feast is set: Mayst hear the merry din."

Grace Wittridge picked up the voice of the narrator. "He holds him with his skinny hand." I reached out and stopped Lettie. "There was a ship," I said.

"Hold off! Unhand me, graybeard loon!" Lettie pushed my hand aside and jumped away.

"Effsoons his hand dropped he," Mrs. Wittridge continued. "He holds him with his glittering eye The Wedding Guest stood still, And listens like a three years' child: The Mariner hath his will."

We spent a lot of afternoons like this. Lettie's mother always seemed so captivated by our playacting, even though halfway through our dramatics her eyelids would droop and she'd fall asleep. While Mrs. Wittridge dozed, we'd quietly do our homework. Sometimes I'd draw. And when she awoke, my sketches seemed to intrigue Grace Wittridge.

"Sara, these are brilliant! Look at how you captured the mischief in Lettie's eyes. Mrs. Fine must be," she began to cough and Lettie looked up, "thrilled," Mrs. Wittridge finally said. Mrs. Fine was our art teacher at BrownWood. I smiled and said, "She says I draw OK."

"Does not," Lettie interrupted. "She says Sara's the most talented painter she's seen in her twenty years of teaching art!"

"Lettie!" I said.

"Don't be so modest, Saralee."

I put my head down, swinging my hair forward in an attempt to cover my red face. Lettie and I were sprawled at the bottom of Mrs. Wittridge's bed. Winkie was stretched alongside Mrs. Wittridge with his head buried under her pillow. Grace Wittridge pushed herself up with one hand, reached over and brushed my hair out of my face, and said, "You do like to paint, don't you Sara?"

"Very much," I said, looking up at her.

"Well, I can't draw a thing. But I love your sketches. Look at this one," she said, holding up a portrait of Winkie. "You've caught his grin. People don't think animals have expressions, but they do." She smiled and scratched Winkie on the side of the head. Winkie turned his head to the other side and sighed. She continued to thumb though the drawings. And as she looked over each one she said, "But you see differently. Even your choice of colors is amazing. Ever think of art school?"

I hadn't thought of much else.

"Of course, she'd like to go to art school," Lettie said, "Wouldn't you, Saralee?"

"Yes. But I don't think we can afford it."

"But Sara, there are scholarships. The Maryland Institute of Art? Your parents can help." Mrs. Wittridge coughed again. I looked down and again felt the heat rush to my cheeks. When her coughing had subsided, Lettie held a glass of water to her lips and said, "I don't think so, Mummy. They don't seem to care much about her painting. Well, Malqueen does. But then Malqueen isn't a blood relative."

"Lettie!" Grace Wittridge said as water dribbled down her chin. "That's a terrible thing to say."

"But, Mummy, it's true."

I pretended to draw, although all I could put down on paper were a few squiggles. After a few moments, I snuck a peek at Mrs. Wittridge. She had disappeared back into her down pillows, and her eyes were closed. But when I looked down at her hands, I saw that her fists were clenched.

The last time I saw Grace Wittridge alive she could not even whisper. Lettie had been out of school for a week, and Mrs. Lindquist, our fifth grade teacher, had given me Lettie's homework assignments to drop off on my way home from school. I hadn't delivered any of them, and I knew I couldn't put it off any longer. I dragged my feet all the way down Roland Avenue until I reached the wrought iron gates of the Wittridge Estate. The mansion sat on top of a moderate hill and far enough back from the main road so that it didn't appear as large as it really was. It had been in the Wittridge family for generations, and yet for all its grandeur, it was a comfortable house; a house where people were allowed to put their feet up on polished coffee tables; a house where dogs left teeth marks on the legs of Chippendale chairs; a house where Lettie and I played hide-and-seek inside antique wardrobes filled with taffeta and silk ball gowns. And, according to my parents, it was a house worth a fortune.

"What kind of taxes do you think they pay on that place?" Mother had once asked Father after they had attended a dinner at the Wittridges'. "An eight-bedroom Georgian mansion sitting on five acres in the city?" Father shook his head. "I don't even want to think about it."

Whenever I visited Lettie, I would run from the main gate all the way to the front steps of the house. That run would be interrupted with shouted "hellos" to the many gardeners who spent all day clipping hedges and pruning trees. At the front door I'd collide with a tangle of volunteers, either on their way in or on their way out. And on Tuesdays and Thursdays I'd run into either Mr. Klein delivering flowers or Mr. Beck delivering a stack of packages for Mrs. Wittridge. But that last day, as I slowly climbed the brick steps and followed the path to the front door, I saw no one. I reached the door, hesitated, and then finally rang the bell. A red-eyed Cerise answered the door, looked out over my head, and then finally looked down at me.

"I have Lettie's homework," I said, holding up the papers. "Mrs. Linquist asked me to—" Cerise grabbed me by the collar of my school uniform and dragged me inside.

"Where have you been?" she said, rummaging around under her sleeve and finally extracting a balled-up tissue.

I watched her blow her nose and then stammered, "I meant to come earlier but—"

"It does not matter. You are here now. Miz Wittridge is not having a good day," she said as she pushed me down the hallway. "She is on the oxygen all the time now." Cerise stopped outside Mrs. Wittridge's room. "Go on in there," Cerise said as she looked down at me, "and pretend not a thing is wrong." She opened the door and pushed me inside.

Someone had overzealously sprayed Lysol in the room, and I tried hard not to gag on the cloying scent of an artificial pine forest. As usual, Lettie was next to her mother, rambling on and on about her science project, a project we had finished last week. Lettie's father sat on the other side of Mrs. Wittridge holding his wife's hands but watching his daughter. An unusually subdued Winkie was also on the bed with his head resting on Mrs. Wittridge's stomach. When he saw me, he winked, and his face stretched back into a smile. But he didn't move and he didn't raise his head. The only thing that betrayed him was his sausage tail as it swished back and forth on the silk bedsheets. Mrs. Wittridge turned her head in my direction. I walked over to the bed, and when I was almost able to touch the bedspread, Mrs. Wittridge smiled. I smiled back and leaned closer. Lettie was saying, "Doesn't she look better today, Saralee? Much better than yesterday. Her new medicine is working quite well, I think. Tomorrow I'm going to see if we can go outside and sit in the garden. Wouldn't you like that, Mummy? We could pick some roses for Cerise to put in the dining room." While we listened to Lettie talk, I followed Grace Wittridge's eyes. She looked from me to the picture I had painted of Lettie that sat on the floor next to her dresser and then back to me. She did this several times until I finally nodded. She sighed and closed her eyes.

I stood next to Mrs. Wittridge and watched her sleep until Cerise finally stuck her head back in the room and said, "Sara, it's time to go now." Mr. Wittridge leaned over, patted my hand, and said, "Thank you." Lettie smiled at me and said, "Come tomorrow, Saralee. You can help us pick the roses." I backed out of the room. But as soon as Cerise had closed the door, I realized I had left my book bag inside. "Cerise, I left my books in the room."

"Wait a minute," Cerise said as she blew her nose again, wiped her eyes on her sleeve, and motioned for me to be quiet. She silently cracked the door, tiptoed into the room, and retrieved my bag. But before she closed the door she paused, and we both stared back into Grace Wittridge's bedroom and watched as Lettie continued to talk to her mother.

I don't remember the walk home. I do know that I made a beeline for the study and Father.

He was writing his sermon for Sunday, and when I came in he put his pen down and smiled. "What's this? Come to help me address the multitudes?"

I ran over and climbed up into his lap.

"Sara, are you all right?"

I buried my head in his shoulder and said, "I saw Mrs. Wittridge today."

Father sighed and stroked my hair. We sat in silence. He rocked me back and forth in his old wooden swivel chair, and we both listened to the twangy tick of the grandfather clock that had sat in Father's study for as long as I could remember. The clock was painted vermillion with gold inlay and chimed "Yankee Doodle Dandy" on the hour. Father had told me Grandfather, the same one in the painting with that heartthrob Sitting Bull, had won it with a straight flush from the owner of the Blue Bison Saloon in Missoula, Montana. From time to time, Mother would pass by it and say to Father, "William, are you sure you want that clock in here? It's such an odd choice for an Episcopal priest's study." Father would just laugh and say, "It's part of the old Wild West, Caroline. It's history." But Mother would lower her voice and say, "It may be history, William, but Father did win it in a *card game*."

The clock broke into its honky-tonk rendition of "Yankee Doodle," and Father and I jumped. We both giggled at the banjo tone of the tune.

I had once overheard our next-door neighbor, Mr. Merrill, telling his wife, Miss Marie, that "that goddamn clock needs a good tune-up." Malqueen and I were in the garden and Mr. Merrill and Miss Marie were getting into their car. Mr. Merrill said, "That's the damnedest sounding clock I ever heard. Marie! You ever hear such a sound? Sounds like a goddamn kazoo." Mrs. Merrill, who was always embarrassed by Mr. Merrill's colorful language, said, "Shhhhh, Pete. Keep your voice down. The Reverend will hear you."

"Don't care if he hears me. He knows how I feel about that goddamn clock. Never heard such a pitiful sound in my life. Goddamn shame he lets a god—"

At that point, Malqueen put her hands over my ears.

"It's OK, Malqueen," I said. "Father told me Mr. Merrill's deaf and that's why he talks so loud. I don't mind."

Malqueen took her hands away and said, "Ain't how loud he talks. It's what he says when he says it. Miss Marie got the patience of a saint to be married to that screamin' Mr. Take-the-Lord's-Name-in-Vain man."

I thought about Mr. Merrill, and I said to Father, "You know what? I think Mr. Merrill's right. It does kind of sound like a kazoo doesn't it?"

"Why do you think I like it so much?" Father said. "No matter how my day goes, I know that every hour on the hour that clock will make me laugh."

I smiled back up at him just as the clock began six loud ponderous bongs. The telephone rang as the last bong reverberated through the study.

Father yanked the phone to his ear, cleared his throat, and boomed, "Reverend Gorman here." I loved Father's voice. It was deep and mellow and rhythmic. When he was tired, it turned into a raspy growl. I told Malqueen I thought he sounded like George C. Scott. But Malqueen disagreed. "Back home," she said, "he got what we call a *bourbon voice*. Good voice for ministering. Even better voice for the ladies."

In church, he would often lower his voice to a whisper, making the congregation lean forward to catch what he was saying. His low, melodic voice would take on the beat of a metronome, and he would gently rock the congregation through" Almighty God, we entrust all who are dear to us to thy never-failing care and love, for this life and the life to come; knowing that thou art doing for them better things than we can desire or pray for..." And just when they were ready to nod off, he would syncopate his rhythm and thunder, "Glory be TO the Father, and TO the son, and TO the Holy Ghost," jerking his parishioners up out of their pews. It was not a technique normally used in the Episcopal Church. Malqueen, who attended her own church on Sunday, The Almighty Baptist Church of the Wayside on St. Paul Street, would sometimes catch one of Father's sermons on her way home from church. Afterward, she would chuckle and say, "Never seen so many white people jumpin' up and down in my life. Alls you needs is a few 'Amens', Reverend Gorman, and you'd have a genuine Southern Baptist service." And Father would laugh and say, "I'm working on that, Malqueen."

Years later I realized that Father had been elected bishop for many reasons: he was smart, he was funny, he was compassionate, and thanks to Mother, he had made the right social connections. But I also suspected he was elected bishop for that voice.

I now listened as his voice whispered condolences into the telephone. When he put the receiver down, he hugged me tighter. I waited. And when he finally did say something, I covered my ears. He took my hands away from my ears, and I heard him say, "Sara, she was very sick. Sara? She was in a great deal of pain."

I wouldn't look at him, and when he tried to turn my head I said, "No." He continued to rock me back and forth, and I saw his lips move in prayer. But all I heard was the ticking of the clock as it broke the silence with its "tank tock, tank tock, tank tock." Father's silent lips continued to move, and eventually, sounds from outside filtered in through the open window—the clatter of steel-wheeled roller skates as they rolled down the pavement, the repetitive plop of a ball bouncing off a curb, the grinding of a car unable to start, and finally, the click of Mother's heels on tile.

"William, are you just about finished?" Mother stuck her head inside the study door. "We still have to start organizing the—" Father shook his head at her. Mother looked at my face and then back at Father and said, "What on earth?"

"Grace Wittridge."

"Oh no," Mother said as she came into the study and sank down onto the sofa. "Why is it the good ones always die young? All that work for the poor. All those fund-raisers and committees for hospitals and schools and charities. Rich and privileged but not a mean bone in her body." Mother got up, patted me on the head, and then turned to Father. "Who's doing the service?"

"Apparently I am. John Wittridge just called and asked me to." Mother's face brightened, and she jumped up and grabbed the legal pad on my father's desk.

"Redeemer?" she asked.

"Have to be. The crowd will be huge."

"Julia Albright for the solo?"

"If we can get her, and call Tom Clarke. He should be able to..." Father stood up and set me gently on my feet. I found myself on the sofa where I watched my parents work. Father moved to the telephone and Mother made list after list. I had seen them do this many times before. They were a good team, and they had learned how to remain detached even as they immersed themselves into the details of the rite of death. But I could not. I slipped out of the study, unnoticed by my mother and father, and found myself in the kitchen with Malqueen.

"Some mopey face you wearin'," Malqueen said as she stirred a pot of stew.

"Mrs. Wittridge just..."

Malqueen put the spoon down, walked over to me, and wiped my face with the palms of both of her hands. Up to that point, I hadn't realized I was crying. Then she put her arm around me and said, "Miz Wittridge was real sick, Sara. Real sick. I tol' you that from the beginning."

"I know. Father said the same thing."

Malqueen sat me down in a chair in front of the kitchen table and walked over to the counter. I watched as she sliced a big piece of devil's food cake, plopped it on a plate, and pushed it toward me. I ignored the cake and looked up at her.

"Why, Malqueen? Why her?"

Malqueen looked out the window, sighed, and then picked up a dishrag and began wiping the counter. "Don't know. The Lawd musta had a good reason. Think what a beautiful angel Miz Wittridge gonna make. And in all them poofy ballgowns she used to wear." Malqueen smiled. "Specially that pink one with the big skirt and the little red hearts all over it she wore to the Heart Ball. Reminded me of Cinderella. She wear that gown and she be the most dazzling angel in heaven. Don't you think?" I didn't answer. "Anyways," Malqueen continued as she leaned over and pushed the cake a little closer to me, "When the Lawd rings your doorbell you can't be sayin', 'Wait a minute Lawd, I'll be there in a minute.' You dealin' with the Lawd, not the Fuller Brush man."

I stared at the cake.

"That's right. When the Lawd calls you gotta answer, Amen. And the angel of the Lawd called unto him out of heaven and said, 'Abraham, Abraham,' and he said, 'Here I am.'" Malqueen looked over at me. But I still didn't say anything. "Had a good soul, Miz Wittridge did. And you knows what they say 'bout good souls. Only the good die young," Malqueen rattled on. "Yep, only the good die—"

I took my fist and slowly pushed the cake off the counter. I watched as it teetered on the edge for a few seconds before it smashed onto the floor. Pieces of blue willow plate, carrying chunks of devil's food cake, shot out across the tiles. Malqueen stopped wiping, but didn't look up.

"MOTHER said the same thing. Do YOU really believe that?"

"That the good die young?" Malqueen eyed the brown exclamation marks left on the white tiles by the flying plate. "Good a reason as any, I guess. Why else would mean ugly people still be livin' and breathin' on this earth when Miz Wittridge gets called to our Savior?"

"Your Savior, not mine. You'd think the Lord would want her to stay on earth and help out some more. Wouldn't that make more sense?"

"The Lawd don't hafta make sense, Sara. He the Lawd."

"Well, if HE doesn't have to make sense, then what good IS He?"

Malqueen finally looked up and threw her wet dishrag at me. "Hush. Don't you let your father hear you talkin' bout the Lawd like that. Who you think you are anyway? You can't question the Lawd. If a man like Job don't question the Lawd, then a no-nothin eleven-year-old like you can't question HIM either. 'Sides you know well as I do that 'God did not create death, nor does he rejoice in the destruction of the living—'"

"Don't quote scripture to me. If God's not responsible, then who is?"

Malqueen walked over to the pantry and took out a broom. "Sometimes lots of people," she said, shoving the broom in my hand. "Sometimes nobody." She folded her arms in front of her and stared out the window. "Jus' happens. And there ain't nothin' any of us can do 'bout it."

"I wish I'd never known her."

"You don't mean that."

"I do."

"And Lettie? Wish you'd never met her either?"

I put my head down and stared into my lap.

"Go on," she said, waving her hand at the chocolate on the floor. "Clean up this here mess. And after you finished cleanin', you call Lettie."

But I didn't. Instead, I went up to my room and collected every picture and painting I had ever drawn for Grace Wittridge and dumped them all into the garbage can for the next day's pickup.

The Church of the Redeemer was standing room only for Grace Wittridge's funeral. Everyone who was anyone in Baltimore society was there. But even though the Blue Book was well represented, they weren't the only ones paying homage to Grace Wittridge. I spotted Mr. Chin, who owned the laundry; Mr. Klein, who operated the florist shop; Mr. Franke, the butcher at Eddie's Supermarket; Miss Grey, who ran the Nearly New Shop; Grace Wittridge's entire household staff; and the household staffs of every family who lived in Roland Park. And of course, Mother and Father, being the coordinators of Grace's service, had been at the church since the crack of dawn. I had overheard Mother tell Father the day before that, "We had better get there early. After all, we do want this one to go off without a hitch. It needs to be a showstopper." I had never heard her refer to any funeral as a "showstopper" before. But Father seemed to agree with her because he had answered, "Absolutely. Grace Wittridge deserves the best."

"Of course she deserves the best," Mother had agreed. And as he left the study and walked away, she added, "...and just think of all the important people who will be attending."

Barbara, Malqueen, and I were lucky to get a seat at all. Barbara, who was eight months pregnant at the time with Randall Jr., was having trouble getting anywhere. By the time we got to the church, every pew was filled. But two men, who noted Barbara's condition, gave up their seats for us. And so, the three of us jammed ourselves into a space for two. We had only been seated for a few moments when a murmur began at the back of the church, grew louder, and then spread all the way to the altar. People were nudging each other and whispering. Barbara turned around to see what was going on, elbowed Malqueen, and said, "I don't believe it." Malqueen followed her gaze and said, "Praise the Lawd. Neither does I." I looked over to the center aisle and saw what all the commotion was about. Cerise, resplendent in a black-and-white suit, had Winkie by the collar. She and the dog, with their heads held high, and looking neither left nor right, were slowly walking up the middle aisle of the Church of the Redeemer. When they got to the family pew, Cerise slid in alongside Mr. Wittridge and Lettie. Winkie jumped up next to Cerise. And after adjusting her wide-brimmed black-veiled hat, Cerise stretched one arm around Lettie and the other one around the dog. The undercurrent of whispers continued until Father finally appeared in front of the congregation, raised his arms in welcome, and boomed, "I AM the resurrection and the life, saith the Lord: he that believeth in me, though he were dead, yet shall he live: and whosoever liveth and believeth in me, SHALL...NEVER...DIE."

Father outdid himself that day. It was the most talked about funeral in Baltimore society for years to come. I don't remember what Father said because I was too busy trying to catch a glimpse of Lettie. But because we were so far back in the church, all I could see was the purple feather in the crown of Cerise's pointed hat, an occasional flash of Lettie's orange curly hair, and the tip of one of Winkie's pointed ears. When we stood for the recessional, I leaned out into the aisle to make sure Lettie saw me. I wanted her to know that even though I hadn't been able to call her I did care. But when she walked past me her eyes were unfocused. Her father held her tightly by the hand as she repeatedly stumbled down the aisle as if she were tripping over rough seams in the rug. Barbara whispered to Malqueen, "Do you think they drugged her?" And Malqueen whispered back, "Lawd, I hope so." I watched Lettie's back as she stumbled down the aisle, out the front door of the church, and into a halo of bright sunshine.

After the funeral, Mr. Wittridge closed the house on Roland Avenue and took Lettie to Europe. I got postcards from all over the Continent. But the cards weren't signed, and there was no message written on any of them. I wondered why Lettie didn't write anything on the cards. Eventually, I overheard Mother and Father talk about Lettie's strange silence.

"But, William, it isn't normal. She hasn't spoken in three months!"

"Caroline, the child's only eleven. She just lost her mother. There is no normal behavior for that."

"But really, William. To go from a nonstop prattler to complete silence? Don't you find that unsettling?"

"Of course. Why do you think John Wittridge took her to Europe?"

"For therapy? As in psychiatrists? Why didn't you tell me?"

"Caroline, John took her to Europe because Grace thought it would be best for Lettie. He didn't mention psychiatrists or therapy. He just wanted to get away. And he wanted to keep their whereabouts quiet. I do have your word that this goes no further than this room?"

"William. I'm your wife! Of course it will go no further than this room."

Mother kept her word. It didn't go any further than that room. The trouble was that room was where she held her Ladies Monthly Prayer Luncheon.

Malqueen referred to Mother's meetings as those "monthly backstabbin' prayer fests." She was so disgusted with them that she made up all the food the night before and then left the house. That meant that Barbara, Natalie, or myself had to help Mother serve food and tea. Out of the three of us Barbara was the only one qualified for the job. Natalie had spilled grape jelly down the front of Frances Lymington's silk blouse (I believe on purpose) and had been banished from the luncheons ever since. I was too young and too shy to be of much use either, but I was pressed into service whenever Barbara couldn't be there.

The Ladies Monthly Prayer Meeting was always held in what the family called the formal sitting room. Mother had crammed this room full of Aunt Rebecca's antiques. This room was special because everything in the room matched. Nothing else in our house even came close. After the "chrome and 'luminum" discussion, Mother just gave up. She relied on the kindness of relatives, departed and still breathing, to help her furnish the five-bedroom Victorian we called home.Once I received a beautiful antique mahogany make-up table, which Mother coupled with an old oak mirror and a tapestry-covered stool. It was my first grown-up piece of furniture—a place for me to primp, experiment with makeup, and wish away my many imagined defects in the mirror. I was so excited by the table that I grabbed Natalie as she was walking by my room and said, "Look, Natalie, isn't it beautiful? What style do you call this? Is it Chippendale? Or is it Queen Anne?"

Natalie had looked at me and then looked over at the table and said, "I believe it's the same period we all have, kid—Louie-the-dead-relative's furniture."

This was why the formal sitting room meant so much to Mother. Even though the furniture was from Aunt Rebecca's estate, it all matched. Even the rug had been part of Aunt Rebecca's decorating scheme. Frances Lymington, who had more money than she knew what to do with, had even commented on that rug.

"Caroline, when did you get this rug?" she had asked as she tapped her foot on the medallion in the middle of the carpet. "I do believe this is a Persian."

Mother had smiled sweetly and said, "Just recently. Care for another petit four, Frances?"

We never used that room unless it was for an important church function. Mother was always afraid someone would spill something on "the Persian." But right before the Ladies Monthly Prayer Meeting, Mother would order the Locust Point sisters to clean the room from top to bottom. I never did know the real names of either of the sisters because they just called each other "sister." And Mother never called them by name either. "Ladies, don't forget to do the baseboards this week," she'd say, "Or next week, ladies, I'll want you to concentrate on the windows in the study."

Malqueen referred to them as "sausage" and "baloney" under her breath, which I thought was terribly unkind. But in all fairness to Malqueen, they didn't like her any better and went out of their way to avoid her.

I asked Mother why "the sisters" hated Malqueen so much, and Mother had said, "Hate is a very strong word, Sara. People sometimes fear what they don't understand. I prefer to think of them as just fearful and ignorant."

When I had asked Malqueen about the way the sisters treated her, she had just shrugged and said, "They ain't never been more than four blocks from where they was born. They believe what the people around them tell them to believe. But your Mama's wrong. People do tend to hate what they fear."

In spite of "the sisters'" odd behavior, they turned out to be great house-keepers. The rectory sparkled during the years they cleaned for us. But even though they were top-of-the-line dust busters, every time Mother had a Ladies Prayer Luncheon scheduled she felt the need to remind them "that rug came all the way from Persia." The Locust Point sisters would look at each other and then down at the rug and resume their cleaning. It wasn't until years later when I finally understood Malqueen's observation on the smallness of their world.

I was passing by the sitting room on my way to make a call when I overheard Mother's standard, "Now ladies, don't pull too hard on the vacuum. After all, this carpet came all the way from Persia." As soon as Mother left the sitting room, one of sisters said to the other, "Sister, now did Ed Jr. tell us that Persia was in northern or southern Maryland?"

"Why, I believe Ed Jr. told us that Persia was somewhere near that Deep Creek Lake place. Remember he told us there was a big Indian population near there."

"Where they weave baskets and make the rugs?"

"Yes."

"Funny name for a town isn't it? Almost sounds foreign."

"Foreign? Like outside the country? You got some imagination, sister. Who in their right mind would buy a carpet from outside the country!" Their laughter was drowned out by the roar of the vacuum cleaner as it began its assault on "the Persian."

Mother now stood in the middle of that Persian rug and began the meeting.

"Ladies, may I have your attention? Thank you. As you've noticed Barbara isn't here to assist today. I don't have to remind you that she's due any day now." Mother paused for applause. "So, until the blessed event occurs, my youngest daughter, Sara, will be serving tea." Mother walked over and stood behind me. I felt her squeeze my shoulders, and then she leaned down and whispered, "And don't spill anything on Frances." I turned crimson and busied myself with arranging Grandmother's Limoge teacups. The meetings always began with a prayer, and while our heads were bowed and we were supposed to be communing with God, I overheard Mrs. Thomas whisper to Mrs. Leach, "Where's the other daughter...the Valkyrie?"

"Stop it, Ellen! You'll make me laugh," Mrs. Leach said.

"Well? Where is she? Why is the runt substituting today?" Mrs. Thomas whispered back.

"I don't know. I think Frances banned her from ever serving again. That was Frances's favorite blouse, you know." Mrs. Leach leaned over again and said, "Don't I know it. She wore it enough. Did she ever clean it? Besides, as far as Frances is concerned, no one can hold a candle to Barbara."

"Well, they are family," Mrs. Thomas said, giving Mrs. Leach a knowing look.

Mrs. Thomas and Mrs. Leach realized I was staring at them. They quickly bowed their heads. Mother ended the prayer and moved over next to me. I looked up to see Frances Lymington bearing down on us. I poured tea and listened to Frances interrogate Mother.

"What have you heard from John?" Frances asked as she dropped four sugar cubes into her cup.

"Why, not a thing."

"Now, dear," Frances looked over her head. "A little bird told me he was in Switzerland. Some mental problem with the daughter?"

"I really wouldn't know, Frances."

"Oh, I think you do."

"Frances, I really don't know." My mother tried to turn away, but Frances clamped onto her elbow and held fast.

"Caroline, Caroline, Caroline. We've never discussed the new window have we? Perhaps now would be a good time to talk about the Lymington stained glass window for the church?" Mother's mouth flew open, and I saw her eyes dart around the room, seeing if anyone else had overheard their conversation. Mother had been trying to raise enough money for a new stained glass window for six months, and I knew from conversations at the dinner table that she was still thousands of dollars short of her goal.

"Frances, don't think you can wheedle information about John out of me through bribery," Mother began as Frances steered her out of the room and into the hallway. I tried to read their lips but became distracted by the conversation between Mrs. Thomas and Mrs. Leach.

"Look at her," Mrs. Thomas said, nodding over to Frances Lymington. "She'll be on the phone with her travel agent before you and I get home. Ever since Seth died she's been trolling for a man."

"Especially a rich man," Mrs. Leach added. "I hear John Wittridge is worth millions."

"More than that. Too bad about the little girl, though. What's her name?" Mrs. Thomas asked.

"Lettie. Absolutely deranged, I hear. John is beside himself with worry. I heard they even tried 'shock therapy' treatments to make her talk."

I put the teapot down, picked up a plate of cucumber sandwiches, and offered one to Mrs. Leach. Mrs. Leach looked down at the top of my head and said, "Thank you, dear," and then turned again to Mrs. Thomas. "Oh my God! I hope not!" Mrs. Thomas lowered her voice so that I had to lean in to hear. "Remember Binky Bunderwald's first cousin? An absolute loon. Thought he was a pig or something. Anyway, after he had those shock treatments he walked lopsided, as if he was stepping up stairs. But, of course," Mrs. Leach raised her eyebrows, "there were no stairs."

"Gracious! Did one of the probes get stuck in his head?"

"Probes? They don't stick probes in your head when you have shock treatments. They wrap you in a wet blanket and run electricity through your body. Probes. Really, Carolyn, where do you get your information? You ought to read more than *Vogue* now and then."

I put down the tray of sandwiches, ran past Frances Lymington and Mother, up the stairs, down the hall, and into my room. I gathered all the postcards I had received since Lettie had left—postcards from Paris, London, Rome, and Geneva—and arranged them in front of me on my bed. What did this mean? What was she trying to tell me? I didn't know.

I even asked Malqueen what she thought about the postcards and Lettie's silence.

"Just thinks she's all talked out," Malqueen said as she rubbed flour on a rolling pin.

"Then you don't think she's crazy and in some hospital getting wrapped in wet blankets and shot through with electricity?" Malqueen looked up at the ceiling and said, "Oh Lawd, give me strength. Who told you that?" she asked as she began rolling the pin over the dough.

"Well, I overheard it at the prayer luncheon."

"Prayer luncheon," Malqueen said, pounding her fist into the middle of the dough. "That's a joke. Women have too much time on their hands. Shot through with 'lectricity," Malqueen mumbled. "I'll tell you what I think. I think the person who said that should be shot," she said, slamming the pin down on the dough and rolling it back and forth, "though not with 'lectricity."

"Do you think she'll come back?" I asked.

"I think one day," Malqueen said, tapping me on the shoulder with the rolling pin. "Lettie will walk right back into this here kitchen. And when she does, she'll act like she's never been gone."

Malqueen was right. It was exactly one year and a day after Grace Wittridge's death. Malqueen and I were in the kitchen making biscuits and arguing about how much flour we needed to add to the already sticky concoction. I saw Malqueen stop in mid-stir and smile. I turned around and saw

Lettie—or at least someone who resembled Lettie. This Lettie was a good two inches taller. Her short curly orange hair had grown longer and darker. And her resemblance to her mother was breathtaking.

"Hello, Malqueen. Hello, Saralee," she said.

"Lettie!" I screamed, throwing the flour down and running over to hug her. When we separated, we looked at each other and laughed. We were both covered in white powder.

"When did you get back?" I asked.

"Today. I came right over."

I dragged her over to the kitchen table. "Malqueen said you'd be back. Didn't you, Malqueen?"

"I guess I did. How you doin,' Miz Lettie?"

Lettie looked at both of us with Grace Wittridge's eyes and just said, "Better." Malqueen jumped up from her stool and said, "Now you've got to stay for dinner tonight 'cause I'm makin' your favorite honey chicken with rice and fresh peas. And your favorite dessert. Devil's food cake."

"Please, stay Lettie. I'll go tell Father and Mother. They'll be so happy to see you. They don't even know you're back. Please, please say you'll stay."

"Well, I'll have to call my father. But I'd love to stay, especially if Malqueen is making honey chicken." Malqueen grinned and wiped her hands on her apron. I grabbed Lettie's hand and pulled her out of the kitchen. I knew Malqueen had a lot of work to do. She had to ditch the meat loaf she had been making for that night's dinner and get started on the chicken and the devil's food cake.

Chapter Four

———————— • ————————

"Absence from those we love is self
from self---a deadly banishment."

Shakespeare

I got Lettie back about the same time I lost Natalie. The year Lettie was in Europe had been very lonely for me. I had friends at school and I had Malqueen at home. But I missed Lettie. And I missed her mother more than I was willing to admit to anyone including myself. After Grace Wittridge's funeral, I had vowed never to paint again. But that promise was broken almost immediately when I found myself adding horns and a mustache to a sketch I had just drawn of old Miss Quincy, our math teacher. I tried to stop myself from doodling next to my unsolved algebra equations, but I couldn't. My unconscious mind would trick me. I would start daydreaming, and before I knew it, I had half a sketch in front of me. I finally gave in and set up my easel again.

Malqueen and I were usually the only ones in the rectory between three and six. Father had a parish to run and was working on a special project for the Diocese. Mother helped him in the parish and also volunteered. They both left the rectory before eight and didn't return until after six. To make things even more hectic, Bishop Jennings had just announced his retirement, and it was rumored that Father was seriously being considered for the job. I was used to having this time to myself to paint, and I was very surprised when one afternoon Natalie came home from school early and wandered into my room. She still intimidated me, but by age eleven I had finally taken Barbara's advice. When she began teasing me, I'd just look at her, yawn, and say, "Oh really?" And then walk away. She kept trying to get a reaction out of me, but I wouldn't give in, and eventually she stopped. So I was surprised when a voice from the hallway said, "So how's the Rembrandt of Roland Park?" Natalie came in and leaned over my shoulder. "What's this supposed to be? A bad portrait of our lovely Malqueen?" I folded my arms and waited.

"You made her look too pretty," she said. "Her mouth's too small, and her nose isn't right."

I swished a brush in paint thinner and said, "I'm still working on the nose, and her mouth's not too small. Anyway, that's how I see her." I turned away and Natalie laughed, flopped down on my bed, and said, "And just what will you do with all that talent?" I thought I hadn't heard correctly. I turned and said, "What?"

"You heard me. What are you going to do with all that talent?" I stared at her waiting for the other shoe to drop, but it didn't. Instead she said, "If I were you, I'd do everything and anything I could to get out of this house as soon as possible. Your grades aren't bad. You can get a scholarship." Natalie turned her head and stared out the window. "I know I'm getting out of here as soon as I can. And I'm not doing it like Barbara either."

I put my brush down on the easel and sat down beside her on the bed. "Barbara fell in love and got married," I said. "What's wrong with that?"

"She never fell in love; she was talked into it. She should have gone to college with her brains." I didn't say anything, but I had to agree with Natalie on that point. Barbara had breezed through BrownWood with straight As. All through school Natalie and I had to listen to the same comments from her former teachers.

"Are you Barbara's sister? What a pleasure it was to teach that young lady. So bright. Let's hope you do as well." And, of course, neither of us did.

"What will you do?" I asked. "Try for a language scholarship?"

"With my grades? Fat chance."

Natalie had always been an average student at BrownWood in every subject except languages. By ninth grade she was speaking both French and Spanish. Father and Mother sent her to Paris for three months on an exchange program when she was fourteen, and when she came back she was fluent in French. Between tenth and eleventh grade she studied German and Italian. Father likened her talent to that of a musician with perfect pitch. She could listen to a foreign phrase once and be able to understand and duplicate the phrase right down to the regional accent of the speaker. I'm not quite sure what my parents had in mind for Natalie after she graduated from high school. No one ever mentioned college. I suppose they assumed since she was so beautiful she'd marry well. And she could have, because she certainly had plenty of admirers.

"What will you do?" I repeated.

"I'm not sure. But I'll figure out something." And she did. Natalie graduated from BrownWood on a Friday, and by the following Monday she was on a train to New York. Mother found a note on the hall table that simply read:

Dear Mother and Father:
I have gone to New York. Don't worry. I have a job interview.
Your daughter
Natalie

"William, she can't go to New York by herself!" Mother was frantic. "You've got to go after her. Bring her back."

"Caroline, she's eighteen," Father said calmly. "Legally she can do what she wants. I wouldn't worry too much about Natalie. She'll be back when she can't find a job. After all, what skills does she have? She doesn't even know how to type." I was eavesdropping at the top of the stairway, and before I could stop myself I yelled down, "She does speak four foreign languages."

"Sara?" Father said, peering up into the darkness. "Well, yes, she does. But where will that get her? She needs a degree to either teach or even get a job as a translator. I can't think of any other job that would hire her just because she speaks four languages. What's she going to do? Work in a French restaurant?" Father patted Mother on the back. "Don't worry, Caroline. I can't see Natalie waiting tables in New York."

"What could she be thinking?" Mother shook her head.

"Don't worry. Just wait and see. She'll be back next week." I watched Father stride off to his study. Mother looked after him and then down at the note. She carefully folded Nat's letter, placed it in her pocket, and slowly followed Father into his study.

But Father was wrong. We didn't see or hear from Natalie for six weeks. And when she did come home it was to pack her belongings and move to Paris for good. She showed up on the same day the church broke the news to the press that Father had been elected the new bishop of Maryland.

I was in the kitchen with Malqueen when Natalie sashayed in through the swinging doors wearing her new TWA stewardess uniform. Malqueen and I stared.

"My, my, both of you speechless, "Nat said. "I must have made the right decision." Malqueen snapped out of it before I did.

"Your parents know you're home?"

"Not yet. I couldn't find them. Where are they?"

"Father was elected bishop today. Didn't you hear it on the news? They're in Washington," I said. Nat sat down on a stool in the kitchen.

"No, I haven't listened to any news. I came straight from the train station." She turned to Malqueen. "So, she finally got what she wanted, didn't she?" Malqueen didn't answer. Instead, she put her hands on her hips and demanded, "Why're you doin' this?"

"Doing what?" Becoming a stewardess? I'm doing it for me."

"Knows that. Everything you do is for you. But why you 'tentionally causin' heartache?"

"Finding a job is causing heartache? I'm surprised, Malqueen. I thought you of all people would be happy to see me go."

"Don't matter what I think. Matter what your parents think. Don't you think they worry 'bout you?"

"As a matter of fact, no, I don't."

"Then you dumber than I thought you was."

"All my parents have ever wanted me to do was to stay in Baltimore and marry some stupid blue blood like Barbara's husband, Randall. No thanks. I want my own life."

"Ain't saying you can't have your own life. I'm talking 'bout how you went about it. Leavin' a note on a table? Not calling for more than a month? Your mama was beside herself."

For the first time, Natalie looked up at Malqueen. "Oh really? That's hard to imagine. Mother beside herself with worry over one of her children? And Father? Was he beside himself too?"

"He said you'd be back in a week," I blurted out.

Malqueen winced at that comment and quickly added, "He hoped you'd be back in a week."

"No, he didn't. I've been an embarrassment to him since I was thirteen. Well, he doesn't have to worry about me now. I'm moving to Paris. Now that he's bishop he can trot out Barbara and Sara when he needs to show off his family." Natalie got up and walked to the door.

"But Nat," I said. "The consecration's next week. You have to be there."

"I'll be in Paris next week." Natalie once again started for the door, but suddenly she turned around, came back, and kissed me on the cheek. "Au revoir, kid," she whispered in my ear. Then she quickly walked away and said over her shoulder. "Adieu! MAL...Queen." We watched her disappear through the swinging door.

"What did she mean Malqueen? How does she embarrass Father?"

"She don't. I don't know where she got that. She's confused that's all... confused." But Malqueen kept staring at the door where Nat had just made her exit. And I couldn't help but note that it was Malqueen who now looked confused.

"Malqueen, what'll we tell Mother and Father about Natalie?"

Malqueen continued to stare at the door. Finally she looked at me and then walked over to the phone.

"We ain't telling 'em," she said as she started dialing. "Talk 'bout shootin' the messenger." Malqueen tapped her foot impatiently as she waited for the person on the other end of the line to pick up.

"Who are you calling?"

"I'm calling Barbara," Malqueen said as she continued to tap her foot. "She's the only one I know can calm your mama."

Malqueen was right about that. In Mother's eyes, Barbara was perfect. She had been an obedient child, a smart student, and a well-mannered teen. She wasn't as beautiful as Natalie, but she was attractive, well spoken, and socially connected.

She had married Randall at twenty, had produced two sons by the time she was twenty-five, and had moved into a mansion in the elite neighborhood of Homeland, thus fulfilling all Mother's expectations for her by the ripe old age of twenty-seven. Mother's conversation with the ladies at her prayer luncheons were peppered with comments like, "Betty, you remember my daughter Barbara. She lives down the street from your son Edward in Homeland" and "Alicia, I know you've run into my oldest daughter Barbara at Helman Prep. She has two boys in the lower school too." In Mother's eyes, Barbara's marriage had elevated not only Barbara's social standing in Baltimore but also Mother's. I wasn't too sure what Father thought of Barbara's marriage. He and Randall rarely discussed anything besides sports and cars; sports because Father knew Randall loved the Orioles and cars because Randall ran two Cadillac dealerships. The only thing Mother didn't like about Randall was his car commercials.

Every time one of Randall's commercials would air, Mother would get up and change the channel. Father, who rarely watched anything on television, and who was usually doing paperwork when it was on, would look up and say, "Now, Caroline, that's Randall's dealership. Why are you turning it off?" And Mother would try to look innocent, change the channel back, and say, "I didn't realize you were watching that channel, dear." Then we'd all be forced to watch Randall as he sat in the front seat of a brand new Cadillac surrounded by three or four blonds in bikinis. He would tell the audience that Cadillacs were classics only to be owned by "those who deserved one." He would wave his hands in the air and say, "All this can be yours for a small down payment." He never said anything at all about the car. But Randall was no dummy when it came to selling cars. He knew his clientele was male, married, and middle-aged. "Buy this car," Randall would murmur into their subconscious, "and you too can have half-naked young girls undulating on your leather interior."

As Randall got older and fatter and balder, Barbara suggested that perhaps it was time to let a "professional" actor represent the car dealerships. But Randall wouldn't hear of it. "What! Have some stranger talk about my cars? Impossible."

Malqueen used to shake her head at the commercials and say, "He just likes bein' round them half-clad burnt-skinned beauties. Probably has all their telephone numbers in a little black book in the glove compartment of one his Caddy-lacks. Man's body looks like a beach ball with a bowling ball stuck on top. Thinks he still looks like Paul Newman. Old swivel-head turned out zactly like I thought he would."

Malqueen's telephone call did the trick and Barbara came right over. When Mother and Father came home, she led them into the study and explained what Natalie had done. Afterward, Barbara came back into the kitchen and filled us in.

"I actually think they took it pretty well," she told us. Malqueen and I waited for her to continue. "I mean, Father was very calm."

"How 'bout your Mama?" Malqueen asked.

"She was quiet."

"Are they going to let her stay in Paris?" I asked.

"Well, as Father pointed out to Mother, there's really not a whole lot they can do. She's eighteen. Besides, Father thinks she'll tire of it. He still thinks she'll come home." Barbara tapped her finger on the counter. "By the way, did she leave an address or phone number?" Malqueen and I shook our heads no.

"Well, then I guess we'll have to wait for her to contact us," Barbara said as she made her way out the door.

Mother got a note from Natalie a week later. In it she congratulated Father for his election to bishop, and she included her address and phone number. Mother called her at the Paris number and begged her to come home for the consecration. Natalie said that it was impossible. She was new and she was "on call," which in airline lingo meant she had to sit by the phone and wait to be called out on a trip. Barbara also called her in Paris and urged her to attend the consecration, but Natalie still insisted she couldn't be there. Both Mother and Barbara thought it was a disgrace that she missed the "most important day in Father's life." Father said nothing.

Natalie did keep in touch. She sent chatty postcards to Mother, and she sent Barbara and the boys presents from all over the world. But I was the only one she wrote letters to. She told me how happy she was and how much she loved her job. She described her boyfriends, who were always named Francois, or Jacque, or Georges, as being handsome and rich. She loved living in the City of Lights, and told me how much I would love the Louvre and the Jardin des Tuileries. But after two years in Paris, she was forced to transfer back to the United States. TWA had to close the base in Paris for financial reasons, and in order to keep flying, Nat had to transfer to New York. She was excited about Manhattan, but I could sense she missed the glamour of Paris. I didn't realize how much I missed her until she missed my graduation from BrownWood. I did get a letter. In it she apologized for not being able to be there. "I have to fly to Sydney that week," she said. "Remember what I told you about getting out of the mausoleum? Did you hear from the Maryland Institute of Art yet? I'll call you when I get home in three weeks. And Sara, I'm very proud of you. Love Natalie."

Mother and Barbara were amazed at her absence from my graduation.

"It's not like she's in Paris," Barbara said. "She's only a three-hour train ride away. What's with her anyway? It's like she wants nothing to do with us anymore."

"It certainly is puzzling," Mother said. "Do you know I left five messages with that roommate of hers and she still hasn't called back. First, she misses your father's consecration and now this. I just don't understand."

I was probably the only one in the family who didn't mind Nat not being there. I would rather have been in Australia too. But I did want to see her. There were some things that I just couldn't write in a letter. I wanted to thank her in person for that last year before she left home, for telling me she thought I had talent and encouraging me to go to art school. But most importantly, I wanted to thank her for showing me what sex was all about.

Chapter Five

⸻ • ⸻

"No matter how much cats fight,
there always seem to be plenty of
kittens."

Abraham Lincoln

Like most people my sex education was comprised of a variety of experiences, the most memorable one being Natalie's rendition of Ken and Barbie on a date. But there were other influences too. Clyde Boy's marriage to Miss LilyPuss was one, and Malqueen's theory that sexual attraction is tied to smell was another. I also learned some things all by myself, primarily from peeping through keyholes, trying to listen in on adult conversations, and reading books I didn't understand.

The keyhole peeping occurred when I was eight. I had come home from school just like any other day, thrown my books on the steps, and headed toward the kitchen and Malqueen's cookies. Usually at that hour the house was empty. But when I passed Father's study, I heard low murmuring voices and what sounded like giggling. I turned my body toward the kitchen, but my feet took me right up to that study door. I put my ear to the wood and heard the unmistakable sound of Mother's light laughter. I knew I wasn't supposed to, but I couldn't help myself, and I kneeled down in front of the door and looked through the keyhole. I didn't see anything at first but a row of Episcopal hymnals. Then slowly a leg appeared in front of the books. It just floated into the frame and propped itself up on the edge of Father's desk. I knew it was Mother's leg because I recognized the shoe the foot on the leg was wearing. When the shoe flew off, it headed right for me and I ducked. It thudded against the door, and I heard more laughter. I waited several seconds and then looked back into the keyhole. Two hands were now slowly rolling down the stocking on the leg that was still propped up against the desk. I heard what sounded like a low groan or growl from some other part of the study, but I couldn't see the other person. I stuck my eye as far into the keyhole as I could, bending down in a crouching position to try and see more of the room than just the desk, the books, and the leg. As I turned my head around, I could just make out Father's shoes off to left side of the sofa. I pressed my body as close as I could get to the door and twisted my head until I was almost upside down. And just when I thought I could make out the side of Father's face, I felt a hand clamp over my mouth, and I was dragged backward into the kitchen where I was dumped unceremoniously on the floor.

"Just what were you doin'?"

"Uh...I...uh...I—"

"I knows what you were doin', and you should be 'shamed of yourself. How many times have I told you," Malqueen said, jerking on the front of my navy blue sweater, "not to go peekin' in keyholes and listenin' at doors?"

"Uh...it's really not what you think, Malqueen. I didn't see anything... really."

"Then why was your eyeball rolling around that keyhole like you was lookin' into one of them submarine periscopes?"

"I didn't see anything, Malqueen...honest. I heard voices, and since nobody's ever home at this time, I just wanted to see who it was." Malqueen finally let go of my sweater.

"Thought I raised you better than that. Spying in keyholes like a sneaky old lady. Actin' just like that nosy sister of yours. What's the matter with you?"

"I'm sorry," I sniffed. "I just wondered who it was."

"It was your mother and father trying to finish some of their work in the privacy of their own study. They don't need a Miss Busybody sniffing around the door. Why didn't you just knock?"

"I don't know."

"I don't know...Hmmph. You do know. And I think you best go to your room and think about what you done. I have a mind to tell your parents what I seen you doin'—"

"NO!" I said a little too loudly as I ran from the room. "Don't tell. I won't do it again." I turned around and saw Malqueen watching me as I paused at the bottom of the steps, picked up my books, and ran up the stairs to my room.

The memory of Mother's leg haunted me all evening. I knew I had seen something important. But in my eight-year-old mind, I didn't have a clue as to what any of it meant.

The marriage of Clyde Boy and Miss LilyPuss occurred about two months later. I had adopted a stray cat that had shown up one afternoon in our garden. Mother didn't allow animals in the house, saying they carried fleas and worms and all kinds of unhealthy parasites. But the rest of the family felt sorry for Clyde Boy. He was charcoal gray, and half of his left ear had been torn off in a fight. He was skinny, he limped, and the tip of his tail dangled like a broken flower stem when he raised it in greeting. Malqueen fed him and every night I left my window open just enough so he could leap from the old oak tree in the front of the house into my room. During the day he patrolled the neighborhood and usually ended up sunning himself on the slate path in our garden. The object of his affection was a white Angora named Miss LilyPuss, who lived next door with Mr. Merrill and his wife, Miss Marie. Miss LilyPuss was an indoor cat, but Miss LilyPuss was sneaky and very good at getting out the door before the very nearsighted and elderly Miss Marie even realized she had gone. And Miss LilyPuss always ran away to our backyard.

Malqueen was fascinated by Clyde Boy's persistent attempts to "date" Miss LilyPuss. We'd see her tail before we ever saw her—a white plume rising up over the fern at the bottom of the garden waving languidly as she moved up the garden path. Once in sight it was hard to miss her because Miss LilyPuss was the size of a Jack Russell terrier. On summer days when all our windows were open, I could hear Miss Marie and Miss LilyPuss discuss the luncheon menu.

"How is mama's baby? Is she hungry? Is she hungry?"

"Yeowllll...yeowllll."

"Does that mean tuna? Or chicken?" Miss Marie would ask.

"Breep...yeowlll."

"Oh tuna? Well, let's see. Yes, here's a can."

"Eeeep...Eeeep."

"There now, are you happy, my precious? Mmmm...yummy."

As a result of Miss Marie's love and kindness, Miss LilyPuss's stomach dragged along the ground when she walked, and it took at least three tries for her to be able to leap up onto our fence. Because of her size, her balance wasn't all that good, and on many an occasion when she'd try to lick her tail, Malqueen and I would watch her teeter forward and then keel over backward and land in Miss Marie's roses. Mr. Mitchell, Miss Marie's husband, summed it up best.

"Goddamn cat is too fat. Look at it, Marie. It's so fat it can't see its own feet—let alone the mice. What good is a goddamn cat that can't catch mice?"

And Miss Marie would just say, "Oh don't listen to him, precious baby. Mama loves her."

Malqueen and I watched as "precious baby" sauntered up the walk.

"Look at her sway them hips," Malqueen said. "She's the Mae West of cats."

As Miss LilyPuss continued her rumba around the garden, I darted around the kitchen jumping up and down trying to see where she was headed. "Where's Clyde Boy, Malqueen?"

"He's over by the trash can. But he don't know she's there yet. Wait a minute...Now he's sniffing the air...Now he knows...just jumped up on the trash can lid...He's watchin' her tail come up the path."

Even though Malqueen had explained to me that Clyde Boy was trying to "date" Miss LilyPuss, I also knew that whenever Miss LilyPuss and Clyde Boy ran into each other, Clyde Boy ended up getting hurt. Miss LilyPuss would only let him get within striking distance and then she would lash out with her best right paw and knock him clear to the ground. Since he was half her size he didn't stand a chance. But he kept trying.

"Why does she hate him so?" I asked Malqueen.

"Just like people," Malqueen shrugged. "Sometimes you meet someone for the first time and you don't like 'em at all. Ain't their fault. Just somethin' bout 'em you don't like. Then sometimes you meet somebody and you feel like you've known them forever."

"But Malqueen, why?"

"Nobody knows for sure. But I believe it have somethin' to do with smell."

"Smell?"

"Yep, smell."

"You mean like Mother wearing Channel No.5 when she goes out?"

"Sorta…only this is a natural smell. Like the way the clothes smell on the line after they dried in the sun."

"I don't get it. Why would the smell of dried clothes attract someone?"

"OK, maybe not dried clothes. But I bet you'd like somebody who smelled like chocolate chip cookies." I thought about that and realized I probably would.

"So, what you're saying is Miss LilyPuss doesn't like the way Clyde Boy smells…right?"

"Somethin' like that," Malqueen said, looking out the window. "However, that don't mean she won't change her mind."

Apparently that afternoon Miss Lily Puss did just that. "Where is he now?" I asked Malqueen.

"He's on the side of the shed…looks like he's ready to pounce." We watched her round the corner just as Clyde Boy reared up and leaped in front of her. But instead of knocking him senseless, she remained where she was and just looked at him. Clyde Boy didn't know what to do. She had whacked him so many times before that he still didn't believe she wasn't going to hit him. He reared up in the air again and this time landed right next to her. Miss LilyPuss leaned over, sniffed his head, and gently licked the side of his face. Then she got up, flicked her tail in Clyde Boy's direction, and walked behind the hydrangea next to the shed. Clyde Boy, still wearing that stunned look on his face, looked over at us and then over at the bush. Within seconds he sprinted for the bush. A few minutes later I saw her tail rise high above the greenery.

"Uh oh," Malqueen said, leaning into the window to get a better look.

"What, Malqueen, what?" I wasn't tall enough to see behind the bush. "Is she punching him again? What's she doing, Malqueen? What's she doing?" I started to run for the back door to the garden. Malqueen caught me and pulled me back. "I don't think you need to be out there right now," she said.

"Why not, Malqueen? I always chase her away when she starts to hit him."

"Because she's not hittin' him right now…that's why."

"Well, why not? What's she doing?" Malqueen looked back out the window into the garden and then looked down at me. "Uh…they gettin' married."

"Cats don't get married...Besides, she hates him."

"Don't mean nothin.' Lotsa people hate each other and still get married. And what makes you think cats can't get married? How you think they have kittens?"

I didn't have much time to stand there and think about what Malqueen was saying because right about then both cats started yowling at the top of their lungs.

"I knew it," I said, trying to push past Malqueen to get to the garden. "She's killing him. Let me go!" Malqueen maintained her firm grip on the elastic waistband of my pants.

"You going nowhere. They fine. They just singin', that's all."

"Singing? You're crazy, Malqueen. He's in pain. I just know it. She's hurting him. She's trying to kill him!" Malqueen dragged me over to the other end of kitchen, and after a few moments the yowling stopped.

"What's going on now, Malqueen?" I said, trying to stand up on a kitchen stool to see out the window. "I know she's killed him, Malqueen," I said, jumping up and down. "He's dead and you wouldn't let me save him." Malqueen sat me down on the stool and said, "Clyde Boy's fine."

"But Malqueen—"

"Clyde Boy's definitely not dead," she said to me. "Now start your homework." I opened my notebook, but before I could do anything, the kitchen door swung open and Father stepped into the kitchen.

"What was all that racket outside?" he asked Malqueen.

"Just Miss LilyPuss and Mr. Clyde Boy gettin' to know each other better," Malqueen said as she put a pot on the stove.

"Getting to know each other?" Father looked puzzled. "She hates him."

"Father, Malqueen said they got married," I said jumping off the chair and looking out the window into the garden. "But I don't think so. He was screaming so loud I just know she killed him."

"Reverend, I told her he was fine," Malqueen said. Father and I jumped as the yowling started up again.

"Father, she's killing him," I grabbed at his hand. Father looked at Malqueen.

"I'm telling you everything is all right, Reverend. Come over here and you can see for yourself."

Father held me with one hand and stood up on his toes and looked over into the garden. Then he pushed me back to the kitchen table and sat me down on the stool and said, "Sara, Malqueen's right. Clyde Boy is just fine."

"But why are they making so much noise?"

Father looked at Malqueen and cleared his throat. "Well, Sara—"

"'Cause they doin' the hokey pokey," Malqueen interrupted.

"Hokey pokey?" Father raised his eyebrows.

"Reverend, what does every married couple you know do after they speaks their vows?" Father thought about that and began to smile.

"Oh, that hokey pokey. Of course!" Father looked over at me. "Don't worry Sara, Malqueen's right. Clyde Boy's just fine. "Why, right now," Father said, waving his arm in the air, "they're shaking it all about."

"Are you sure?" I looked at Father.

"Absolutely," Father said as he and Malqueen put their right foot in and their right foot out.

"Do you swear he's not dead?" I looked at Malqueen who was busy putting her left foot in.

"I swear he ain't dead," Malqueen said, crossing her heart and shaking her foot alongside Father. "No sir, he ain't dead at all." Then she looked over at Father who was now putting his left foot in and said, "But I do believe he be in heaven." Father didn't even turn around. He hokey-pokeyed right out the kitchen door. I heard him laughing all the way to his study. And Malqueen covered her mouth and snorted into her hand. I glared at Malqueen.

"What's so funny?"

"I'm just thinkin' about that dance, that's all. Malqueen pulled me to my feet and tried to get me to dance. I resisted but I didn't hold out too long. We sang and danced, and for the moment I forgot about the antics of Clyde Boy and Miss LilyPuss

When I was eleven, our sixth grade class was herded into the projection room at BrownWood and shown a film called *Now You Are A Woman*. It was the first year that private schools decided to add sex education to the curriculum. I knew that public schools had been showing this film for several years because

Molly O'Norton, who lived down the street and went to Johnson Elementary, had asked me if I'd seen it yet. When I told her I hadn't, she had laughed and said, "My father says private school is just for snobs—that it isn't any better than public school...and he must be right. That school you go to doesn't even teach you about getting your period."

I had told her that the correct name for "period" was menstruation and if she didn't know that, then the film she had seen must not have been that good after all. Molly ended our argument the way she always did. She stuck her tongue out at me, turned around, and ran home.

Most of the girls in my class had older sisters, and that was why we already knew what a menstrual cycle was. Lettie, who didn't have any sisters to walk in on, was the only one who sat through the movie with her mouth open. After the film ended, we were each given a book also entitled *Now You Are A Woman*. But unlike the movie, which was more of a how-to guide, the book discussed the emotions involved in becoming a woman. It used phrases like "butterflies in the pit of your stomach" and "the urges of spring." This made us look at each other and ask, "What urges? And why would we get butterflies in our stomachs?" The book didn't answer "the big question," the one we all wanted answered, which was, how do you get pregnant in the first place? Barbara later told me that it was Frances Lymington who fought the sex education course at BrownWood. Frances was a benefactor and influential member of the school board and said, "Explaining pregnancy to girls that young is just asking for trouble. The less they know the better."

There were several versions floating around school of how babies arrived. Mary Lou Farnsworth's sister told her that after you got married you could order a baby from a catalog like L.L.Bean. The babies always arrived at night via UPS. But Coffey Darlington said that was a bunch of hooey. She said you didn't have to be married. You could get pregnant if you were menstruating and you kissed a boy. The baby grew in your stomach and had to be cut out by the doctor. Juliet Warrenton agreed with her but said that you had to do more than kiss a boy; you had to have sex with him before you could get pregnant. But she didn't know what sex was. And Marion Evansford said sex was when the woman and the man got real close and he put his "thing" into the woman. But we couldn't figure out where he was supposed to put it, and so nobody believed that version because it was just too gross. We weren't a worldly group of girls, even though we would come of age during the sexual revolution of the sixties. We would have to wait until after we graduated from our all-girl convent-like high school before we discovered the joys of free love.

I had tried to read *Now You Are A Woman* again after I got home. But the book was so boring I fell asleep. One minute I was reading about "the urges of spring," and the next minute Natalie was shaking me.

"Come on, Sara. Wake up. Dinner's ready," she said, giving me a hard shake. I felt the book leave my hands.

"Well, well, well...what's this?" Natalie said, thumbing through the book.

"Give me that," I said, lunging for the book. Natalie being taller and bigger held it up over my head.

"Oh, please. *Now You Are A Woman?*" she said. "This is a terrible book. Where did you get this?"

"Give me my book back," I said, jumping up and down.

"Listen, kid, I don't know who gave you this, but there are better books out there than this." I stopped jumping and looked up at her.

"I mean...do you understand any of this?" Natalie asked.

"Natalie, it's just a book about getting your period. They gave it to us in school."

"No kidding?" Natalie sat down on the bed. "They didn't give us anything when I was your age. This sure is vague. Do you understand what they mean by the 'urges of spring'?" I shrugged my shoulders. "I didn't think you did." Natalie threw the book on the bed. "Come on, Barbara's yelling for us again. And when we finish dinner, I'll explain what 'the urges of spring' means. I followed Nat down to dinner.

Mother, Father, Barbara, and Randall Jr. were seated at the table. Lately, Barbara had been spending more time at our house than she did at her own. She ate with us at least four nights a week. Mother and Father didn't seem to notice. But Natalie would always bring it to everyone's attention.

"Back again so soon, Barbara? Weren't you just here last night?"

"Randall's working late again," Barbara said as she shoveled peas into Randall Jr.'s mouth. "I think it's better for the baby to be surrounded by family than sitting at an empty table by himself."

"Of course it's better," Mother said. "It's good for a child to learn proper dinner table behavior when he's young."

Malqueen entered with the mashed potatoes just as Randall Jr. blew green goo out his nose. Natalie and I laughed, Malqueen ran back to the kitchen, and Father shut his eyes.

"Barbara, quick, wipe up that mess. He's getting mashed peas all over the tablecloth," Mother said. "Where's Malqueen? Malqueen!" Malqueen stuck her head in the room and looked at Mother.

"Malqueen, can't you get some towels or something to wipe up this mess? Before it soaks into the table linen?"

"I could but that baby's ready to explode. She been stuffin' him since early today. I'm afraid it's going to start coming outta the other end too."

"Please," Father said, throwing his fork down in disgust. "Can't we talk about something besides Randall Jr.'s digestive track?"

Mother looked at me. "Sara, go in the kitchen and get some towels to wipe up Randall's spit."

"Why do I have to go?" I said, looking at Father.

"Because I told you to," replied Mother.

I looked over at Father, who was trying to put a piece of meat loaf into his mouth but kept putting it down every time he looked at Randall Jr.'s pea-spattered face.

I got up and went into the kitchen. Malqueen had the towels in her hand. I took them from her and walked into World War II.

"He's only two. He can't have the manners of an adult," Barbara said.

"I don't ask that he have the manners of an adult. I ask that if you are going to have dinner with us every night that at least he has the manners of a human being and not an animal," Mother said.

"Animal? You're calling your own grandson an animal? He's your flesh and blood. How can you say that? He's a baby. Have you forgotten that babies throw up?"

Natalie had stopped eating and her head bobbed back and forth as if she were watching a tennis match. Father rubbed his forehead and raised his hand.

"Enough," he said. "Barbara, I realize that Randall Jr. is only two. However, I think we've been very patient with him and the way he…well…he throws up every night at the dinner table. Maybe if you fed him in the kitchen before we sat down to eat. He could still sit at the table—"

Barbara started to wail. We all looked at her. The sight of Barbara crying was even shocking to her own son, who stopped blowing peas out his nose and started to scream himself. Malqueen came rushing in.

"What happened?" she said as we all stared at Barbara. When we didn't answer, Malqueen put her arm around Barbara and led her off to the kitchen. She nodded over to me and said, "Bring the baby."

I got up and tried to lift Randall Jr., but he was so heavy I had to roll him out of his high chair and drag him into the kitchen. I tried not to touch any of the sticky green goo that covered him. As I dragged him over the carpet, kicking and screaming, I heard Mother say to Father, "William, this can't go on. We have to talk to her, and we have to talk to Randall." I pulled Randall Jr.'s body through the swinging doors and into the kitchen. Randall spotted his mother and threw up again.

Barbara was still sobbing as Malqueen held a cold cloth to her forehead.

"There, there...I know you need to get it all out, but I'm afraid all this sobbing is going to bring on the migraine. Barbara's chest stopped heaving up and down.

"What am I going to do, Malqueen?" she asked.

Malqueen ran the cloth under some more cold water and put it back onto Barbara's forehead. "That's what you've got to decide," she said as Barbara took a Kleenex and blew her nose.

I dropped Randall Jr. in the middle of the kitchen and said, "Decide what, Malqueen?"

Malqueen looked over at me and then over at Randall Jr., who was on his stomach swimming for his mother.

"Never you mind. Get that baby and take him outside."

"Oh, Malqueen. I always have to watch him. Why do I—"

"You just do it, that's all."

I turned Randall in the opposite direction so that he was now swimming toward the screen door, which led to the garden. He had his eyes shut and was screaming so loudly that he didn't know he was headed in the wrong direction. Barbara and Malqueen were talking so quietly I could barely hear what they were saying. I caught the words "Why does he do this to me," from

Barbara. And I heard Malqueen say, "You knew what he was when you married him. He ain't gonna change now." Malqueen said something I couldn't hear, and Barbara said, "But I can't do that, Malqueen...I'm three months pregnant." I must have been paying too much attention to the conversation because before I knew it Malqueen had the screen door open and was shoving both Randall Jr. and me out the door.

"Stay out here till I call you," Malqueen said.

I looked around the yard and said, "And what am I supposed to do with him out here?" Malqueen threw the towels at me, slammed the screen door in my face, and said, "Clean the baby up...That's what you can do."

"How do you expect me to do that?" I asked.

"I don't care. Just clean him off."

I watched Barbara and Malqueen talk through the kitchen window. It wasn't fair that I always got stuck with Randall Jr. Natalie never had to watch him. I wanted to be in the kitchen and find out what was going on. I looked over at Randall Jr. who was now pulling Malqueen's parsley out of the ground and stuffing it in his mouth. The pea goo had hardened and he was crusty with green peas. I also detected a familiar smell emanating from his diaper. I stood up. Clean him up? I thought. How? I looked around the garden and spotted a hose that was coiled beside the shed.

"Randall?" I called lightly. "Oh, Randall...come over here and see Aunt Sara. She has a nice surprise for you...a nice, wet surprise." Randall didn't mind the hose at all.

That night, after Barbara had retrieved Randall Jr. from the garden and gone home, I went back to the peace and quiet of my room only to find Natalie waiting for me.

"So, did Barbara decide to leave him?" Natalie asked.

"Leave who?"

"Randall, you dummy...her husband."

"I didn't know she was unhappy with Randall."

"You're such a weird little kid...For someone who's always eavesdropping, you're so dumb!"

I walked around my bed and sat down on the other side.

"Well, how am I supposed to know anything? Every time I try to find out what's going on, they send me out of room. Sara, take the baby. Sara, get the towels, Sara, do this. Sara do that. And how come you never have to watch that little monster?"

Natalie turned around, looked at me, and laughed. "That's easy. She doesn't trust me."

"Barbara?"

"Actually, none of them…Father, Mother, Malqueen and, yes, my loving sister, Barbara." Natalie went over and took my Barbie doll off the shelf.

"Do you still play with this?" she said, holding the doll up in the air.

"Sure."

"Where's the 'smoothie?'" she asked.

"Smoothie?"

Natalie pulled Barbie's dress up and said, "Her boyfriend, Ken. You know, the one with no sex organs."

I pointed to the opposite shelf. Natalie went over and got Ken. She stared at the two dolls.

"Natalie, is Barbara going to divorce Randall?"

"Nah, Mother and Father will step in and counsel them first. They'll even drag in Randall's parents. Divorce is still pretty taboo in the church. That is, if they can even find Randall."

"Find him? Is he lost?"

"You could say that. He usually disappears for two or three weeks… Then he must realize what an idiot he is and he comes crawling home."

"How many times has he left?"

Natalie started to count on her fingers. "Let's see, first there was the redheaded receptionist…then the blond secretary…oh, and I forgot the brunette car washer…and I think there was another blond in there somewhere. So what's that? Four?"

"He's run away four times?"

"Yep."

"Poor Barbara."

"Poor Barbara? No, Sara…the one thing Barbara isn't…is poor. The Lymington family is loaded. When Randall's parents croak, he stands to inherit a mint. And if Barbara keeps bowing low three times whenever Frances Lymington enters the room, she'll get Frances's millions too."

I sat on the bed and tried to absorb all this new information. I knew that married men did cheat on their wives. I had heard Father and Mother complain about couples in counseling who "had not honored their marriage vows," and I had also been to enough Ladies Prayer Luncheons to overhear Mrs. Leach tell Mrs. Thomas that Richard Childs was "fooling around" again with MaryAnn Morgan, a woman who was not his wife. The problem was I didn't know what "fooling around" meant.

While I thought about Barbara, Natalie was busy searching my room. Finally, she found what she was looking for.

"Got it," she said, pulling Barbie and Ken's pink Cadillac from under the bed.

"What're you doing?"

"I'm going to show you what happens on a real date," Natalie said as she put Barbie in the passenger seat and placed Ken behind the wheel of the car.

"OK, let's pretend Barbie and Ken are out on a date," Nat said, twirling a white curl around her finger. "In fact, Ken wanted to take Barbie to the movies, but Barbie was late because she couldn't get her eyeliner on right and she discovered she had a ketchup stain on her white blouse and she had to change and..."

I started to fidget.

"Well, never mind why she was late. But now they can't go to the movies because they missed the show. Now pay attention, Sara, this is important. You won't read about any of this in that pathetic sex manual." Natalie pointed to the *Now You Are a Woman* book that she had carelessly thrown back onto my bed. I looked at the smiling girl on the cover and then back up at Natalie. The girl on the cover was pretty and perky and looked like she had just finished milking the cows. But even at the age of twelve, I knew that if she walked into a high school mixer she'd be stuck sitting behind palm fronds studying her nails as my beautiful and exotic sister bewitched every testosterone-oxygenated prep-school boy in sight.

"Sara? Are you paying attention?"

I looked up at Natalie and shook my head yes.

"OK, so now they can't go to the movies. And Ken suggests they go to 'the park' and make out."

"What's making out?"

"God, you're hopeless. Are you sure you're twelve? You are so backward. I have my work cut out for me tonight. Making out is what guys live to do. It's really just a lot of kissing and touching and stuff."

"Touching? Where?"

"Don't rush me. I'll get to that in a little while." Natalie pushed the car down the length of the quilt and parked it at the very end of the edge of the bed. She moved Ken's arm around Barbie and turned their heads toward each other to make them look like they were kissing. Natalie sat back to examine her handiwork. Then she leaned forward and snaked Ken's arm under Barbie's blouse. I watched in fascination.

"Ken," Barbie shrieked in a high falsetto, "you pig! Get your hand out from under my blouse!"

"But baby..." Ken murmured in a deep low voice, "you know I love you."

Barbie leaned back and punched Ken in the head so hard he flew out of the car and cartwheeled over and down the edge of the bed. Natalie smiled and rearranged Barbie's clothes. Then she leaned down and helped Ken drag himself, hand over hand, back up the bedspread and over to the car. Natalie repositioned Barbie so that one arm rested on the back of the driver's seat and the other arm hung languidly outside the car window. Ken crawled around the car, put his head under her hand, and said, "I'm sorry, baby. You know I love you." It took Barbie several seconds to respond. Finally, she turned her head, looked down at Ken, and patted him on the head. Natalie rubbed her hands together and moved over to the other side of the bed. I leaned forward to get a better view. Ken kissed Barbie on the fingers and slowly worked his way up to her elbow. Barbie whispered "Oooh" when he got to her elbow and "Ahhh" when he reached the inside of her upper arm. Suddenly, Ken leaped into the backseat, pulling Barbie on top of him. Barbie and Ken kissed passionately for several minutes, and then Barbie said halfheartedly, "Stop...Oohh, Ken...No!" Ken paid no attention and continued to kiss Barbie. Pretty soon Ken's shirt flew out of the car. I peered over Natalie's shoulder to get a closer look into the backseat. Ken was once again rooting around under Barbie's blouse. Barbie let him undo the third button before she kicked him in the stomach and sent him back up in the air and over the end of the bed. Natalie hummed "Ain't She Sweet" to herself as she rebuttoned Barbie's shirt and placed her demurely back in the front seat. Meanwhile, Ken had landed on his head in the trash can. I dug him out of last night's homework and eagerly handed him back to Natalie. Natalie paused for a moment and stared at Ken before she put him back in the driver's seat. Finally, Ken leaned over and said, "I'm sorry, baby. You know I love you."

"If you loved me," Barbie said, putting on fresh lipstick, "you wouldn't ask me to do those things."

"I know, baby...you're right. It won't happen again." Ken fiddled with the car radio and Natalie hummed Nat King Cole's "Unforgetable."

"Oh, Ken," she sighed, "isn't this the most romantic song?"

Ken slowly slid closer to Barbie until his fingers just touched her neck. Gradually, his hand traced the side of Barbie's face. Barbie sighed again. Hesitant, but unable to resist, Ken leaned over and kissed Barbie behind her ear. Barbie leaned toward him and said, "Ooooh, Ken."

I crawled around the other side of the bed where I could get a better view of Ken sucking on Barbie's neck. Natalie sat back, surveyed the scene before her, and then placed Barbie's hand on Ken's crotch. I didn't have time to blink. Within seconds, Ken was catapulted out of the car and landed on the bookshelves across the room. I ran to get him again, and as I handed him back to Nat, I noted that Ken had no shirt on and his pants were undone. His hair was sticking straight up in the air and he was missing one shoe. He was in bad shape; and yet, he still braved the climb up the bedspread to get back to Barbie. I couldn't help but feel sorry for him.

"Ken, look at you," Barbie said. "You're a disgrace."

"I'm sorry, baby. Can I get back in the car?"

Barbie studied her nails. "What's the magic word?"

"Please?"

"Please what?"

"Please," Ken said as he hung onto the driver's side of the car. "May I get back in?"

"Well, I suppose so...but don't touch anything; you're filthy." Ken sat as far away from Barbie as possible in the front seat. He kept both hands on the steering wheel and watched Barbie smoke a cigarette out of the corner of his eye. Finally, Barbie offered Ken a drag off her cigarette. Ken took the cigarette and Barbie leaned over and stroked Ken's cheek. Ken leaned in like a wounded dog.

"Are you going to be a good boy now?" Barbie asked.

"Sure, baby. You know I love you."

"Because if you're a real good boy," Barbie said as she scooted over to Ken's side of the car, "I may let you—"

"NATALIE!"

All four of us jumped. Mother stood in the doorway.

"Just what are you doing?"

"Uh...I'm showing Sara, uh...how I used to pretend I was on a date when I played with dolls, Mother." Natalie looked directly at Mother and smiled. Mother looked over at me. I smiled too.

"I don't know why I think there's something fishy going on here, but..." Mother stared at both of us. We both smiled again.

"Anyway, it's getting late and you both have school tomorrow. Gracious, what an exhausting day...meetings and more meetings...and then Barbara and that child of hers...What's wrong with that child anyway? And Randall? I just don't know. And your father and I have an important conference tomorrow. It just never stops." Mother paused and rubbed her forehead. Then she seemed to realize who she was talking to. "Natalie, are you going to that mixer at Helman Prep on Friday night?"

"Yes, I'm going with Richard." Natalie got up off the bed. "You know his mother, Eudora Chason."

"Eudora? Chason?" Mother's face went blank as she thought about the name. "That's right, I remember...the wine people." Mother smiled at Natalie but then frowned. "Well, that's all very well, Natalie, but he'll have to come to the house to pick you up this time. You can't meet him at the Oswalds like the last time. You know how your father is."

Natalie locked her arm into Mother's and walked her out of my room but then leaned back in and said, "Bonsoir, mon petite soeur, and don't forget what I just showed you."

"Good night," I said as the door closed. And I heard Mother say, "Sweet dreams, girls" from somewhere down the hallway.

I put the car and the dolls back in their places, undressed, and got under the covers. I felt something hard under my back and discovered it was the *Now You Are A Woman* book. I held the book up and stared at the smiling Heidi look-alike as she sat in a field of yellow and white daisies. Had she ever been on a date with Ken? Did she jump around in the backseat of a pink Cadillac and "ooohh" and "aahh," while Ken's hands mysteriously disappeared under her blouse? Somehow I didn't think so. By comparison my sister had a date every single weekend. Did this girl with her ivory soap complexion even go on dates? Maybe all she did was sit around and get those "urges" the book kept talking about. How was I to know? Who should I believe? A book? Or my sister? I turned out the light, held the book against my chest, and snuggled down under the blanket. But I was too excited to sleep. I was still awake when I heard Father's heavy footsteps as he walked past my door and down the hall to my parents' bedroom. Did he and Mother have "dates" like Barbie and Ken? I pulled the covers over my head and finally fell asleep. But Ken drove his pink Cadillac into my dreams almost immediately: tall, blond, and handsome, wearing khaki pants and a pale blue button-down shirt. And when he leaned closer to kiss me and whispered, "You know I love you baby," I realized we weren't alone. Lounging in the backseat in a red satin gown was my sister Natalie, smoking a cigarette and laughing.

Chapter Six

•

"Nil desperandum"—Never despair
Horace 65-8 BC: Odes

In spite of all the conflicting information Lettie and I received about the mysteries of womanhood, we did survive adolescence and dating. We quickly found ourselves in our senior year waiting for something more important than a date for the prom: acceptance to the college of our choice. Lettie had only sent out one application and that was to Johns Hopkins. Her admission was guaranteed. She was a straight-A student, her father sat on the board of directors at Hopkins, and she had the money to pay for her own education. I, on the other hand, had none of those things. I desperately wanted to go to the Maryland Institute of Art. But while my grades were good, I wasn't a straight-A student, and I knew my parents couldn't afford to pay tuition. My art teacher, Miss Fine, knew all this and helped me put together a "killer" of a portfolio. She kept reassuring me that there was no way the Institute wouldn't accept me.

"Sara, you're too good. They can't turn you down."

"But am I good enough to get a scholarship?"

"Of course you are. But a lot will depend on your family's finances."

At the last minute Miss Fine did suggest I apply to two other art schools "just in case." I didn't want to think about "just in case" at all, but I did what she suggested. I was accepted at all three, but only one offered me a full scholarship, and it wasn't the Maryland Institute of Art.

"Sara," Lettie yelled as she ran down the front steps of BrownWood and over to the main gate where I stood. "Wait up!" she said, running up behind me. "What's with you the last couple of days?"

"With me? Nothing," I said as I walked a little faster.

"Oh, come on. You always wait for me after school, and the last two days you just disappeared. What's up?"

"I had a dentist appointment Monday, and I had to get home early Tuesday to help Malqueen."

"And why didn't you call me back last night?"

"I forgot."

"Sara, this is me, remember? I know you. You're squinting at me, and that means you don't want to tell me something."

"Really, Lettie, I'm squinting because I don't have my glasses on. You know how nearsighted I am."

"Nearsighted, smear-sighted. You don't need glasses to see a foot in front of your face; you need glasses to see twenty feet down the road. Besides, that's a different kind of squint."

"Now you're a squint expert? Where do you get this stuff?" I said, walking still faster.

"Where do I get it?" Lettie said, grabbing my arm. "I get it from you. Your face is like a mood ring."

"My face is not a mood ring, Lettie. It does not turn colors." I spun around and started to walk again.

"OK, so it doesn't turn colors," Lettie said, running behind me. "But when you're happy, your eyes get real wide and you look directly at me. And when you're unhappy, you squint and stare at the top of my head."

"I think you've been reading too many of those medical texts."

"I don't need a medical text to see that something's bothering you. I'm your best friend. Are you going to tell me or not?"

I took a deep breath, stared at that mystical place at the top of Lettie's head, and said, "I didn't get a scholarship to the Institute."

"What?" she said, grabbing my arm and bringing us both to an abrupt stop. "That's not possible."

"I got the letter two days ago. It's possible." I began walking again.

"Wait a minute. You said you didn't get a scholarship. But you did get accepted, right?"

"Oh, sure. I was accepted. A lot of good that does me. I was also accepted at the University of Missouri and the University of Utah. Out of the three, the only one that offered me a full scholarship was the University of Utah. Which school do you think my parents will want me to go to?"

"Oh no!" Lettie said, shaking her head. "You can't go to the University of Utah. You're going to the Maryland Institute of Art, and I'm going to Hopkins. That's always been the plan. Utah is too far away. Besides, what kind of art program do they have anyway?"

"Apparently a good one," I said still unable to look at her. "Miss Fine said it was one of the best in the country."

Lettie reached up and grabbed my scarf, pulling me back toward her. She reached up, took my head in both of her hands, and turned it around to look at her. "Tell me you won't go to Utah," she said.

"Lettie," I said, pulling away, "you know my parents. I may not have any choice."

We walked in silence. "Did they give you a reason about the scholarship?" Lettie finally said. "I mean, did they tell you why—"

"Just that they only give out a certain number of them and that there were other students who needed a scholarship more than I did."

We continued to walk on in silence. I stole a look at Lettie and caught her talking to herself. Whenever Lettie had a problem, she discussed it with herself. And it didn't matter where she was or whom she was with.

We had been in Eddie's Supermarket one afternoon, and Lettie couldn't decide if she wanted tomato or vegetable soup. I had left her in front of the Campbell's display to go get bread and had returned to find her deep in discussion with the red and white cans that lined the soup shelves. A white-haired lady, who was using her shopping cart as a walker, stopped next to Lettie. Lettie continued to talk and the woman pretended to read the ingredients on the can of soup she was holding, but from time to time she glanced in Lettie's direction. Finally, she slowly maneuvered her cart around next to Lettie's, leaned over, and said something to Lettie. Then she swung her cart around and shuffled back down the aisle. Lettie was laughing as I tossed the bread into the cart. "What was all that about?" I asked as we made our way to the checkout line.

"That lady told me to stop talking to myself," Lettie said as she put the soup on the conveyor belt. "She said it was OK for someone her age to do that because people expected it. But when my age did it, well, they just thought you were nuts."

"What did you say?"

"I told her I wasn't talking to myself. I was discussing it with my mother."

When she saw the look on my face, she playfully hit me on the shoulder and said, "Oh, come on, Sara, I'm just kidding."

But I wasn't so sure.

Lettie mumbled to herself all the way to Roland Avenue, our point of separation on our walk home from school. I said, "See you," and she said, "I'll talk to you tomorrow." And as we went our separate ways, I thought I heard Lettie say to herself, "But Mummy, I want her to go to the Institute..."

I tried to bring up the subject of college that night at dinner. Father and Mother had arrived late, and they were exhausted from a seminar they had attended at the Diocese. Barbara was there with the new baby and Randall Jr., who, much to Father's relief, had finally stopped throwing up at the table. The conversation that night revolved around Barbara and the work she was doing for Mother.

"Barbara, did you call Mrs. Thomas about the clothing drive?"

"Yes, Mother I did. She's not very organized, is she? I had to remind her three times where the drop-off point was."

"I know," Mother sighed. "But she means well. What did Brian Watson say about the..."

Mother and Barbara went on discussing the drive as Malqueen came in with the standing rib roast. Father immediately sat up straighter, leaned in to catch a whiff of the beef, and said, "Doesn't that look delicious, boys?"

Randall Jr. bounced up and down in his chair, and the baby smiled as a thin, slimy piece of viscous mucous stretched from the corner of his mouth to the tablecloth.

"Quick, Barbara, wipe that drool from his mouth before it lands on the tablecloth," Mother said. "And Randall, stop bouncing in that chair. That's a habit you should break him of, Barbara," Mother said, snapping her napkin into her lap.

"They're just excited," Barbara said, wiping the baby's mouth and steadying Randall Jr. with her other hand. "They're little boys. Besides, Father started it."

Father was still transfixed by the rib roast and ignored Barbara's remark.

Mother glared at Barbara and said, "William? Grace?"

Father tore his gaze from the meat, bowed his head, and said "O most merciful Father, who of their gracious goodness hast heard the devout prayers of thy Church, and turned our dearth and scarcity into plenty; We give thee humble thanks for this special bounty; beseeching thee to continue thy loving kindness unto us, that our land may yield us her fruits of increase, to thy glory and our comfort; through Jesus Christ our Lord. Amen."

As we responded "Amen," Malqueen brought in the potatoes and the peas. When she passed by me, she nudged me on the shoulder.

"I have some news," I said as I passed the peas to Barbara. "I got responses from the colleges I applied to."

Father and Barbara looked up.

"Well? What's the verdict?" Father asked as he salted his beef.

"I got into all of them."

"That's terrific," Father said, coming around the table and kissing me on the cheek. "Caroline, did you hear that? All of them!"

Mother finally looked up.

"How many did you apply to, dear?"

"Three."

"Three?" Barbara asked. "Why three? I thought you only wanted to go to the Maryland Institute of Art?"

"Well, Miss Fine thought it best to cover all my options."

"Smart woman, that Miss Fine," Mother said, waving her fork in the air. "Best to have contingency plans."

"What kind of scholarship did the Institute offer?" Father asked as he passed the peas to Mother. I took a mouthful of mashed potatoes and mumbled, "Nothing." Everyone stopped eating and looked at me.

"Did you say nothing?" Mother asked, still holding the bowl of peas.

"Well, they only have a certain number they can offer. I guess I just didn't..." my voice trailed off.

"Did any of the schools you applied to offer you a scholarship?" Mother asked.

"One."

"And that was?"

"The University of Utah," I said.

Barbara and Father stared at me.

"Did they offer you a full scholarship?" Mother asked.

"Yes."

"Well, I don't see what all the glum faces are for," Mother said as she looked around the table and heaped peas on her plate. "Of course you'll go to the college that offers you the best deal. I hear Utah is a nice state."

"If you're a Mormon," Barbara said, wiping away more drool from the baby's face.

Malqueen, who had disappeared back into the kitchen when I had begun my "college" discussion, suddenly burst through the swinging doors carrying a basket of rolls in one hand and a set of tongs in the other.

"Don't think that Utah such a great place to be sending a young Christian lady, do you Reverend?" She clicked the tongs a few times, leaned over him, and plopped a roll down on his plate. "Them Mormons have more than one wife," she continued, walking around the table and over to me. "Like them Arab princes in the desert. Harems they call them. Seen it on the TV." She dropped a roll on my plate and moved over to Barbara. "We don't want our Sara livin' in one of them harems," she said, pointing the tongs in his direction. "Now do we, Reverend?"

"Malqueen," Mother interrupted, "Sara, is not going to end up in a harem. Utah does have a lot of Mormons, but they outlawed polygamy a long time ago. Besides, I think you have your cultures mixed up. Mormons don't keep harems."

"That ain't what I heard," she said as she put the rolls down and held her hands over Randall Jr.'s ears. "That TV show said Utah was a regular Sodom and Gomorrah. Some of them Mormon fellas even married several of their own kinfolk." Malqueen uncovered Jr.'s ears and continued on around the table. "I don't even thinks they marry their own kinfolk anymore in West Virginia, do they, Reverend?" Malqueen dropped a roll on Randall Jr.'s plate and looked over at Father.

"Actually, I think they still do," Father said. "Caroline, didn't you have a cousin who married—"

"William!" Mother interrupted again. "We don't need to discuss some distant relatives of mine who reside in West Virginia. We're talking about Utah and your daughter's education."

Malqueen had finally arrived behind Mother's chair. She picked up a roll with the tongs, lowered her voice, and whispered to Mother, "Once they gets you in one of them harems, I hear they make the wives dance the hoochy-koochy wearin' skimpy little see-through tops and pants."

"Malqueen! That's enough!" Mother said, turning around to look to her. "Mormons do not dance the "hoochy-koochy wearing see-through tops!" Randall Jr.'s eyes widened.

"How would we know, Caroline?" Father said, leaning back in his chair and pointing his fork at her. "That temple in Utah has more secret rooms in it than Tutankhamen's Tomb. I've never been able to understand why certain rooms aren't open to the public." Father put his fork down and reached for the butter. "I mean, what are they hiding in there?" Father picked up his fork again and speared a potato. "Imagine a bunch of Episcopalians trying to do that. We'd be accused of elitism and—"

"William, you're rambling," Mother snapped. "We're not discussing the Mormon religion, although," she conceded, "you do have a point. We're discussing Sara and where she's going to attend college. Although, I really don't understand what's to discuss. She was offered a full scholarship to Utah, and that's where she'll go. That's the practical thing to do...isn't it, William?"

Father was still stuck somewhere in the temple. It took him several seconds before he said, "Yes, of course, dear."

Malqueen still stood behind Mother with Mother's roll mashed between the tongs. I appreciated her efforts, but I could see she was only making matters worse. I tried to signal to her to stop, but she ignored me and said, "Maybe Sara doesn't want to go away as far as Utah."

Mother's mouth twitched as she put her fork down and looked over at Father.

"Well, Caroline," Father said, "It is rather far. Maybe Sara doesn't want to be that far away," he said, looking over at me and winking. "Maybe I don't want her to go that far away either."

I smiled at him.

"William," Mother said, watching the two of us grin at each other, "while we may not want her to be that far away, we do want her to get the best education, don't we?" Father stopped smiling at me and looked at Mother.

"Now, it seems to me this Miss Fine knows what she's talking about. Frances Lymington thinks the world of her. And if Miss Fine thinks Sara is talented and she thinks the University of Utah has a lot to offer her, then how can we refuse to let her go? After all, we can't afford to pay her college tuition, or least we couldn't the last time I checked our bank account." Mother raised one eyebrow at Father who immediately looked down at his plate. "She was offered a full scholarship. That's an incredible opportunity for her. And not to use it would be very wasteful...don't you agree?"

"Well, I suppose so—"

Malqueen dropped the last roll onto Mother's plate. We watched as it bounced off the rim of the china, rolled off the table, and landed on the floor.

"Malqueen," Mother said, ignoring the fallen bread, "the potato bowl is empty. Would you get us some more, please?"

Malqueen opened her mouth to say something, looked at me, and changed her mind. "I ain't sure there're any taters left, Miz Gorman," she said as she made her way back into the kitchen. "See...I'm measuring real careful these days..." Malqueen kept her voice low as she walked toward the kitchen and kicked open the swinging door. "Only makin' just enough for one serving per person because I don't want anyone thinkin' that we're—" The door whooshed shut behind her but not before we heard the word "wasteful."

"Good heavens," Mother said, looking at Father. "Sometimes that woman..."

But Father didn't answer. He just chewed his roast beef and stared at his plate.

Randall Jr. broke the silence.

"Mama?"

"Yes, dear?" Barbara said.

"What's the hoochy-koochy?"

"It's just a silly dance, dear."

"Can you teach me how to do it?"

"No, dear, it isn't a very nice dance."

"But I like to look at ladies with see-through tops on."

"Randall," Barbara said nervously, pushing his hair out of his eyes. "Have you been looking through the Sears catalog again?"

"No. I've been looking at the naked ladies in those magazines Daddy keeps in the bathroom."

Mother dropped her fork, and Father choked on his standing rib roast. Barbara put her head down and said, "Junior, eat your peas."

Later that night in the kitchen, Malqueen, Barbara and I tried to figure out where I could come up with the money to get me into the Maryland Institute of Art. Barbara had her calculator out and was adding up all my expenses.

"No room and board bill at least," Malqueen said.

"That helps," I said. "But the tuition is three thousand dollars a year. Where am I going to get twelve thousand dollars? Plus money for books, and art supplies, and who-knows-what-else I'll need in the next four years?"

"Calm down," Barbara said. "How much have you saved from baby-sitting?"

"Babysitting? I babysit for you for free! The only money I have is the five hundred dollars Aunt Flo left me plus two hundred dollars I saved from working for Lettie's father last summer."

"He paid you two hundred dollars? To do what?" Barbara asked.

"Work in the mailroom."

"He had you delivering mail?"

"Why not?"

"Well, the man owns the company, Sara. He could have put you in a nice office where you answered the phone or learned about investments or something...but the mailroom? Did he make Lettie work in the mailroom?"

"Barbara, I was grateful the man offered me a job at all. What's wrong with the mailroom?"

"Well, for starters, it's dirty. And I really—"

"We got more important things to discuss than Sara's summer job in the mailroom," Malqueen interrupted. "Which, by the way, I think was good for her. Ain't nothin wrong with gettin' a little dirty." Malqueen frowned at Barbara and turned to me. "I got four thousand dollars saved you can have."

"Oh, Lord, Malqueen...that's the money you've been saving for the Baptist Retirement Home. I can't take that."

"You can if I give it to you."

"I can scare up at least two thousand," Barbara said. "And I know where I can get the rest of the money."

"If it's from a certain woman with the initials F.L. I don't think that's such a good idea."

"Why not, Malqueen? She's has more money than she knows what to do with. Besides, I can handle her...She likes me," Barbara said.

"She likes you because you're beholden to her. You makin' deals with the Devil and you gotta stop."

"But Malqueen, it got the boys in Helman Prep and—"

"Barbara, Malqueen's right," I said. "I don't want Frances Lymington's money. I'll figure something else out."

"But it's really coming from me," Barbara said.

Malqueen and I exchanged looks and finally I said, "I really appreciate the offer, Barbara. But I think Malqueen's right."

"Fine. Cut off your nose to spite your face," Barbara said, getting up to leave. "The truth is you don't have enough money. And no one will give you a student loan unless Mother and Father cosign, which they aren't about to do because you have a full scholarship to Utah."

The baby started to scream in the next room, and Barbara jumped up and ran out of the kitchen to find out what was going on. I looked at Malqueen and said, "She's right, you know. I don't have enough. Maybe I should start thinking about Utah."

"You worked too hard to get into that Institution of Art. Don't quite seem fair," Malqueen said.

"Well, as you've always said, Malqueen, 'Life ain't fair.'" Malqueen looked out the window and shook her head. "Yes, I guess I did say that," she said. "But I never meant for that to apply to you."

The next day I actually sat down and read the brochure from the University of Utah. Miss Fine was right. The University did have a great art program. Besides, the mountains were beautiful, and, according to all the literature, the skiing was excellent. So what if Utah was three quarters of the way across the country? I could still fly home for holidays. So what if I couldn't ski? I could learn. So what if I couldn't see Lettie every week? There were phones. Mother was right. Utah was practical. But as I sat in my room and tried to talk myself into being practical, I found myself looking longingly at the Institute's catalog. I tossed the brochure on Utah and I prayed for a miracle.

The miracle turned out to be John Wittridge with a little help from an angel. He paid us an unexpected visit the following evening. We had just finished dinner, and I was helping Malqueen clear the table when the doorbell rang. Mother went to answer the door.

"Why, John. What a pleasant surprise."

"Good evening, Caroline. I'm sorry to drop in unannounced like this, but I have some important business to discuss with you and the Bishop...and Sara."

"Business with us?"

"Yes. Are the Bishop and Sara home?"

"Yes, they are. Here, let me take your coat."

I had heard the doorbell, and I was already standing in the hallway. I went over and kissed John Wittridge on the cheek. Mother went to get Father.

"How's my favorite mail lady?"

"OK. What kind of business do you want to discuss? Another job?" I asked as I led him down the hall and into the study where we caught Father and Mother whispering to each other. Father stood up and shook John Wittridge's hand.

"John, how good to see you. Care for a drink?"

Mr. Wittridge declined. After we all sat down, Father said, "Now what's this about a business deal?"

"Well, actually it involves Sara and Grace," Mr. Wittridge said, folding his arms and looking at me. "As you know after Grace died, Lettie and I went to Europe for a year for a change of scenery. And after we came back, Lettie and I just never got around to going through Grace's things." John Wittridge stood up and leaned against Father's bookcase. "So we just left her room the way it was. Cerise did go in to clean from time to time. But even Cerise didn't like to spend a lot of time in Grace's old bedroom. Just too many memories... just too tough..." John Wittridge's voice faded. We remained silent and after a few minutes he looked up at us and continued. "Last week, for some reason, Lettie announced that it was time for us to go through her mother's room. I wasn't exactly thrilled with the idea but Lettie was insistent. Cerise offered to help, and so the three of us spent all day yesterday sorting through Grace's things. It wasn't an easy day." John Wittridge paused again and stared at the clock from Montana.

"John, I wished you had called me," Mother broke in.

"You're very kind," John Wittridge smiled. "But Lettie wanted to do this her way. Anyway, I'm glad we did. Because we almost missed something very important." John stopped and looked at me. "Cerise found this letter tucked inside a book of poetry." He pulled a folded up piece of paper from his pocket. I recognized Grace Wittridge's pink embossed stationery. "I'd like to read it to you." Mr. Wittridge put on his reading glasses and began to read the letter.

"My dearest John,

You and I have said all there is to be said about Lettie after I'm gone. I know you will do your best, and I know Lettie will grow up to be a wonderful young woman. But there is something else that I need you to do...something that has just come to my attention...something very important to me. Please set up a trust for Sara Gorman's college education. I want her to have the sum of twenty thousand dollars to be used for tuition, books, art supplies, and food and lodging. I know her heart is set on attending the Maryland Institute of Art. She has great talent and she should get a full scholarship. But in the event that the administrators at the Institute are blind, then I want her to be able to go there anyway and not worry about money. You must convince her to take this money for art school. And more importantly, you must convince her parents that this is a request they must allow her to accept. Tell her—" Mr. Wittridge looked up. "I'm sorry, but the letter is unfinished." We sat in stunned silence. Finally, Mother said, "Twenty thousand dollars?" And Father added, "John, you're very kind, but Sara did get a scholarship to the University of Utah. We can't allow her to accept this money when—"

"But she didn't get a scholarship to the Maryland Institute, did she?" John asked.

"No," Mother said. "But twenty thousand dollars is—"

"Caroline, I have no choice. Grace's request is specific. The money is for Sara for a college education at the Maryland Institute of Art. This is what Grace wanted, and if that's what Sara wants, then the money's hers."

"John," Mother said, getting up and walking over to him. "This is a tad embarrassing. We just cannot allow Sara to accept money from you." Mother paused and looked at me. "And quite frankly, I'm sure Sara will agree that it just wouldn't be right." Mother, Father, and Mr. Wittridge turned to look at me.

During the reading of Grace's letter, I had begun to smell gardenias, which had been Grace Wittridge's favorite fragrance. The scent grew stronger and stronger, and as the scent grew so did my confidence. The three of them stared at me and waited for an answer. I stood up, smiled at John Wittridge, and said, "Thank you, very much, Mr. Wittridge. I'd be most grateful to accept Mrs. Wittridge's kind offer."

"Sara!" Mother said, jumping up.

"Really, Sara!" Father stood up too. "Your mother is right about this. You just can't take money from the Wittridges—"

I had my hand on the doorknob and my back to them when I said, "Oh, yes, I think I can." But then I turned around and said to John Wittridge, "But I will only accept it as a loan. I intend to pay it back. This is a business deal...agreed?"

John Wittridge smiled at me and nodded. "Come to the office tomorrow, Sara, and we'll work something out." Then John Wittridge turned to my parents. I didn't wait to hear what they were going to say. I ran out of the study and into the kitchen where I grabbed Malqueen and danced her around the room.

"Lawd! What's got into you?" Malqueen said out of breath.

"Grace Wittridge left me money to go to school," I said, telling her what had just happened in the study.

"Praise be. Leave it to Mrs. Wittridge to find a way from the grave. Didn't I always tell you she'd be the most important angel in heaven?"

"Actually, you said she'd be the most beautiful angel in heaven."

"Don't matter. She came through and all the way from up there," Malqueen raised her hands to the ceiling. Then she got a worried look on her face and said, "What did the Reverend and your Mama say?"

"Well, they're not happy with me right now. I think they're still in shock. John Wittridge was still talking to them when I ran out. I just hope he—"

Malqueen and I heard a door open. We both stuck our heads out into the hallway and spotted John Wittridge heading for the door. Father and Mother were nowhere in sight. Malqueen ran ahead of him and got his coat, and I opened the door.

"I'll see you tomorrow, then Sara? About ten?" he asked as I walked out behind him.

"Ten? Sure, that's fine with me," I said as we walked to his car. When we reached the navy blue Mercedes, he turned to me and said, "Sara, you don't have to pay me back. This is what Grace wanted. It's a gift from us."

"I know exactly what it is," I said as he got into his car and slammed the door. He started the engine and put the car into gear. I waved to the back of the sports car as he roared up the street. And long after the lights of the Mercedes had disappeared over the hill, I was still outside looking up at the night sky. I thanked Grace Wittridge for her gift...not for the money that would pay for the school I had always hoped to attend, but for a generous daughter who could duplicate her mother's handwriting well enough so that her best friend could follow her dream.

I didn't exactly run, but I did move out rather quickly. Mother and Father, who were still embarrassed and somewhat perplexed by my eagerness to "accept money from the father of my best friend," weren't all that surprised when I announced I had found an apartment and was moving out. Mother made the comment, "And what will you live on? More Wittridge money?"

Barbara, who was still peeved with me because I wouldn't take Frances Lymington's money, said, "How can you take HER money and not take mine?" But before I could answer, Malqueen had jumped in and said, "Cause Miz Wittridge ain't the Devil, and Mr. Wittridge don't expect nothin' in return."

Father remained silent on the subject of tuition and money. He did ask to see the Institute's catalog, and he also wanted to know what classes I was going to take in the fall. He was visibly relieved when I told him where I was going to live and who my landlord was. And after he helped me load the car, he slipped me a hundred-dollar bill and told me to tell Lightning "Hello."

Chapter Seven

---•---

"It is the stars, the stars above us,
govern out conditions."
Shakespeare

I first met Leopold "Lightning" Grabowski at Memorial Stadium when I was eight years old.

"Lightning," Father had said, "I'd like you to meet my daughter, Sara."

"Come out, come out, little girl. I can't shake your hand if yoose hides behind your father." I peeked around Father's leg.

"There, that's better. What'll it be? One dog? Two dogs? Sauerkraut? Mustard?"

I smiled and nodded.

"Good! A little girl with a big appetite. Wants the works on her dogs." He whipped up two dogs before I could blink and had turned to the next customer. His ability to move the line at "lightning" speed had earned him that nickname. But for all his speed, we never felt rushed. He talked from the time you placed your order to the time he handed you your wrapped dog. He had a phenomenal memory and remembered the details of everyone's life: your children's names, your bad back, and even who you voted for in the last election—and God help you if it was a Republican. He teased, and argued, and flirted, and made everyone feel special. And even when I hadn't seen Lightning for a whole year he still remembered me.

"Well, if it isn't the little girl with the big appetite. Where you been?"

I had to explain I didn't get to go to all the games with Father, only the ones no one else wanted to go to. Lightning smiled and said, "Seeya next week then."

"Next week? How do you know I'll be here next week?"

"Odds are bad. Colts are favored to win by three touchdowns. Fans like a close game." He was right. I was back ordering more hot dogs the next week.

I lost track of Lightning when he personally stopped selling his Polish dogs at the stadium and became the Polish Hot Dog King by opening stands all over Baltimore City. I didn't run into him again until ten years later, that first week of college, when I answered an ad tacked to the student union bulletin board for a loft in Fells Point.

I was nervous when I went to see the apartment because I knew landlords didn't like to rent to students—especially students without jobs. The bus let me off two blocks away, and I took in the neighborhood as I searched for the address I had copied from the bulletin board. The street was lined with tiny little row houses with freshly painted shutters. Eucalyptus wreaths hung from doors adorned with brass kickplates. And in every window a white sticker stated that this house is protected by Chyron Security Systems. Here and there a white formstone row house stood out in defiance. The building I was looking for blended better with the renegade formstone and stood in contrast to the quaint little houses with their brightly painted doors and their designer wreaths. It was big and gray and looked just like an old factory, because obviously nothing had been done to it to make it look like anything else. I walked toward the building and almost tripped over a three-legged, shaggy, black-and-white mutt who darted in front of me, stood in front of a fire hydrant, and peed. I jumped in time, and the dog missed christening my shoes by inches. A woman in a faded blue flowered housedress and yellow scarf tied around pink curlers leaned out her front door and yelled, "Jack-Kay! Baaaad Dog! Stop pissin' on people and get your shaggy ass over in this here house!" Jackie the dog gave one last shake in my direction and then tore off across the street, past the woman, and disappeared into the darkness of the house. The woman stared at me and finally said, "You plying for the 'partment?"

"Yes."

"You gotta ring that bell on Mickey Mouse's nose." I looked at the door, and sure enough someone had stuck a decal of Mickey Mouse over the buzzer.

"Thanks," I waved to her as I pushed the button.

"Sorry 'bout Jackie. Only does that to pretty girls."

"Great," I thought, some reward for being attractive. I waved to the woman again and yelled, "No problem." She waited as I pushed the buzzer again. This time I got static, and a man's voice said, "Yeah?"

I cleared my throat and said, "Hello? I'm here to see about renting the loft?"

I heard a buzz, a click, and then the door popped open. I stepped back to thank the woman in the doorway and saw that she had disappeared back into her formstone cave. I turned and walked into what could have been a lobby but was probably some kind of front office when the factory was operating. But when I looked closer, I realized that everything—floor, walls, and ceiling—was covered in yellow tile, making the entry area to the factory look less like the front office and more like a men's room. There was a staircase and an elevator to the right and a metal door to the left. I waited. Finally, the door screeched opened and Lightning Grabowski stepped out. I recognized him immediately because even though he was thirty pounds heavier and looked like he hadn't shaved in a week, he still looked the same. What was different was how he was dressed. I had always seen him in a white serving apron at the stadium. But today he looked like Ernest Borgnine in a beautifully cut Hugo Boss suit. He obviously didn't know who I was because as he handed me the rental application, all he said was "Arentcha a little young?"

"Eighteen," I answered as I read the application.

He shook his head and muttered, "God Almighty, eighteen. Listen, I gotta get outta here soon. I'll show ya the loft, and yoose can fill out the form upstairs."

I followed him into the steel cage and watched as he pulled the doors together, inserted a key, and hit the button for three.

"Elevator only operates with this key," he said, holding it in the air. He stared at me again and mumbled, "Yeesh, eighteen," as we lurched upward. The elevator shimmied to a stop. I knew before he even opened the doors that this was where I was going to paint. I walked into the loft like a six-year-old being led into Disney World for the first time. Sunlight poured into the room from every possible angle. Lightning shielded his eyes as he stepped into the room.

"Whew! Too goddamn bright in here for me." He waited while I stood transfixed in the middle of the loft.

"Oh, no," he sighed. "Let me guess. Not only are ya only eighteen, but you're a student too, right?"

I still couldn't answer.

"Look, if you're a student, I don't think you'll be able to afford this place. It's four hundred bucks a month. I don't wanta be nasty but can you afford that? And I mean by yourself. I don't want one of those hippie communes up here."

I continued to stare and walk around the loft.

"Listen, Miss, I don't have much time," he said, looking at his watch. "Can you or can you not afford four hundred dollars a month?"

"I can afford it," I said, awakening from my trance.

Lightning stared at me and then sighed. "OK, fill this here form out and we'll see."

I sat down on the floor and filled out the form in record time. I handed it back to him and looked out the window. I watched him out of the corner of my eye, and when I saw him smile, I knew he had remembered. He put down the application and said, "So, the little girl with the big appetite became an artist?"

"Not yet, but I'm working on it."

"How's your father?"

"He's the Bishop now."

"That's right. Seen it in the paper. Top dog in the 'Piscopal Church. Always liked your old man...seemed like such a regular guy. Never forget the first time he told me he was a priest. I started callin' him Father Gorman and he almost had a cow. Course I'm Cattlick, so I just assumed he was too. He had to explain to me that "Piscopal priests can get married and have kids."

"Good thing they can or I wouldn't be here. How's the hot dog empire?"

"Done for. Sold the business when the Food and Drug Administration wanted to put labels on all the food."

"Ah...the secret ingredient?" When I was eight, Father had explained to me that the reason Lightning's Polish dogs were so good was because they were homemade and contained secret ingredients.

"Well, that wouldn't a hurt too much. It was the fat content I was afraid of. Those dogs were ninety-nine percent fat. Can you imagine me trying to sell them now at the new stadium to all those skinny ladies in spandex?"

"They were the best hot dogs I ever ate in my life."

"Course they were; flavor's always in the fat. Anyways, I got a hunch and I decided to dump the dog business and go into real estate. Bought and sold a lot of waterfront property. I own this here building and 'nother one downa street." He looked at the application again. "So, how do I verify a trust fund?"

"Call this number," I said, handing him John Wittridge's business card. "He'll vouch for me...at least for the next four years."

"What happens after that?"

"Well, if I'm not a successful artist, then you can throw me out."

He eyed my backpack and asked, "You got any of your pixtures in there?"

"No," I said. "But just give me a few minutes and I can whip something up." I opened the bag and pulled out a sketch pad and a nib of charcoal. I made several broad strokes before he said, "Whatcha drawin?"

"You."

He stood up straighter and tried to hold in his stomach, a feat which left him red in the face. Within a few minutes I had a finished caricature. I ripped the page off and handed him the sketch. He grinned from ear to ear.

"Ain't that somethin'," he said pleased with himself. "Can I keep this?"

"Sure," I said, putting the pad back into my bag. "Consider it collateral. Now do I get the loft?"

"You got the loft for four years," he said, throwing me the keys. "And the odds are in your favor," he added looking at the sketch, "that you'll still be here in ten."

Chapter Eight

─────────────── • ───────────────

"God hath given you one face, and
you make yourselves another.".
Shakespeare

I discovered the neighborhood was tailor-made for me. In the morning, mothers walked their children to St. Stephens Catholic School, in the afternoon iron workers bought cod fish cakes at the Fish Market on Main Street, and at night everybody gathered at one of the many family-owned bars, drank Bud, and complained about how high their taxes were. The once all-blue collar community was now being renovated to accommodate doctors and lawyers who discovered how convenient this location was to their downtown hospitals and businesses. On the weekends, Fells Point teemed with tourists from out of town, and at night it exploded with drunken college students who liked to pee in my neighbor's window boxes. It was an ever-changing eclectic mix—perfect for an artist.

Lightning had bought up most of the waterfront in Fells Point back in the late fifties, when the area still catered to sailors and fishermen. Over the years, he had sold off bits and pieces of real estate, and it was now rumored that he was a millionaire several times over. When Lightning wasn't at the track, or in Atlantic City, he was in his favorite hangout, the Blue Parrot, a bar he owned one block south from my loft. He had bought the bar in December of 1960. Nothing had been changed in the place since the day the previous owner had handed Lightning the keys. The sole window in the bar was still outlined in fake green garland and intertwined with red and green flashing lights. A plastic Santa hung from an anchor on the backside of the door, and Christmas cards from years past were tacked all over the walls. Santa and his sleigh lit up the wall over the mirrored bar, and a faded cardboard Frosty the Snowman swung from a nail on the front of the bathroom door. When I asked Lightning why he never bothered to take down the decorations, he had shrugged and said, "It makes the bar look more festive. Besides, I'd have to put them back up in a couple of months anyway."

If anything made the bar festive it wasn't the decorations but the real blue parrot that sat on its perch over the bar and made insulting comments to anyone who stepped foot on the premises. The regulars were used to the parrot's insults and either ignored him or insulted him back. I believed then, as I do now, that the damn thing actually understood what went on around it because the parrot didn't just yell out generic insults. He yelled out insults that were uncannily appropriate. For instance, the first time I walked into the bar he yelled, "JAIL BAIT! VIRGIN ALERT!" While I wasn't exactly jail bait at that time, I was a virgin. When my status in that department changed, somehow the parrot knew, and he began greeting me with "ART BABE."

He called Lightning "MAVERICK" or "MONEY BAGS." When Lightning lost at the track, the bird knew and shouted, "LOSER," and when Lightning won, the parrot would scream, "MONEYBAGS BUYS A ROUND!"

Lightning had inherited the parrot from the previous owner of the bar who had to leave town in a hurry when Baltimore's finest discovered that there were several outstanding warrants for his arrest, so we never really knew where the parrot had come from. We all fed the bird, but the bartender, Iron Man, so named because he was a retired ironworker from Bethlehem Steel, was the bird's caretaker by default. Iron Man was the only one who would change the paper in the bird's cage, and he only did that when the bird yelled, "HEY! THERE'S POOP IN HERE!" But no one in the bar would admit to teaching the bird any of the insults he yelled. "HEY, FAT ASS!" was his favorite comment but he was also fond of "BLUBBER BUTT," "BIG HOOTIES," "SPANKIN' THE MONKEY," and "LITTLE WILLY." Needless to say, only those with the thickest of skins stayed to finish their beers. Most of the insulted tourists ended up in the yuppie bar down the street from us—a renovated wonder which had comfortable leather bar stools, imported beer, and no parrot. And that seemed to suit Lightning just fine.

My art career started in the Blue Parrot. Lightning hung the caricature I had done of him on the wall. As soon as it went up, the customers started to talk.

"It sure does look like him."

"Actually, the picture looks better."

"No it don't. Look at that pot belly. . .and he needs a shave!"

"Yeah, but then why does he look so…what's the word for lookin' like a king?"

"Regal?"

"Yeah, regal. How come he looks 'regal,' and he's fat and he needs a shave?"

"Don't know how she does that. It's the same with the pixture of the damn bird."

I had actually painted the "damn" bird for a portrait class. And after I had gotten my grade, I gave the picture to Lightning for the bar. He was so pleased with it he actually took down some of his precious yellowed Christmas cards from ten years ago to create a space to hang it. The parrot had taken one look at the picture, thrust out his chest, and screeched, "I'M HOT!"

The parrot picture got me more work and eventually catapulted me into the pet portrait business. I painted Persians on red velvet cushions, Rottweilers in rhinestone-studded collars, Cockatoos on swings, and even a Python wearing a blond wig and boa (the pink furry kind) as the snake dangled from its owner's ficus tree.

My ability to make my subjects look like themselves and yet look better was my greatest talent as an artist, or at least that's what my instructors said. I knew I would never be thought of as a great "Artiste" because I had been told time and again by well-meaning teachers that I was much too commercial for that. But that was fine with me. I didn't need to make a serious statement in the art world. I just needed to paint.

I segued from animals to people the year I graduated from the Institute, operating my portrait business out of my loft in Fells Point. Within two years, I had clients from all over the country. And I now found myself, ten years later, in the delightful position of having more jobs than I could handle. It had taken me ten years, but my success as a portrait painter had enabled me to finally pay back John Wittridge.

While I loved what I did, I sometimes missed the animals. They never criticized my work, they couldn't talk to me while I painted, and most of the time, they didn't have buck teeth.

This is what I was thinking when the phone rang as I was trying to put the finishing touches on a portrait of Angel D'ellensio, the mayor's ten-year-old daughter. Angel's front teeth were almost horizontal to her lower lip.

I had painted all around them, trying to figure out how to make her look cute as opposed to just plain goofy. I tried to ignore the phone, but after the tenth ring, I finally gave up and yelled, "WHAT?" into the receiver. I was annoyed with myself as much as with whoever was on the other end of the line. Usually I unplugged the phone when I was painting because I was tired of telemarketers trying to sell me vinyl siding for my rented apartment. There was a silence on the other end of the line.

"Who is this?" I asked impatiently.

"Is this Sara Gorman?" a woman asked.

"Yes, it is. Who are you and what do you want?" I picked a hair off the canvas.

"Uh…sorry to bother you, but my name is Ruth Myers. I'm Natalie's supervisor in New York. Are you her sister?"

"I am," I said, putting down my brush. "Is something wrong with Natalie?"

"Uh, actually she's doing much better now. But yesterday her roommate came home from a trip and found her unconscious on the bathroom floor. Her roommate got her to the hospital and they pumped her stomach out—"

"What? Did you call my parents?"

"Natalie didn't list your parents as a contact. She just listed you."

"What's wrong with her?" I asked, sitting down on the chair and staring at Angel's picture.

"Miss Gorman…I don't know how to say this except just to say it. Natalie tried to kill herself. She swallowed an entire bottle of Valium along with half a bottle of vodka."

There was silence on both ends of the telephone. Neither of us knew what to say next. Finally, Ruth Meyers said, "I know this is a shock. I've already explained to Natalie that because her roommate informed the company, she has to go through counseling before she can return to work. She wants to go home for treatment. She said you'd take care of it."

"I don't live in New York, Miss Meyers. Surely you know the hospitals there better than I do."

"Miss Gorman…she doesn't want to go back to her apartment in New York. She wants to go home to Baltimore. She said you'd know what to do."

I looked at the phone and thought, "Me?" but instead said, "Of course," as I wrote down the name of the hospital and how to get there. I hung up and spent the next ten minutes pacing back and forth. My sister tried to kill herself? Miss Self-Sufficient? Why?

I picked up the phone to call Barbara but put it back down when I remembered that Randall was on the lam again. Barbara had gone to bed with another one of her migraines last night, and anyway she was still angry that Natalie had refused to visit us this past Christmas. Although, I didn't know why she even bothered anymore. Every year for the last ten years, either Mother or Barbara had tried to get Nat to show up for Christmas, and every year Nat had found some excuse. I stared at the phone and I decided I really didn't want to listen to Barbara go on and on about "Natalie's strange and selfish behavior," and I guessed that Nat wouldn't want to listen to it either. Then, I picked up the phone and dialed Mother and Father and once again put the phone down before it started to ring. They weren't home. They were in San Francisco at a yearly conference for Episcopal bishops. Besides, Ruth Meyers just said Natalie didn't even list them as contacts. She must have her reasons. But why me? I finally stopped pacing and dialed Lettie.

"Oncology. Dr. Wittridge's office."

"Maureen? It's Sara Gorman. Is Lettie available? I'm afraid it's something of an emergency. I hate to bother her but—"

"Stop apologizing," Maureen laughed. "She always wants to talk to you. Hold on. She just got out of a meeting."

I listened to "Raindrops Keep Falling on my Head," for five minutes before Lettie got on the phone.

"What's up? You backing out of Friday night?" I had completely forgotten about Friday night. Since Lettie had gotten married, she had made it her life's goal to find a husband for me. Unfortunately, the men Lettie fixed me up with usually didn't interest me at all.

In our junior year of college, Lettie had met and married Oscar Stein. He was ten years her senior, Jewish, and a child psychiatrist at Hopkins.

When Lettie and I had first started college, we had thought we would get together all the time. But all either of us could manage with our schedules was once a month and sometimes not even that. It was at one of those lunches that Lettie told me about Oscar.

"So are you dating anyone?" Lettie had asked, adding sugar into her tea.

"Dating? Are you nuts? All I do is paint animals and go to class."

"Well, you could meet someone at school."

"I've met plenty of people at school but at the moment no one I want to go out with. What's with you? You're starting to sound like Barbara."

Nothing. It's just…well," Lettie looked up from her soup, "I have."

"Have what?"

"Met someone."

"As in a man?"

"Of course as in a man. What did you think? As in a dog?"

"You have to study all the time. How could you meet someone?"

Lettie leaned forward. "He's a pediatric psychiatrist, and I met him when I interviewed him for a project…and Sara, he's wonderful," Lettie sat back from the table and absolutely glowed. I had never seen her so ga-ga before, especially over a man.

"Well, that's great. When do I get to meet Mr. Wonderful?"

"How about now?"

"Now?"

Lettie turned around and waved. A man who had been lurking in the doorway for the past ten minutes waved back and made his way over to our table. Lettie introduced us.

"Sara, I'd like you to meet Oscar Stein. Oscar, I'd like you to meet my very best friend in the whole world, Sara Gorman."

"Oscar," I said, holding out my hand.

"I've heard a lot of good things about you, Sara," he said, taking my hand.

"Please sit down."

Oscar was bald, short, and serious. But as we talked, I discovered why Lettie thought Oscar Stein was so wonderful. He was smart, kind, and responsible. And from the way he looked at her, I knew he would never leave her. He was everything she needed in a husband.

While Lettie was busy discovering Oscar, I was busy discovering birth control pills and musicians. Lettie didn't say too much about my love life, but of course, my sister Barbara did.

"Sara, just what is it with you and musicians?"

"What do you mean?

"You go through at least two a month."

"Oh, Barbara, I do not."

"You do too. Why can't you date someone with a steady job?"

"They have steady jobs."

"Sure. All night long in bars. How about someone who works nine to five?"

"I've dated men who have day jobs."

"Yeah, right. They were musicians who worked as waiters during the day, right?

I shrugged and tried to change the subject.

"Sara, I worry about you. You're twenty-eight years old and you've never had a serious relationship."

"That's not true."

"Oh really? Well, who have you dated for more than six months?"

"Ricky."

Barbara threw her hands up in the air. "That was a relationship?"

"Well, it lasted for more than a year."

"I still can't believe you actually were involved with someone named Ricky Wick. Your taste in men is very strange."

"Barbara, that was his name. He can't help what his parents named him."

"Well, that should have been a clue right there. What kind of parents would name their child Ricky Wick?"

I hated to admit it but Barbara was right. I did have strange taste in men. His name should have warned me off, but then I signed all my paintings Saralee. My clients were always shocked when they met me for the first time—they all thought I was Asian.

Ricky had hair down to his shoulders, a nose that only Pinocchio's mother could love, and smoked dope from dawn to dusk. He was also the best bass player I had ever heard in my life. Our relationship ended when his band went on the road and he got to open for Metallica. Ricky's career took off, he became a rock star, and I never heard from him again.

"Sara? Are you still there?" I couldn't believe I was daydreaming about my love life when I was supposed to be getting help for Natalie. "Yes, I'm sorry. Lettie, I need your help. Nat's in a hospital in New York," I said. "Apparently she tried to kill herself."

Lettie listened while I explained what Ruth Myers had told me.

"I have to go get her, and I have to arrange for some kind of help. Do you think Oscar would know who to call?"

"I'll call him right now. I'm sure he knows someone. Sit tight for a few minutes and I'll call you right back."

But it was Oscar who called me back. "Sara? I want you to call a Dr. Len Sullivan at this number. He'll tell you exactly what to do."

"Thanks, Oscar. I just didn't know who else to call." I hesitated for a moment and then I asked, "Oscar, you're a shrink. Why would she try something like this? I mean, she's so sophisticated and beautiful and—"

"Sara, let's leave all that to Len. Just remember that how you see Natalie might not be how Natalie sees herself." I thought about that for a few seconds and finally said, "Do you think I should call my parents in San Francisco?"

Oscar sighed. "How old is Natalie now?"

"Thirty-six."

"I think you should first call Dr. Sullivan. I suspect he'll tell you to go get your sister, check her into Pratt, and then you can ask her that question."

I did what Oscar suggested and gave Len Sullivan the name of Natalie's attending physician in New York. He arranged to admit Natalie to Shepherd Pratt, Baltimore's finest psychiatric hospital, the next day. I called Amtrak and made reservations for my trip to New York and back. Then I went to the bank and withdrew money. I should have been home before dark, but my thoughts were so jumbled that I just kept walking. I walked along the brick path that hugged the shoreline and remembered Nat's blond ponytail swinging behind her as she ran up the stairs at the old rectory. I stopped at the main pier and watched the boats come in as I remembered Natalie laughing as she ran out the door and down the front steps to join friends on her way to school. I sat down on a bench and watched the sun slip into the Bay as I remembered how beautifully defiant Natalie had looked in her brand new uniform the night she had left for Paris. But the one thing I couldn't picture was my sister washing down a bottle of Valium with a bottle of vodka.

I got back to the loft as the pale white light of the full moon crept up the side of my wall and hugged the corner of the first skylight in the ceiling. I sipped a glass of merlot, looked up at the moon, and thought some more about Natalie. I realized that Nat had cut herself off from everyone in the family except for me. She had stopped writing to Barbara and to Mother, and yet she still sent me long letters. She refused all invitations to come home to visit, and yet she had snuck into Baltimore for a weekend with me right after I had graduated from the Institute. And when Mother or Barbara suggested they visit her, she told them she was working a trip and was going to be out of town, all the while begging me to move to New York and set up my portrait business there.

If any of this concerned Father he didn't say. By the time I was an established portrait painter, he was consumed with the duties of being bishop. He and Mother had moved to a larger, more gracious-looking house in Guilford, which was right down the street from Barbara. Father had hesitated over the move, saying, "But, Caroline, I liked the old rectory just fine." But Mother had insisted. "Really, William," she had told him. "The church expects you to accept this house. It's more befitting your position as bishop. Besides, the Diocese needs the old rectory for another priest and his family. It would be an insult to refuse their offer."

My contact with my family hadn't been much better than Natalie's. I avoided family functions like the plague and had stopped attending church when I had started art school. When I did go to church, usually at Christmas and Easter, I went to the Baptist service with Malqueen.

I sat on the floor, sipped wine, and stared into the window at the woman I had become. I still had chocolate brown hair, but it now hung well past my waist and was streaked with Clairol #100, a color not quite gold but close to it. I had Mother's thin lips, which could make me look quite stern at times, but I also had huge deep-set eyes, which gave me a wide-eyed innocent look. When I was younger, people said I resembled Barbara. But now that I was older, people told me I reminded them of Natalie. The truth was I looked like both of them.

I watched as the moon swallowed pane after pane of skylight overhead. I realized how very little I knew of Natalie's day-to-day existence. What had pushed my sister this far? Why had she cut herself off from her family? Who was Natalie? The moon eventually fell off the end of my building, pulling the plug on the soft white light that had kept me company. I sat in the dark until my hands grew cold and my nose started to run. I pulled my sweater around me and walked over to the portrait of Angel D'ellensio and lifted off the cover. I flipped on a lamp and stared at the portrait of the mayor's young daughter, and I wondered why her father would spend the money to have her portrait painted but wouldn't spend the money to get her teeth fixed.

I went to New York the next day and found Natalie sitting in a wheel-chair outside the room I was told she'd be in. Like a sleeping swan, she had tucked her head down into her collar, effectively hiding her face. Somebody had tried to get her fabulous platinum hair into a classic chignon. They hadn't been successful. The knot dangled off to one side, and several long strands of hair drooped sadly over one shoulder.

"Natalie?"

"Let's go," she said, not making eye contact with me as she got up out of the chair.

"Whoa!" a voice from the nurse's station said. "Now, miss. You know we can't let you walk out of here. Sit down and we'll get someone to push you to the front door." Natalie sat back down.

"I'm her sister," I said. "I can push her."

"You'll have to wait just a minute. Let me make sure all her paperwork is in order." The nurse walked over to the nurse's station and came back with a release form. She handed me the form.

"You need to sign this. It says once you walk out of here she's your responsibility." I looked up at her.

"It's really only for insurance purposes," she said in a kinder tone. I looked over at Natalie who was again buried in her coat. I signed quickly and handed the form back.

Once Natalie and I were seated on the train back to Baltimore, I asked her who she wanted me to call.

"No one," was all she said as she pulled the collar up over her face and disappeared into her coat. I pretended to read the newspaper but spent most of my time staring out the window. We arrived at the station at rush hour. I had planned to hail a cab, but as we were walking toward the taxi-stand I heard a familiar voice yell, "Sara! Over here! Over here!" I looked up and saw Lettie waving from the front entrance. I waved back, relieved that Lettie had been kind enough to meet us. Natalie stopped, but I pushed her forward as I whispered, "Nat, Lettie and Oscar found the doctor and the program for you. I didn't know whom else to call. They won't tell a soul. I promise."

Natalie let herself be led to the car, and as soon as Oscar saw us, he ran to Natalie and helped her into the car. We drove up Charles Street and through Shepherd Pratt's Tudor gatehouse in silence. As a child I had always been fascinated with the gatehouse because it looked like it had been plucked right off of the pages of a Grimm's fairy tale. I imagined a wart-nosed witch living inside and orange-haired boil-ridden trolls patrolling the stream that ran underneath the gatehouse. I couldn't remember who had designed Shepherd Pratt, but it seemed incomprehensible that the same person who had designed the modern square red-bricked hospital had also designed that mysterious entrance. As we passed through the arch, I cracked my window and inhaled mold, mildew, and dead leaves. I looked back down at the gatehouse as we drove up the steep hill to the hospital. The stream winked back at me, reflecting small pinpoints of light in the afternoon sun, and the shadows of the old oak trees that surrounded the gatehouse, elongated, finally plunging the magical little entrance into the darkness of the woods. When I turned around, I saw that Oscar had been watching me in the rearview mirror. He smiled and said, "You spotted snakes with double tongue, Thorny hedge-hogs, be not seen; Newts; and blindworms, do no wrong; Come not near our fairy queen."

"Not bad for a shrink," I said.

"What? You think doctors only read medical journals?" he said, laughing. "I just can't go through that gate without thinking of fairies and elves."

"Funny," I said, "I was just thinking of trolls and witches."

"And I always think of Snow White and the Seven Dwarfs," Lettie said, turning around to face us. We all looked over at Natalie who had buried her face into her coat.

When we reached the hospital doors, Oscar once again ran around and helped Natalie out of the car. Lettie and I followed behind. Dr. Sullivan met us when we checked in. He talked quietly to Natalie for a few moments and then signaled to a nurse. A wheelchair appeared, Natalie was guided into it, and before I had a chance to say good-bye, she was gone.

"Come on," Lettie said. I'll buy you a cup of coffee. You can fill out those stupid forms in the cafeteria."

I stood in the middle of the reception area holding the forms in my hand. I was supposed to fill them out and hand them back to the nurse behind the desk. I followed Lettie and said, "I should be treating you to coffee. I'm so grateful you met us at the station."

"You seem to forget we're best friends. She's your sister. You needed help. There's nothing more to say." Lettie threw her coat on a table in the corner and said, "I'll get the coffee…be right back."

I tried to focus on the forms, but I still hadn't been able to make any sense out of them by the time Lettie came back with our coffee. I gave up and pushed them aside.

"When can I see her again, Lettie?"

"Probably not for a day or two," Lettie said, reaching for the forms. "Len will let you know. They like to get them settled first. What kind of health coverage does Natalie have?"

"Beats me. I guess I'll have to call her supervisor or something."

"Don't you have her purse?"

I had forgotten I had been toting Nat's purse around since New York.

"I do," I said, opening the bag and looking for Natalie's wallet. I found a wallet overflowing with business cards.

"Look at this…three different cards from nail salons, a card for massage therapy, two cards for cosmeticians, and five different hair stylist cards." I looked up at Lettie and said, "Do you think she spent enough time on herself?"

Lettie shrugged. "She's in a job where she has to look good every day."

"I know Lettie but—"

"Saralee, not everybody can roll out of bed like a certain artist I know and work at home in their pj's all day."

"When have you ever caught me in pajamas?"

"Last Friday. Remember? I stopped by to see if—"

"Oh, well, that…I wasn't feeling well that day."

Lettie took a sip of coffee and said, "Keep looking for her health card."

I finally found it and read the information off to Lettie, who filled in the forms for me. I thought we had finished when Lettie slid a form across the table and said, "This is one I can't fill out. You have to sign on the bottom line and initial where the X is." I looked down at the form and back up at Lettie who said, "It has to be done, Sara. She needs help."

I took the pen from her and signed the form that gave my permission to commit my sister to a mental institution.

"I went home that night and didn't sleep at all. I tossed and turned and felt guilty about not calling my parents and Barbara. The order was all wrong. I was the baby in the family, the one everyone else was supposed to look out for. And yet, here I was making decisions for an older sister. Why had Natalie even put me down as a contact? Why not Barbara? Or Father and Mother? I just didn't know.

I got up as the first shaft of light lasered through the skylight and hit me in the eye. I made coffee and watched a local early morning television program until the coffee was finished. How could these people be so cheerful at six in the morning? I turned the TV off, sipped coffee, and wandered over to my easel. Angel and those awful teeth were still there. I shook my head. I should just tell the mayor that I couldn't do the portrait...make up some excuse...plead an illness in the family...that was true. I didn't know how long Natalie would have to spend in the hospital. Hell, I didn't even know if Natalie was going to get better. Angel's sad eyes looked back at me. Why on earth had I taken this commission? The poor child deserved better. In frustration, I blindly reached for a brush and wiped out her teeth in one stroke. In my hurry to get Natalie, I hadn't cleaned my brushes, and the brush I had picked up still had some silver paint on it from yesterday. Cursing my forgetfulness, I threw the brush down in disgust. But when I looked up at the portrait again, it had been transformed. Instead of an awkward ten-year-old in desperate need of orthodontics, a shy, sweet-looking young girl in braces stared back at me. I laughed out loud because it was so simple. Now all I had to do was sell it to the mayor and his family.

The mayor lived in a Georgian mansion in Homeland, a well-to-do area located in Baltimore City. I had called and left a message that his daughter's portrait was finished. One of the mayor's many assistants called me back and asked me to join the mayor and his family for cocktails that evening. It seemed the mayor wanted to toast the unveiling of the portrait. I hoped he still felt like toasting after he saw it.

I had tried to see Natalie that day, but the day nurse had told me Natalie had requested no visitors. So I left Pratt and arrived at 12 University Parkway early. I was nervous, and I was trying to get my spiel down pat. I took a deep breath and walked to the front door. The door opened before I even had a chance to knock. It was Angel, teeth and all, in a state that can only be described as hysterical. She took one look at me and the wrapped package in my hand, burst into tears, and ran up the stairs. A woman I recognized as her mother ran after her. I was left holding the portrait, so to speak, in the foyer of the mayor's home, but I didn't have to stand there too long.

"Miss Gorman?" The mayor appeared and offered me his hand.

"Mayor D'ellensio," I said. "Have I come at a bad time? Would you like me to come back?"

"Not at all! Angel will be down in a few minutes. You know how pre-teens are. Everything is life and death at that age." He smiled and ushered me into an adjoining room. I put the portrait down alongside a Chippendale sideboard and sat down in a blue-flowered chintz-covered wing chair. The mayor sat down on the white loveseat across from me. I wondered if the mayor knew how good he looked against that white background. He was casually dressed in a black turtleneck and black wool slacks. His thick black hair, which was streaked with white at the temples, had been combed away from his face revealing a nose that could only be described as Roman. When he smiled, he flashed brilliantly white straight teeth. He was an extraordinarily handsome man.

"What would you like to drink?" he asked.

"White wine, if it isn't too much trouble."

"Chablis or chardonnay"

"Chardonnay, please."

"Alfredo. Chardonnay for Miss Gorman, and I'll have my usual."

I hadn't noticed the short, thin man in the corner until the mayor had addressed him. Alfredo, in his white pants and white serving coat, appeared to have stepped out from inside the wall.

"So, Sara, how's your father?"

"Fine. Busy. He's at a conference in San Francisco at the moment." Alfredo returned and handed me my wine. The mayor took his drink and we both took a sip. Alfredo blended back into the white colonial molding. After ten minutes of social talk, Angel and her mother had still failed to appear. The mayor excused himself, and I heard him run up the stairs. I also heard muffled shouts and more crying from the upper floors. Then I heard silence. I looked over at Alfredo. He didn't blink an eye. I rehearsed what I was going to say as I unveiled the portrait, but before I could finish my thoughts, Angel, her mother, and the mayor returned.

"Well, now. How about some champagne for this momentous occasion?" The mayor nodded to Alfredo, who left the room once again and returned with a bottle of Tattingers. He poured three full glasses and a small amount in the fourth glass. He gave the small one to Angel. There was no doubt Angel was miserable. Her eyes were red, her face was swollen, and those teeth were even more pronounced than I remembered.

"I guess we should have a drum roll," the mayor joked. "Miss Gorman, if you'll do the honors. I'm so excited," he said, rubbing his hands together. "I've decided to hang the portrait in my office downtown." I looked at Angel and saw two big tears roll down her cheeks.

I picked up the portrait and placed it on top of the sideboard.

"I should say before I take off the wrapping that this is my interpretation of Angel. Therefore, I have to remind you that you may not be pleased with what I've done. I take certain liberties and I—"

"Come, come, Miss Gorman. We've seen your work. We know what to expect." The mayor smiled at his wife who refused to look at him and instead put her arms around her daughter.

I removed the packaging and lifted the paper. The effect was immediate. The mayor leaned in closer and said, "What the hell? Mrs. D'ellensio clapped her hands and laughed, and Angel screamed, "Thank you, Papa!" and ran to her father. The mayor looked over Angel's head at his wife and said, "Did you know about this?" Mrs. D'ellensio shook her head and looked at me. I tried to look innocent and said, "Is something wrong?"

Angel released her father and ran to me. "Thank you, thank you, Miss Gorman! I love my portrait." Angel held both my hands and with "thank you" jumped up and down.

"You're quite welcome, Angel."

"Papa didn't want me to get braces. He kept telling me how beautiful I was...that I looked just like my Grandma D'ellensio, his mother. Mama and I couldn't convince him that I needed them. Angel pointed to a photo on the table, and I looked at the picture of Angel's grandmother. There was a remarkable resemblance. Angel's grandmother was a very handsome woman. But I did note that she wasn't smiling in the picture.

"You painted me with braces," Angel said, "and look how much better I look. Right Mama?" Mrs. D'ellensio put her arm around her daughter.

"Yes, you do look much better, and I think your father can finally see that too, can't you Tony?"

The mayor looked uncomfortable. He put on his glasses and leaned in for a closer look.

"Mayor D'ellensio," I said, tapping him on the shoulder. "Stand back here with Angel and your wife. The perspective is better. You need to be at least five feet away from a painting to get the full effect of it."

The mayor took off his glasses, rubbed his eyes, and stepped back. Finally, he turned to his wife and daughter.

"I guess I've been outvoted."

Angel jumped up and down again, and Mrs. D'ellensio smiled at her husband.

"Perhaps now we can have some peace and quiet in the house? Eh?" the mayor asked looking down at Angel. "No more tears and yelling?"

Angel ran to her father and hugged him and said, "Absolutely, Papa, absolutely."

I left the D'ellensio house with a check in my purse and a smile on my face. The dilemma of Angel's teeth had been satisfactorily resolved for me. Now if only Natalie's problem could be solved as easily.

Chapter Nine

———————— • ————————

"But I don't want to go among mad
people," Alice remarked. "Oh, you
can't help that," said the Cat: "we're
all mad here, I'm mad you're mad."

Lewis Carroll

I left the mayor's house determined to see Natalie. I checked in at the front desk of the hospital and was told someone would be with me in a few moments. An hour later, after I had finished reading the paper and completed the crossword puzzle, a middle-aged woman in a white coat finally came and got me.

"Miss Gorman?" she said, extending her hand. "I'm Linda Mankowitz. I'm the head nurse in charge of Natalie's floor."

"How do you do," I said, taking her hand. "I'd like to see my sister."

"You're aware that Natalie doesn't want any visitors?"

"Yes, I am," I said, looking directly at her. "Are you here to tell me I can't see her?"

"Actually, I'm here to tell you that Dr. Sullivan OKed your visit," she said as she fidgeted with a ring of keys she had fastened around her waist. "Give me two seconds and I'll meet you by the elevators." With that she walked away. I threw down the paper, slid my purse over my shoulder, and headed for the elevator bank. I heard her keys before I saw her.

"I have to warn you, Miss Gorman, you may see some disturbing things on your way to your sister," she said as she pushed the button for the elevator. "Just keep in mind these people are seriously ill. They're here because they can't function on the outside. They're here because they need help."

We rode in silence to the fourth floor. When we got off, we walked down a yellow-painted corridor until we reached the first of many locked steel doors. Linda Mankowitz reached for a key and opened the door. She waited for me to go through and then turned around and locked the door behind us. I didn't panic until the third door.

"Miss Gorman, are you all right?"

"How many more doors?" I asked as the room spun before me.

"Just one more," she said, grabbing my arm and pushing me forward. "It helps if you walk through the door and keep walking. Don't look back for me. I'll catch up."

"OK," I said, taking big gulps of air as I walked as fast as I could down the hallway.

"Your reaction is quite normal, you know," she said once again at my side. "In fact, you should be proud of yourself. Most people panic at the first door."

"Really?" was all I could manage to get out.

"What you need to remember is that we're not locking you in. We're protecting our patients." She paused and looked at me. "They tell me the locked doors actually make them feel safer."

As I followed her down the hall, I tried not to stare at a woman who dangled puppet-like over the back of a sofa in the hallway, her eyes following our feet as we passed by, or a small, brown, wrinkled man who wore two cardboard boxes on his feet like skates and chased behind us all the while yelling, "Double Lutz...watch me do a double lutz!"

When we finally arrived at Natalie's room, Linda Mankowitz stuck her head in the door and said, "Natalie, your sister's here." Then she turned to me and said, "When you're ready to leave, just tell the nurse at the mid station over there and she'll get someone to take you back down."

"Thank you," I said.

"You're welcome. Good luck."

I watched her walk briskly back down the hall, capturing Mr. Cardboard by the arm and propelling him back down the hall with her. I took a deep breath and walked into Natalie's room.

Natalie sat in a chair by the window. Pieces of loose hair that had escaped from her chignon floated around her heart-shaped face, like dust motes in the afternoon sun, descending and ascending on the whim of a sudden draft. She stared out the window at a deserted tennis court, keeping her hands folded and uncharacteristically still in her lap. She hummed under her breath.

"Nat?"

Natalie didn't answer.

"Nat? It's me, Sara."

Natalie's hum got louder, but it wasn't a tune I recognized.

"Nat? Can you hear me?" I jumped as a woman screamed from some-where down the hall. Natalie didn't move.

"Natalie?"

Natalie hummed even louder, but I still couldn't recognize the tune. I looked around her room. There was a single bed in the middle of the room, which had been made up with stiff white hospital sheets. A scarred wooden desk sat in one corner of her room, and an even older pine wardrobe sat in the other corner. I could have been inside any room at the Holiday Inn, except I didn't think any motel chain would ever paint any of their rooms baby-booty pink. Natalie sat in an oversized black vinyl recliner. I dragged over the chair from the desk and tried to talk with my sister.

"Nat? Do you like Dr. Sullivan? Lettie and Oscar said he's the best. I did as you asked. I didn't tell anyone. Actually, I couldn't tell Barbara because you-know-who is missing in action again. I wonder who he's run off with this time? I guess it doesn't really matter anymore. He always comes back and she always forgives him. Barbara's been on the edge since she found out the baby's grades aren't good enough for him to get into Princeton. I can't believe we still call Richard "the baby," can you? And didn't we just go through this two years ago with Randall Jr.? I mean, with all the money Frances Lymington shelled out for private school, you'd think those kids could get into the college of their mother's choice. But then they obviously inherited Randall's brains. If they were as academically smart as Barbara, we wouldn't be having this conversa-tion. Anyway, I expect Frances Lymington will have to get out her cauldron, boil some toads and spiders, and cast a spell on someone at Princeton so that the baby, I mean, Richard, can wear that ugly sweater with the big "P" on it in September. Mother and Father are in San Francisco at a conference. Barbara says they're having a wonderful time. You have to hand it to the Episcopalians; they pick the best places for their conferences. Remember the one they went to last year? Well, maybe you don't. It was held in Hawaii. Can you imagine? Father and Mother came back dancing the hula and singing all those awful Don Ho songs. But then you've been to Hawaii so you already know how wonderful it is." I paused and took a breath. "Father's a whirlwind these days. I hardly see him. And Mother, well you can guess what her life is like now that he's bishop. She's beside herself. They moved into the old McMartin estate in Homeland right down the street from Barbara. But then I guess she wrote you about that. At first Father didn't want to move, but Mother finally convinced him that the Diocese needed the old rectory for a new priest. She said the Diocese had offered him this new house and it would be an insult not to accept it. I'm not so sure about that. We both know how Mother is. Father had a time convincing Malqueen to come with them. The only way Father could get her to move was if he moved all her old stuff over to the new house. Mother was furious. She was ready to donate all the old kitchen stuff, especially the table I used to hide under, to Goodwill. But you know Father. He won and Malqueen moved with them...although I'm not sure how long Malqueen will stay. Malqueen stops by to see me every week. I can't tell if it's me she wants to see or if it's Lightning. You remember Lightning don't you? He's my landlord and he owns the bar that I took you to that time you snuck into town...the one with the parrot? Anyway, Malqueen and Lightning have a great time together. I paint and those two talk for hours about what the Inner Harbor was like thirty years ago. Malqueen brings me apple pies, which Lightning eats, and Lightning brings me homemade sausage, which Malqueen eats. I'm lucky if I get to smell the stuff before it disappears. I am a little worried about Malqueen, although I'm sure you don't care...no love lost between the two of you. She seems out of sorts...said she doesn't have enough to do in the new "hoity-toity" rectory." I paused again to see if I was getting any reaction from Natalie. I wasn't, but the woman down the hall let out another blood-curdling scream, and I decided it was better to just keep talking. "Lettie's pregnant again. This will be number three. Lettie's father loves to tease her about it too. He says, 'Lettie, how come an intelligent doctor like you hasn't figured out how to prevent that yet?' I think Oscar and Lettie want five children. I just can't imagine. Oscar's mother thinks they're both crazy. Oscar was an only child too, and his mother can't understand why two only children who had 'perfect' childhoods would want to have more than one child. She's always asking Lettie why she wants to 'spoil a good recipe.' Oscar hides in his study or runs to the hospital when she comes to visit. Lettie refers to her mother-in-law as the Beast from Philadelphia. And John Wittridge leaves town and goes to his summer home in Hilton Head and plays golf until she leaves. Did you did know that Oscar, Lettie, and her father all live together? I admit, it's an unusual setup. Can you imagine our family doing that? No, neither can I. But right after Oscar and Lettie got married, John Wittridge built a wing onto the old Wittridge estate for himself. He turned over the main house to Lettie and Oscar. He keeps threatening to move to one of those posh retirement communities, where he says, 'I can get some peace and quiet and play golf every day.' But then Lettie reminds him that he plays golf everyday anyway. He'll never leave. I don't think Oscar would ever let him. He adores his father-in-law." Natalie had stopped humming.

"Nat?" I said, leaning forward. "Are you listening?" Natalie tilted her head and resumed her strange chant. I reached in my purse and pulled out the check I had just received from the mayor. "Nat, look at this," I said, waving it in front of her face. "Do you believe people pay me this kind of money just for a picture? Remember back when I was little and you came into my room and told me I had talent? I didn't believe it then…took a long time for me to believe that I did have some talent…took me getting out of the house and living on my own to see what I could do. But you knew even back then." I paused and looked into Natalie's face. "How did you know? What did you see back then?" Natalie stared right through me, and I finally looked down at the check. "Who knew people would throw money at me if I painted their picture?" I laughed. "Anyway, my latest commission was to paint the mayor's daughter, who is a real sweet kid but has these horrible buck teeth that look just like those wax teeth we used to buy at the candy store…you know the ones we wore on Halloween to scare people? Well, I couldn't figure out how to paint her without making her look like Bucky Beaver, when all the sudden I got this great idea, which was to paint braces on her teeth. That way I could straighten those teeth up a little and make her look like the sweet kid she really is. Well, it worked and the mayor's family loved it, and now I'm sitting here waving this big old fat check in front of your face…" I talked for another hour before a nurse came in and told me visiting hours were over.

"Natalie?" I said, leaning over and kissing her on the cheek, "I have to go but I'll be back tomorrow." Natalie had not moved a muscle the entire time I had been there. I stared at her for a few minutes more and said, "Au revoir, ma grande soeur." Then I picked up my coat and walked slowly toward the door. I turned for one last look. Natalie had tilted her head in puzzlement as if she heard something in the distance that she couldn't quite recognize. Then she turned her head to the window and began to hum softly again.

Natalie began speaking again after two weeks, and I was hopeful she would get moved off the fourth floor soon. But, just when I was convinced that her hospital stay would remain a secret, I got caught.

I had just finished visiting Natalie when I literally ran into Barbara.

"Oh, I'm terribly sorry," I said, although I knew I had the right of way. Barbara had cut the corner too sharply.

"Oh, no. Excuse me. It's all my fault. Sara?" Barbara stood in front of me.

"Barbara?"

"What are you doing here?" Barbara asked, straightening her coat.

"What are you doing here?"

"I volunteer here. I'm working. What are you doing here?"

"Visiting someone."

"Oh? Who?"

"A friend."

"Which one?"

"One you don't know."

Barbara took a step closer and stared at me.

"You're hiding something."

"Am not," I said. "Listen, I'm late for an appointment. I'll talk to you later." I began walking toward the exit.

"I know that look," Barbara said behind me. "You're fibbing."

"I'm not fibbing. I'm late," I said. "And by the way, any news from Princeton?"

That stopped her in her tracks and allowed me to gain some distance.

"Frances is working on it," Barbara said. Then, seeing through my ploy, she ran after me and said, "Nice try. Who are you visiting?"

"I told you, no one you know." I headed out the door and ran for the car.

Two days passed before I got a chance to see Natalie again. I signed in and waited for someone to take me to the fourth floor. But instead of a nurse, the receptionist came over and told me Nat had been moved to the second floor and that I could go on up and see her. This was good news. The hospital was set up so that the sickest patients were on the highest floor. The fact that Natalie had been "moved down" meant that she was better. I hopped on the elevator and got off at two. When I got to the nurse's station, I asked for my sister.

"She's in 210," a white coat with glasses said.

I hurried down the hall and into 210 where I found my sister Natalie dressed and looking like a million bucks and my sister Barbara rearranging the room.

I must have stood there with my mouth open because Natalie finally said, "Trying to catch flies?"

"Wha?" was all I could get out as I stared at the two of them. Then I managed to add, "How did you find out?"

Natalie smiled and I saw her take out a lit cigarette from her dresser drawer. She took a puff, put it back in the drawer, and said, "Because you are the worst person in the world to keep a secret."

"I didn't tell," I said. "I swear. Barbara, tell Natalie I didn't tell you anything!"

Barbara was fluffing pillows and pushing the bed two inches to the left. She looked at Natalie and said, "You should have known better, Natalie. The girl's face says it all. She never could lie, even as a child. Remember the time she stole typing paper from Father's office? All he did was look at her and she ended up crying and confessing."

"But I didn't tell you anything," I insisted.

"Not directly. But by the look you gave me, I knew something big was up."

I turned to Natalie and repeated, "Nat, I didn't tell her."

Natalie reached in the drawer and took another drag from her cigarette. She had just managed to get it back into the drawer when a nurse appeared in the doorway.

"Excuse me, but is someone smoking in here?" she asked, looking at the three of us.

We all shook our heads no. The nurse sniffed the air, gave us a disapproving look, and then disappeared down the hallway. Natalie exhaled and said, "Don't blame yourself, kid. Barbara always was a know-it-all busybody."

"Well, excuse me for caring," Barbara said, moving the water pitcher to the other side of the bed. "I know we're not that close anymore, Natalie...but of all the people to call for help...Sara?"

"Wait a minute," I said, throwing my coat on the bed. "I did get her in here and into a program, didn't I?"

"What I heard," Barbara said, pushing the bed back to where it had been, "was that you got those Wittridge people involved in it and they got her into Pratt."

"Wittridge people? You mean Lettie and Oscar? Barbara, thank God they were there. I can't think of a better place to start than with a doctor and a psychiatrist."

"I think a good place to start is with your family, Sara. Did you even think to call me or Mother and Father?"

"Yes, I did," I said, allowing my voice to get a little too loud. "But Randall had just done his Houdini act, and you were arm wrestling with Frances Lymington about money for Princeton. And Father and Mother were in San Francisco at a conference."

Barbara and I had faced off on opposite sides of the hospital bed. Natalie watched us and took another drag from her hidden cigarette.

"Randall has not disappeared," Barbara said, smoothing the sheets. "He's on a business trip. And I do not arm-wrestle with Frances for money."

Natalie started to laugh and said, "Sure, Barbara, he's on a business trip all right...monkey business. And no, you don't fight Frances for money. You beg for it."

"I didn't come here to be insulted, Natalie. I came here to offer my help and to tell you I quite understand why you wanted to keep this quiet."

I looked at Barbara and tried to read her. But, unlike me, Barbara could hide her thoughts. I didn't know where she was going with this. Natalie did.

"So that's why you're here," she said, taking another drag from her cigarette and not bothering to put it back into the drawer. "You don't want anyone to know I'm in here either, do you?"

Barbara sighed and said, "Natalie, I want you to get help."

"I'm getting help," Nat said, looking at me. "Very good help. Sara's right. Oscar did find the best for me. Len Sullivan's a good doctor."

"That's all well and good. But don't you think you'd be better off in New York? After all, you live there. New York must have zillions of shrinks. You are going home eventually, aren't you? Wouldn't it have been better to get help there?"

Natalie just stared at Barbara who remade the corner of the bedsheet.

"I mean, if you need money, Natalie, I can help with your expenses; after all, I am you sister and—"

Natalie and I looked at each other and rolled our eyes. Barbara caught us and said, "I'm only thinking of Natalie's well-being, that's all."

"No, you're not," I said. "You want her out of Baltimore. Why?"

"Surely you can guess why, Sara," Natalie said. "Barbara doesn't want anyone she knows to find out that the Bishop's daughter is in the Whacko Ward. Right, Barbara?"

I looked at Barbara, who folded the blanket at the bottom of the bed into thirds.

"Sorry, Barbara. I can't go. I still have two more weeks to finish before I complete the program. And I have to complete the program if I want to keep my job. Trust me, as soon as I can, I'll go back to New York."

Barbara seemed relieved and said, "I'm not trying to get rid of you, Natalie. Mother and I have been trying to get you to visit us for more than ten years now. But no, you won't come home for a friendly visit." Barbara pulled the spread apart and refolded it. "You'd rather come home and have a nervous breakdown! I find that very telling."

"Barbara, I'm not trying to embarrass Father or Mother."

"Could have fooled me."

"Time out," I said. "How is Natalie trying to embarrass anyone? She tried to kill herself."

Natalie and Barbara looked at each other and then over at me. Finally, Natalie said, "Give it up, Barbara. I'm here for two more weeks and then I leave."

Barbara stopped her fidgeting with the bed and looked at her watch.

"Oh my goodness," she said, "I was supposed to be at a meeting twenty minutes ago. They'll be wondering what happened to me." She grabbed her coat, ran over and pecked both Natalie and me on the cheek, and then took off down the hall. I turned to Natalie and just said, "I'm sorry. I really did try."

"Don't worry about it, kid. It doesn't matter. It's not like I was admitted under a fake name. All she had to do was look at the admitting records." Natalie took another drag from her cigarette. "Besides, I'll be out of here in two weeks."

"Really? They'll let you out in two weeks? I mean, I know you've improved and all, but don't you need more therapy or something?"

Natalie took another drag and said, "All I have to do is complete a six-week program in order to get back to work."

"I know, Nat, but two weeks ago you weren't even talking, and they just moved you down here. I mean, I just think you might need more than six weeks."

"If I do, I'll see someone in New York. Barbara's right. New York is teeming with shrinks."

We heard footsteps coming down the hall and Natalie tossed her cigarette in the drawer just as a nurse stuck her head in the door and eyed us suspiciously.

"Smoking is not permitted inside the hospital. If you have to smoke," she said, looking at me, "go outside." Then she turned to Natalie and said, "And if you need to smoke, there's a room down the hall set aside for patients who smoke."

We watched her back disappear. I got up and put my coat on.

"I'm off," I said. "Do you need anything before I go?"

"Got any cigarettes?"

"You know I gave that up last year."

"Then lend me some money so I can buy some."

I forked over what I had in my wallet, which was twenty dollars.

"Aren't you generous."

"Nat! That's all I have on me. I can get some more tomorrow if you need more."

"Nah, there's nothing to buy in the nuthouse anyway, except cigarettes. Keep your thousand dollars in the bank, Miss Big-Shot Commission."

"Yeah, that's me all right...moneybags," I said, kissing her on the cheek and heading out the door.

It wasn't until I was in the elevator that I realized what Natalie had said to me. The check that I had waved in front of her face that day she had seemed catatonic had been the mayor's check for one thousand dollars. My sister had apparently heard me after all.

Nat was true to her word. The day she completed her six-week employee-mandated program, she left town. I took her to Penn Station and saw her off.

"Will you promise to call me when you get home?" I said.

"Yes, I'll call you as soon as I get to my apartment," Natalie reassured me. "Now, stop hanging onto me and let me get on the train." I kissed her good-bye and watched as she edged closer to the platform as her train pulled into the station. She waved before she disappeared inside the train. I walked along outside the train and followed her search for an empty seat. When she stopped so did I. When the train pulled out, I waved to her until the train rounded the curve and vanished from sight. Then I went back to my loft. While I waited for Natalie's call, I made myself some chicken noodle soup with a healthy dose of sherry poured in it to give it some zip. I felt a cold coming on, and I figured the sherry was medicinal. The phone rang too early, so I knew it wasn't Natalie.

"Is she gone?" Barbara asked.

"Yes," I said. "She should be in New York in about two hours."

"Good," Barbara said with a sigh of relief. "Now I don't have to worry about Mother and Father finding out."

"Would that have been so bad?" I said, slurping soup into the receiver.

"Of course! They would have gone to see her, and then everyone would have known who she was, and Father would have had to explain that she had tried to commit suicide, and, by the way, did she ever tell you why she tried to kill herself?"

"No, she didn't."

"Didn't you ask her?"

"Barbara, for the first two weeks she didn't talk."

"What about the four weeks after that?"

"The subject never came up."

"What do you mean the subject never came up? Didn't you bring it up?"

"No. Did you?

"Me? I came in on the end of this debacle. I only saw her a few times. I thought you'd find out everything."

"Well, I didn't."

"Sara," Barbara said, "sometimes I worry about you. Aren't you the least bit curious as why your sister swallowed a whole bottle of Valium?"

"Yes, I do wonder about that. But I just figured that if she wanted to tell me why she would."

"No clues at all? Did she mention a man?"

"Barbara, what is this? The Spanish Inquisition? I told you she didn't talk about it."

"Sara, you need to find out what sent her over the edge. What if she tries it again?"

I had thought about that, and I didn't like to be reminded of it.

"Barbara, she got the best Baltimore had to offer in the way of psychiatry. She promised me she'd continue her therapy in New York. I have to believe she's telling me the truth."

"Since when has Natalie ever told anyone the truth?" Barbara said as she banged down the phone in my ear. I hung up the receiver and went back to my soup and waited for Natalie to call me from New York. My phone didn't ring again until midnight.

"Hulllooooo...I'm hommmmme."

"Natalie? Where have you been? I've called your apartment twice!"

"Sorry. Made a pit stop at Eighty-Third and Second Avenue."

"Are you drunk?" I asked when I realized that my sister was slurring her words and hiccupping.

"Who me? Nah. Just had a little pick-me-up before I headed home."

"Natalie, you're drunk. Is Sherry there?" Sherry was Natalie's roommate.

"Sherry?"

There was silence on the other end of the line, and I was afraid that Natalie had passed out. But after a few minutes, I heard Natalie scream, "SHERRY!"

I heard the phone drop and then a sleepy voice said, "Hello? Is anyone there?"

"Thank God it's you, Sherry. This is Natalie's sister, Sara. Is she all right?"

"Aside from being drunk, I think she's fine. I've never met anyone who could drink the way she does and not have a hangover the next day."

"What exactly are you saying?"

"Uh...nothing. Just that your sister can hold her liquor."

"No you're not. You're saying she drinks too much. Sherry, how long has Natalie been drinking like this?"

"Look, Sara, Natalie has been drinking like this for as long as I've known her, which is...what? Ten years? But then what does that mean? Lots of people drink. Besides, her drinking never interfered with her work."

"Until six weeks ago," I said.

There was silence on the other end of the line. Finally, I said, "Listen, Sherry, I'm not blaming you for Natalie's problem. I'm just trying to understand it. Did something happen to upset her the night she swallowed those pills?"

"Sara, I swear to God until that night I had no idea that Natalie was unhappy or upset about anything."

"No boyfriend problems?" I asked, sounding too much like Barbara.

"Boyfriend problems? You've got to be kidding. She has to beat them off with a stick. She comes home from work with at least ten business cards every single trip. I tell her the only reason I room with her is to get her rejects."

"Well, that does sound like Natalie," I said and then asked, "Does she ever go out with any of them?"

"Sure. She goes out with them until they get serious, and then she dumps them. Your sister is quite the heartbreaker."

"Well, that sounds like Natalie too."

"Sara, listen I've got to go. I have a 5:00 a.m. sign-in tomorrow. I'd like to get Natalie in bed before my alarm goes off."

"Sorry. Thanks for your help. Tell Natalie I'll call her tomorrow."

"I will. Now stop worrying."

I hung up the phone and immediately began to worry.

Natalie called me at 9:00 a.m. the next morning.

"I hear I gave you a scare last night."

"A scare? I was a wreck wondering what had happened to you. You promised to call me the minute you got to your apartment. Natalie, it was midnight!"

"Well, I did call the minute I got to my apartment. It just took me longer to get there than I thought it would."

"Natalie, you were drunk. And according to Sherry, it's a condition you're all too familiar with."

"Oh, Sara, what does that idiot roommate of mine know anyway? She falls down after one glass of white wine. You should see the times I've had to drag her drunk butt home."

"Nat, I don't care about Sherry. I care about you. Now what's going on?"

"Nothing's going on. I'm back in New York. I'll be back to work in two days. And all's well that ends well."

"Has it ended, Natalie?"

"Has what ended?"

"It's just something Barbara said to me after you left, she said—"

"You listen to what she says? Our dear sister may be bright, but she doesn't have an original thought in her head I don't—"

"Natalie. She said you might try to do it again."

There was silence on the other end. I held my breath and waited.

"Sara, I did not plan to kill myself. It was an accident. In fact, even my esteemed shrink told me I wasn't trying to kill myself when I swallowed those pills and a half bottle of Smirnoff."

"What were you trying to do then?" I asked quietly.

"Trying to get attention? Asking for help? Trying to lose weight through the new pump-your-stomach diet program?"

"Natalie, be serious."

"I am," Natalie said. "I'm very serious. The last thing I wanted to do that night was kill myself."

I took a deep breath, and then I said, "Then why did you do it, Natalie?"

"That, my sister, is classified. Only my shrink knows for sure."

"What are you talking about? You don't know?"

"I know and Len Sullivan knows. But that's my business, and I don't care to discuss it with you."

I was a little put out by that, but then Natalie said, "Listen, don't think I don't appreciate what you've done because I do. I will always be grateful for your help. I just don't choose to talk about it. End of conversation." And with that she hung up.

Natalie stopped writing me letters after that. I would still get an occasional postcard from her, and I always got a card at Christmas, but nothing like before. No news of boyfriends or trips or work. Just a "Having a great time" or "You should see this place" scribbled on the back of the card. One Christmas I got a card with a picture of Natalie and Sherry sitting on what looked like saddles inside a bar with a huge stuffed bear standing beside them. The postcard was from Jackson Hole Wyoming and Natalie had written: "Merry Christmas from Jackson Hole. Just think, this could be the poor old bear who sniffed Mother's crotch at the Quaker prayer meeting."

I put all of her postcards on the refrigerator. I didn't know what I was supposed to do about Natalie. Go to New York, throw her in a taxi, and take her to a rehab facility? Or was I overreacting? Sherry had said Natalie had always been able to drink everybody under the table. But I knew that wasn't such a good thing, and I wondered if I put those postcards on the fridge because I felt so guilty. How do you help someone who doesn't want your help?

"Another missive from our errant sister?" Barbara said as she walked right for the refrigerator to read the postcard.

"Looks like a great place to spend Christmas," I said as I took the dishes from the dishwasher and put them away in the cupboard. "Look at all that snow."

"She should be spending her holidays with her family instead of in a bar with a bunch of strangers." I watched as Barbara picked up an apple and smelled it.

"She's not with strangers, Barbara. She's with Sherry. She's known her for years."

"Your friends are not the same as your family," Barbara said, taking a bite of the apple and staring at the picture.

"That's for sure," I said, backing out of the room. "You can at least choose your friends." I ducked and the apple hit the doorframe.

Chaper Ten

———————————— • ————————————

"We know what we are, but know
not what we may be."
                        Shakespeare

Malqueen lasted less than a year at the new rectory with Mother and Father. I'm not sure Father ever forgave me for my part in her decision to leave, but I do know that Mother was relieved when she finally left.

Malqueen complained constantly about her life at the NEW house. Every visit with Malqueen now began the same way.

"It an insane asylum…that place."

"The NEW house?" I'd say on cue as I tried to paint ears on a senator who must have had some genetic link to Dumbo.

"Course, I mean the NEW house," Malqueen would say as she carefully hung up her coat on a hook on the wall and headed for my kitchen.

"All day long strange people coming and going. Reverend shuttin' himself in the study with those high-up 'Piscopalian mucky-mucks. Reverend don't even have time to eat."

"Now, Malqueen, he must eat. What about dinner?"

"They don't eat at home no more. They got more dinner invitations than the Queen of England." Malqueen pulled out flour and sugar from my cupboards.

"What are you doing?" I asked.

"Bakin' a pie. I bake stuff at that NEW place, but nobody eats it 'ceptin' me. I've gone up two dress sizes!"

"Thanks. If you keep coming over here every week and baking me pies, I'll be going up two dress sizes too."

"You could use it. You're too skinny as it is."

I painted and listened to her bang pans around, and in the middle of it someone knocked on the front door.

"That's probably Lightning," I said. "I think he has radar as far as you're concerned." I went over and opened the door.

"Hi Lightning," I said as he walked in the door and looked around the corner for Malqueen. "She's in the kitchen."

"Who?" Lightning asked.

"You know who," I said. "And she's making a pie."

Lightning's eyes lit up. He handed me a bag and said, "Here's some fresh dogs."

"Thanks," I said, taking the bag and throwing them on the kitchen counter.

"Malqueen, your friend is here."

"What friend?" Malqueen said.

I rolled my eyes at her and went back to my painting.

"Is yoose makin' another one of them apple pies?" Lightning said as he rubbed his hands together and sat down on a stool in the kitchen.

Malqueen stuck her hand into the flour and threw a fistful into a bowl. Then she shook a little baking soda and some salt into the mix and stirred them around with her hand. "I got to do somethin'. Livin' in that NEW house with nothin' to do is drivin' me crazy...cookin' for people who don't eat," she said, slamming the bowl on the counter, "bakin' for people who forget it's there. Life's got to have more to offer than this."

Lightning watched her work and said, "Ever measure anything, Malqueen?"

"Never," she said, looking at him as if he had insulted her.

"I never did neither...kept it all up here," he said, tapping his forehead. "Want me to fry up the dogs for lunch? I brought some fresh sauerkraut too."

"Malqueen stopped her mad swirling and smiled. "Dogs and sauerkraut? Sounds mighty good to me. But I'll fry them up," she said, shaking her hands off and opening the brown paper bag I had thrown on the kitchen counter.

"Sara, you want a dog?" Malqueen asked.

"Do I have a choice?"

"Of course you do," she said as she pulled the dogs out. "To eat or not to eat."

The hot dog ritual was always followed by a discussion on how much Baltimore had changed over the last thirty years.

"Do you remember the old wharf, Malqueen?"

"I remember how it stunk is what I remember."

"How about Harrod Street and all the old department stores?"

"I remember the windows at Christmas and how pretty everything looked back then. Not that I could afford anything, but it was still nice to look at."

"How about the smell of them spices coming out of McCormick's? And that fancy tea room?"

"They didn't let black folks in there back then."

"Sure they did," Lightning said.

"Not in the late fifties," Malqueen argued. "Remember that was before 'The Riots.'"

I yelled from the other room, "Did you ever go there, Lightning?"

"No, but I used to pass by and look in the window."

"Why didn't you ever go in?" Malqueen asked as she opened the oven door and checked the pie.

Lightning held up his calloused bear paw hands and said, "Can you see these holdin' onto one of them teeny-weeny little teacups?"

"Ain't nothing wrong with them hands," Malqueen said, leaning in for a closer look. "They're workin' man's hands. You should be proud of 'em. Shows you got character."

"Yep, that's me. No class...but lots of character."

"Don't talk to me about class. Most of the people I see in that NEW house of the Reverend's are supposed to be loaded with it. But from my view they don't have any class at all. Can't believe how some of 'em act. Always pushin' and shovin' their way in the front door trying to get to the Bishop first. Dog eat dog. Never seen such a vicious crowd! They're worse than that bunch of barracudas that shows up for your Mama's Ladies Monthly Prayer Meetin'."

"Oh, Malqueen," I said. "That can't be possible. Those meetings are like shark fests."

"I used to think they were the nosiest, back-snabbingest, evilest bunch of women I ever saw in my life. But after seein' what goes on in the NEW house, I ain't so sure no more."

"If it's that bad why don't you look for another job?" I heard Lightning ask.

Malqueen's voice dropped so low I couldn't hear what she said to Lightning. I finally yelled from the other room, "Malqueen, that's a good idea. Why don't you find another job?"

Malqueen came storming out of the kitchen.

"Why you sayin' that?"

I put down my brush. I never did get a lot of painting done when Malqueen came to visit.

"I'm saying that because you're obviously unhappy."

Malqueen looked at the floor.

"But I been with the Bishop for more than thirty years."

"That's right. You've earned the right to do what you want to do now... You could even retire." I said this having no idea how old Malqueen was.

"Retire! I can't retire. I'm bored now and I have a job. I need more work."

Lightning had come out of the kitchen eating a doughnut. He looked at the two of us and through a mouthful of chocolate jimmies said, "I have a proposal."

We both turned to look at him.

"I think Malqueen should go into business for herself."

"Doing what?" I asked.

"That's what I'd like to know too," Malqueen said.

Lightning made us wait while he swallowed his doughnut.

"I was thinking about selling your pies."

Malqueen and I looked at each other.

"How?" I asked.

"Well, Malqueen has nothing to do at the NEW house. So why couldn't she bake up a whole bunch of pies every day...all kinds...apple, cherry, lemon meringue." I watched as Lightning's eyes rolled back in his head. "Then I could come and get them and distribute them to the various restaurants in the city. I still got plenty of connections in the food business, and I know restaurants are always lookin' for a good dessert. Besides, we know how good those pies are—"

"That's an interesting idea. But do you realize how much work that would entail for Malqueen? Not to mention the expense of setting up the business and—"

128

"I want to hear more," Malqueen interrupted. "How many pies we talkin' about?"

"Hundred?"

"A hundred!" Malqueen and I said in unison.

"Well, maybe we could start off with fifty and then if the business takes off increase our output—"

"You've thought this through, haven't you?" I asked him.

"I sorta know which restaurants would be interested."

Malqueen looked at me and said, "What do you think?"

"Well, if anybody knows how to make money, it's Lightning, and if anybody knows how to make pies, it's you. If you're willing to work yourself to the bone, then go for it."

"Work myself to the bone," Malqueen smiled. "I like the sound of that. When do we start?"

"When can you get me fifty pies?"

"Pick them up tomorrow," Malqueen said, putting on her coat and heading for the elevator.

"Well, gee, good-bye Malqueen," I said to the back of her head.

"Sorry about cutting our visit short, Sara," she said. "But I got pies to bake."

And bake she did. She had so much business that Lightning had to hire a driver to pick up and deliver the pies for Malqueen. The business started as Mrs. M's Pies and expanded into Mrs. M's Homemade Desserts. Malqueen was so busy I sometimes didn't see her for weeks at a time. But when I did see her, I noticed her eyes sparkled and she looked and acted like the old Malqueen. Everything ran smoothly for six months. Then I got a call from Mother.

"Sara? You have to talk to Malqueen."

"About what?"

"This so-called business she runs out of our kitchen."

"It's a legitimate business, Mother. She supplies some of the best restaurants in town."

"I don't care who she supplies. The delivery trucks block our driveway. Last week the bishop of Virginia came to see us and he had to park all the way down the block because of that truck."

"Mother, just exactly what do you want me to say to her?"

"Tell her to stop this nonsense. She's our cook, not Mrs. Pose." (Mrs. Pose was the queen of cheesecakes in Baltimore and had started her business in a similar fashion.)

"Why can't you tell her that?"

"You know how your Father is about Malqueen, Sara. He'd be most upset with me if I said anything to her."

"I'm sorry, Mother, but I won't do that."

"Sara, really!"

"I said no."

The next call I got was from Father.

"How could you do this?"

"Do what?"

"Instigate Malqueen's desertion."

"Excuse me? Desertion from where?"

"Don't act innocent with me. You know what I'm talking about."

"Father, I'm afraid I don't. What's wrong?"

I heard Father take a deep breath and then he said, "I didn't think you would encourage her to leave. It was probably your mother."

"Father, what are you talking about?"

"Malqueen gave her notice today."

I waited a few minutes before I said, "I'm sorry." And then I added, "But Father, you can't be surprised by this. You know how bored she was in that new house."

"Yes, but I never thought she'd leave me."

"I don't think she left you. She just didn't have enough to do anymore. You know how she is. She's not happy unless she's working all the time. Besides, she was never comfortable there. She missed the old place."

I waited a few seconds and then asked, "Did she say where she was going?"

"Apparently, Lightning...that traitor...found her a storefront near you."

"What! Where?"

"So, I knew something before you did! Well, I don't know for sure. I always get confused in that part of town. But I think it's a building he owns."

"That could be anywhere," I said. "He owns most of Fells Point." But, even as I said that, I had an idea where Lightning wanted Malqueen to move. He owned a building on Broadway, the street that ran through the tourist section of Fells Point. It would be the perfect place for a bakery, and it also had a large upstairs apartment.

"Father," I said. "Don't be upset. You'll still get to eat Malqueen's pies. You and Mother eat out more now than before you became bishop, so the chances of you eating a pie made by Malqueen are greater now than they were before she started her business."

"Somehow that doesn't make me feel better," he said. "I just feel like an important part of my life has ended."

"Well, it has. She was with you for over thirty years."

"I know," Father sighed again.

I waited on the other end of the line and finally he said, "I heard something while I was in the mayor's office yesterday that you might be interested in."

"Oh?" I waited for him to continue.

"Two words. Expansion team."

"You mean we might get football again in Baltimore?"

"It's not general knowledge, so keep a lid on it, OK?"

"Sure. Did he say when?"

"Well," Father continued as he whispered into the phone, "according to my source, it might be as soon as…" Father talked about a new expansion team for the next thirty minutes. Like most Baltimoreans, he had never gotten over the Colts packing up their equipment and moving out in the middle of the night. I listened and at the end of the football conversation he got back to Malqueen.

"I will miss her."

"Of course you will. But she needs to leave. Let her go."

"Better is a poor and wise child than an old and foolish king."

"I hardly think of you as old or foolish, Father."

"He who knows others is wise, but he who knows himself is enlightened. Good-bye, Sara." And with that, he hung up.

Chapter Eleven

—————————•—————————

"Love looks not with the eyes,
But with the mind, And therefore is
Winged Cupid painted blind."

Shakespeare

    I sat on a bench outside Malqueen's Bakery and watched the people as they strolled up and down Broadway. It was October in Baltimore, but it felt like the middle of July. Tourists passed me wearing shorts and sandals. Shopkeepers, trying to save money, had turned off their air conditioners and propped open their doors. I wondered when the first blast of Arctic air would hit us, turning us into weather junkies as we held our breath during the news and waited for the local weatherman to utter the dreaded "S" word.

    But thoughts of snow faded quickly as I tilted back my head and felt the sun warm my cheeks. I had run three miles along the waterfront, and I had ended up in front of Malqueen's store on Broadway, eating a bag of her chocolate chip cookies and trying to avoid Jac-kay, my neighbors three-legged dog.

    "Go home, Jac-Kay," I said to him. "You should be on a leash. You've already lost one leg. If you're not careful, you'll lose the other one. And then what will you do?" The dog looked up at me. "You think it's tough now with three legs? Wait until you only have two. They'll have to tie you to one of those carts with wheels and you'll have pull it around like the Pigeon Man." I nodded down the street, where a blind, legless man surrounded by pigeons begged on the corner of Broadway and Fleet Street. Jac-Kay looked down the street at the Pigeon Man and then back up at me. He barked and stood up on his one good back leg and turned around in a circle.

    "Looks like he's doing OK the way he is."

    I turned around and glanced briefly at the man who had made that comment. The sun was behind him, and I couldn't see his face, not that I wanted to anyway.

    "He should be on a leash," I said as I got up and walked away. Jac-Kay hopped on one leg alongside me.

"Sorry, I thought he was your dog," the voice said. "You're right. He should be on a leash."

I could hear heavy breathing behind me as I walked faster, and as soon as I got the chance, I abruptly turned into a used bookstore off Main Street. I hid behind the card display and waited for the strange man to walk by the store. He never did. Eventually I crept out of the store, checked to make sure "the breather" wasn't still hanging around, and walked back to my loft. That encounter is what Aubrey liked to refer to as our "first date."

The fact that I was still unmarried only bothered two people: Lettie and Barbara. Mother and Father didn't seem to care if I ever "settled down." And Malqueen said, "When the time's right, you'll find somebody. Best not to make any hasty decisions...Look at Barbara."

Lettie still fixed me up but with less enthusiasm and less frequency. Barbara tried to fix me up too. But she spent so much time trying to figure out what "type" of man I wanted to be with that I usually lost interest by the time a specimen was actually produced.

"Do you like tall men?" she would ask.

"Not necessarily," I answered, searching for jelly in her refrigerator.

"How about blonds?"

"Not especially,"

"Redheads?"

"Not that I can remember," I said, spreading peanut butter and jelly on two slices of bread.

"Schwarzenegger build? Or a Woody Allen type?"

"Neither, really."

"How about men in general?"

My sandwich stopped halfway to my mouth. "Barbara, what are you asking me?"

"I'm asking you if you even like men!"

"Of course I like men."

"But what type then?" Barbara said, throwing her hands up in the air.

"I don't have a type. I go on instinct," I said, chewing my sandwich as she put back the jelly and the peanut butter.

"Everybody has a type. You don't like blonds, redheads, muscles, brains, or height. What's left?"

I chewed for a while and finally said, "Dark-haired, short, average... musicians."

"I knew it," she said. "With you it always comes down to the music thing."

It did. I'd go out with the Roto-Rooter man if he could play the piano. But I usually didn't know that on the first date. Lettie always tried to find someone who had some musical ability. One of her best fix-ups was with an accountant she knew at Hopkins, who played the accordion at the VFW Hall in Locust Point, the Polish section of town. The date was rapidly going downhill when the accountant suddenly revealed that he had a gig later that evening. I went with him. He played and I polkaed and we had a glorious time. We dated for about four months until I couldn't stand his repeated efforts to get me to balance my checkbook. I'm one of those people who figures it's the bank's job to keep it straight. I always have a vague idea of how much money I have, but I don't feel the need to know exactly how much.

"How can you not want to know?" he would ask.

"I just don't," I said. "It's all so boring. As long as I can pay my bills I don't care."

Never ever tell an accountant you don't care about how much money you have because it makes them crazy. We parted amicably, and he became a good friend and eventually my taxman.

Barbara called me right after Mr. Accountant and I had called it quits.

"Sara? Don't forget the party is Saturday at 8:00 p.m. It's formal."

"What party?" My mind whirled with excuses.

"My Christmas party. The one I hold every year."

I had managed to miss this event for the last ten years. I hesitated too long and Barbara must have sensed my vulnerability because she said, "And I won't take no for an answer this year. You've weaseled out of my party for the last time. Be there or else."

The last place I wanted to go to Saturday night was Barbara's house. I wasn't in a jovial mood, and I didn't care for my sister's so-called "friends." When I look back, I can only assume that I went out of guilt. I certainly knew it wouldn't be fun.

I put on my one and only long evening dress, a black lace number I had found in the Nearly New Shop in Roland Park, ran my fingers through my hair, and arrived as late as I thought I could get away with. It wasn't late enough. I followed a pack of mink and cashmere coats up the front walk, who bad-mouthed Barbara and Randall until they got to the front door and rang the bell.

"Darling, Randall...how divine you look," squealed a mink.

"Randall, old pal...how's that golf game?" a cashmere asked.

Randall stood in the doorway, looking handsome in his black tux, despite his expanding waistline and his Mr. Weave toupee. He was the epitome of graciousness as he greeted guests and handed the coats off to a maid who had been hired for the night. Barbara had always had a hard time keeping help. It wasn't that she was nasty to them; it was just that she had a cleaning fetish. Her cleaning lady was no sooner out the door and she was recleaning the house. If her circle of friends knew how much time she spent with a dust rag in her hand they would have been appalled.

I realized I was alone with Randall in the hall.

"I can't believe you're here," Randall said, taking my coat. "Your sister will be ecstatic."

"Good, because I can't believe I'm here either."

"Come on. It won't be so bad. If I can survive them you can too."

"Yeah, but you get to run away every six months...The rest of us can't."

Randall looked down at his shoes and then shrugged. "I just don't know what gets into me sometimes. I really try to behave myself, but somehow I always manage to screw up."

"No kidding. You're lucky she always forgives you."

"Don't I know it," he said. "Let's get you a glass of wine, and then we'll find Barbara and let her know you're here.

I noticed that Randall's toupee was slightly askew as we walked into the living room, and I hit him in the side and motioned to his head. As he righted his rug, I wondered why Barbara didn't tell him he looked better bald. Then it dawned on me that maybe this was one of the ways that Barbara got her revenge for Randall's infidelity.

Randall smiled over at me as he escorted me into the room. It must have been the toupee because I suddenly felt a little sorry for him. I smiled back. He was a cad, but he was a grateful cad. And in spite of all his philandering, I knew he still loved my sister.

I made small talk with people I didn't know until I couldn't stand it anymore. Then I swiped a bottle of chardonnay from the bar and snuck off to the library where I pulled a book off the shelf and settled in to read. I had only been there a few minutes when the door opened and a tuxedo backed into the room.

The tuxedo was deeply tanned, and when he realized I was in the room, he said, "Excuse me. I didn't think anyone would be in here." He turned around and started to leave, but before he could get out the door, I said, "Trying to hide too?"

He turned around to face me and smiled. "Was it that obvious?"

"People having a great time at a party don't usually end up hiding in the library." I snapped my book shut and stood up. "Hello," I said, extending my hand. "I don't believe we've met. My name's Sara Gorman."

He smiled again and this time I noticed dimples and fine lines around pale blue eyes.

"Aubrey Landers Struttgard the third," he said, taking my hand.

"You're kidding."

"No, I'm not."

"That's a terribly long name. What did you do in grade school?"

"Oh, when I was little everybody just called me Augie."

"That's worse. Sounds like a dog. You might want to talk to your parents about that."

"I can't," he said, his blue eyes darkening to navy. "They died in a car crash when I was a junior in college."

"I'm terribly sorry," I said. There was an awkward silence broken by laughter outside the library door. "Well, at least someone's having a good time," I said.

Aubrey crossed his arms.

"You don't remember me, do you?"

I took a closer look at his black hair, tanned olive skin, and chiseled features and decided most women would find him very handsome.

"Sorry…I don't. Have we met before?"

"Well, I'm afraid you took me for a masher."

"Now, there's a word you don't hear anymore."

"Stalker then."

"I give up. When did you stalk me?"

"Fells Point...two months ago. You were with a funny-looking three-legged dog."

"You were the heavy breather who followed me down the street?"

"Actually, I wasn't following you. I was on my way to my apartment. And if you had even bothered to look at me, you would have seen that I was carrying two ten-pound bags of sand."

"Oh...well...sorry about that. But I try not to look at strangers on the street. I only talk to the panhandlers and stalkers I know."

He laughed at that and looked down at the book I had been reading.

"*Portraits of the Twentieth Century?*" he said, picking it up and flipping through it. "Interested in art?"

"You could say that," I said and took a swig of wine.

"I just came back from the Caribbean. I'm afraid I'm a little culture starved.

"That explains the tan. What were you doing down there?"

"I own...owned a forty-foot sailboat. I sailed a lot of rich people around the islands."

"Nice job. What happened?"

"The boat sank," he said as he put the book down and wandered over to the window. "The main mast cracked in half during a squall." I listened to him tell me about the boat, and I found myself wondering how old he was. He looked about fortyish; his hair had silver streaks in it and his face was deeply lined. But then the silver could have been premature gray, and the lines could have been from the sun.

"...Anyway, that's what happened. How's your sister?"

"Which one?"

"Natalie."

"Wait a minute. You know Natalie?"

"You don't remember that either, do you?"

"I'm beginning to feel like an amnesia victim. How do you know Natalie?"

"I took her out once."

I choked and wine spurted out of my nose.

"Are you all right?" he said, coming over to me.

"I'm fine," I said, holding up my hand. "I'm still trying to digest the fact that you dated my sister."

"Actually, I didn't date her. I took her out once. We went to a Helman mixer."

"You went to Helman Prep? You're from Baltimore?"

"Of course. You didn't recognize the name Struttgard? As in appliances?"

"Your father is the appliance wizard?"

"Oh, God no. Father's probably rolling over in his grave every time those commercials air. The appliance wizard is the guy who bought the business from us after my parents died. Unfortunate that he was allowed to keep the name what with that getup he wears in those ads."

I could see his point. The appliance wizard sponsored the six o'clock local news. At six fifteen he would leap onto our screens, wearing a traffic cone wrapped in aluminum foil on his head and sporting an oversized purple chenille bathrobe. In his demented Merlin costume, he'd chant "hocus-pocus" over his washing machines and a shirt with $250 printed on (obviously attached to wires) would jerk upward out of the washer and dangle in the air next to the appliance wizard. Then he would tap the shirt with his special magic wand, which was also heavily encased in Reynolds Wrap, and the shirt would spin around to reveal the reduced price of $175 printed on it.

I looked at Aubrey and said, "Yes, it is unfortunate you let him keep the Struttgard name."

"Well, at the time all my brother and I wanted to do was sell the business. I'm afraid we took the first offer...and we didn't read the fine print."

The library door suddenly flew open. We jumped and Barbara burst in.

"There you are, Sara. I've been looking all over for you. I wanted to introduce you to Aubrey, but I see you two have already met." Barbara's eyes darted back and forth between us. "But now that you've met," she said, taking Aubrey's arm, "you've got to circulate. Sara, Frances has been looking for you. And Aubrey, Langley Holmes, you remember him, he's the CEO of Holmes Investments, wants to talk to you." Aubrey looked helplessly back at me and shrugged as she whisked him out of the library. I smiled at him, and as soon as they had both disappeared, I retrieved my coat from the maid and snuck out the back door. The last person I wanted to socialize with was Frances Lymington.

The next day Barbara called and let me have it.

"You snuck out."

"I was tired."

"No, you weren't. I had to tell Frances you were ill."

"Well, at least you didn't have to lie. The thought of talking to Frances does make me ill."

"Sara, really. Frances is Randall's aunt. She been very good to us, and she donates a lot of money to Mother's causes."

"I don't care how much money she donates or whose aunt she is. The woman is a bigot and a bore."

"She's just old-fashioned and set in her ways. You should be more tolerant of older people, Sara."

I knew I could never win this argument. Barbara owed Frances big time and would always defend her. I held the phone away from my ear and listened to "Blah, blah, Frances this, blah, blah, Frances that." When I finally put the receiver back to my ear, it took me a few minutes to realize that Barbara wasn't talking about Frances anymore.

"Well, what did you think?"

"Of what?"

"Aubrey."

"I think his name is too long...and I think he was bored."

"Come on, Sara. He's gorgeous, he's a stockbroker, and he comes from one of the oldest and richest families in Baltimore."

"A stockbroker? He told me he owned a sunken sailboat."

"Oh that. Well, apparently he came back to look for a job. I hooked him up with Larry Holmes."

"Good for you."

"He's perfect for you."

"Barbara, I don't even know him."

"You will. I bet he calls you tonight."

"You didn't."

"Didn't what?"

"Give him my number?"

"Well, maybe I suggested that you weren't dating anyone at the moment."

"Barbara, he's not my type. He's too good-looking, too preppy, and he's a stockbroker."

"I thought you didn't have a type."

"I don't, but he really doesn't do anything for me."

"What do you want him to do? Sara, just give him a chance. For once in your life go out with a man who doesn't wear an earring and have orange hair."

I sighed. "We'll see, Barbara. But who's to say he'll even call? I may not have done anything for him either."

"He plays the guitar."

"Folk or classical?"

"Folk."

"Hmmm…well, maybe. But, I don't know, Barbara. He may already have a girlfriend."

"No girlfriend. I asked around. And I happen to know he was absolutely intrigued, Sara. I'm good at these things. I could see he was very interested."

But Aubrey obviously wasn't interested enough because he never called me. I could tell Barbara was puzzled by this. But after a while she stopped asking me if I'd heard from him. A month passed, and I went about my business as usual. I painted and hung out at the Blue Parrot.

"Hey bird," I yelled to the parrot as I headed to the bar.

"ARTBABE," the bird squawked.

"Hey, Lightning. Hiya, Iron Man…Bud please." I settled on the stool next to Lightning.

"Where you been?" Lightning asked, clinking his glass to mine.

"Painting a portrait of the wife of the CEO of Benton Electronics."

"What's wrong with her?"

"Squinty eyes…and her hair's a mess. Too stiff-looking. Has it all teased up in an old beehive do."

"That ain't been in for years," Lightning said.

"Wait a minute," Iron Man the bartender broke in. "My wife's had that hairdo since we started dating back in '61. Says it's convenient. Don't have to wash it but once a week. She wraps it in toilet paper at night. Says it holds its shape real good."

"I'll have to remember that, Iron Man," I said, looking over at Lightning and winking. "I'm trying to think up an excuse to get her to wear a hat but—"

We were interrupted by a blast of cold air as the door opened and Aubrey came in. He didn't notice me, so I continued to talk to Lightning.

"Jack and water, please." He threw down some bills on the bar and then looked over at the door. He was halfway through his bourbon when he recognized me.

"Sara?"

"Hi," I said and then introduced him to Lightning. "Lightning this is Aubrey Landers Struttgard the third."

"No kidding!" Lightning turned around to look at him. "You the wizard's son?"

"I just bought a washer from that wizard man," Iron Man added. "Best deal we ever got."

"Sorry to disappoint you. But no...my father owned the business before the wizard took over."

Lightning and Iron Man looked disappointed. Aubrey picked up his drink and came over and sat next to me.

"I owe you an apology," he said.

"For what?" I signaled Iron Man for another beer.

"I told your sister I'd call you, and I didn't." Then he hurried to add," It wasn't that I didn't want to call you; it was just that something came up."

I couldn't resist. "And what came up?"

"I got fired."

"Oh," was all I could think to say. I watched as Lightning got up and moved to the other side of the bar where two of his cronies were arguing about the latest football pool.

"Yeah, that's sort of what I said too." Aubrey took another slug of bourbon and again looked at the door.

"Waiting for someone?" I asked.

"Yeah, an old friend of mine. We went to Helman together. Haven't seen him in years."

"So, now that your boat is gone and you just got fired, do you have any idea what you're going to do?"

"I'm thinking of starting my own business. Being a stockbroker was never my thing anyway. My father was the one who wanted me to get a degree in business. He thought I'd make a great stockbroker. Unfortunately, I never did." He waved to Iron Man for another drink.

"What kind of business?"

"Rehabbing."

"You can use a hammer?"

Aubrey laughed. "And a saw and even a screwdriver. I worked in construction for a while when I lived in Mexico, and I helped restore some schools and churches down there. Nothing grand or detailed but enough to know what to do to a row house." I must have looked skeptical because he said, "What? You don't think I can renovate a house?"

"You just don't look the type. I mean, you don't look like a construction worker."

"Why not?"

"Because you're too pretty," I said, getting up to leave. I laid a five on the bar and waved to Lightning.

"Where're you going?" Aubrey asked.

"I have work to do," I said. "Besides, you're meeting someone anyway."

"Why don't you join us? You probably know him," Aubrey said, sipping his bourbon. "Tom Bennet?"

I stopped and turned around. "Tom Bennet as in Reverend Tom Bennet?"

"The one and only."

Tom Bennet was a well-liked and respected Episcopal priest who was now rector of St. David's over in Waverly, a working-class section of the city. He had been a protégé of Father's, and I had known him for years. With that the door opened and Tom walked in. He spotted Aubrey and his face lit up.

"I can't believe you came back," he said, hugging Aubrey.

"Neither can I." Aubrey stepped away and grabbed Tom by the arm. "Tom, look who I discovered hanging out in bars...the Bishop's daughter."

Tom saw me for the first time and smiled.

"Sara! How are you? I haven't seen you in ages. How long has it been? Three years? Four years?"

"Don't ask." I said. "It was probably at a function I didn't want to attend.

"No, it wasn't," Tom said, shaking his finger at me. "I remember! It was at the art show at the Walters'. You were showing your portraits."

Aubrey looked at me and said, "Art show?"

Tom looked at the two of us and said, "You didn't know?"

"Know what?" Aubrey asked.

"This is Saralee, the famous portrait painter."

"Oh, stop. I'm hardly famous," I said, wishing I could hide behind the bar.

"She's famous all right,'" Lightning yelled from the other side of the bar. "She paints Baltimore's rich and famous."

"She even painted the boss here," Iron Man said, pointing to Lightning's picture on the wall. "And, of course, the bird."

Aubrey's eyes went from Lightning's picture to the parrot's as the bird screeched, "I'M HOT!"

Aubrey was looking impressed, and I was getting embarrassed. I decided now was a good time to leave.

"Don't pay any attention to him," I said, edging toward the door. "It was nice seeing you again, Tom…Aubrey." Aubrey continued to stare at me as I worked my way to the front door. Tom walked over to the bar and ordered a drink. When he got to the bar, the parrot began to squawk and jump up and down.

"What's with him today?" Tom asked Lightning.

"I dunno. Hey, blue boy, whatsa matter?"

The parrot looked at Tom and screamed, "PRETTY BOY."

"I'd like to know why I'm Pretty Boy," Tom said to Iron Man. "I mean, if anybody is pretty, it's this one over here." Tom waved a thumb at Aubrey.

I opened the door and said, "He's right. Hey, Bird, I said, pointing to Aubrey. "Here's your PRETTY BOY." The parrot began sliding back and forth on his perch and bobbing up and down. Then he leaned forward, placed his beak between the bars, turned his head toward Aubrey, and said, "UH-OH."

After my encounter with Aubrey at the Blue Parrot, I began to run into him more and more.

"You sure do like those cookies," he said to me as I stood in front of him in line at Malqueen's store.

"I grew up on these cookies," I said, turning around. "How's the rehab business?"

"Good. Had to trade in my car and buy a pickup." He leaned over and looked in the case.

"The apple pie is the best," I said, pointing to the pie on the left. "Then the cherry, then the lemon. What kind of car did you have?"

"Porsche. I like cherry better than apple."

"Then get the cherry."

"Stop tellin' him what to get," Malqueen interrupted as she came out from the back room. "Let him figure out what he likes himself."

"You traded in a Porsche? Must be some pickup."

"I got a used Ford. The Porsche was old."

"I handed the cashier two dollars, which Malqueen tried to give back to me. I shooed her away and waited for Aubrey to order. He ordered the apple, and when he was finished, he tried to pay the girl at the register. Malqueen stopped him.

"That's OK...The pie's on the house."

Aubrey looked up in surprise. "Well, gee, thanks, but I can pay."

"I know," Malqueen said. "Take the money and buy Sara a beer at the Parrot. I like the way you two talk to each other." Malqueen disappeared into the back of the store.

"Now what was that all about?" I asked, looking at Aubrey.

"I don't know. But it's a good idea. Let's get a drink."

We walked slowly down the street, and Aubrey told me he had decided he needed some experience before he went into business for himself.

"I'm hiring myself out to different contractors in the area," he said, sticking his hand in my cookie bag. "That way they get to know my work and I get to work some houses."

"Just what is your work?"

"I can do everything...drywall, floors, painting, electricity. But I really like to do custom trim work...you know, moldings, chair rails, even cabinets.

"What about plumbing?"

"I've done some plumbing."

"I should hire you to fix my sink. Nothing will unclog it, and I'm afraid to tell Lightning."

"What did you put down there?"

"I'm not sure. I may have let a rag slip through. All I know is I can't get the drain to clear."

"Want me to take a look?"

"Sure, "I said, watching him munch on my cookies. "Whenever you get a chance."

"I'm not busy now."

"You sure?" I was trying to remember how I had left the loft this morning.

"I can be bribed with a beer."

I decided the loft was presentable and said, "Deal."

Aubrey didn't say a word as I led him through the yellow-tiled foyer and into the caged elevator. When we got to the third floor, he stood with his mouth open.

"This is all yours?"

"Great, isn't it?" I threw my keys on the table and Aubrey followed me in.

"Is there anybody else in this building?"

"Just Lightning. He lives on the second floor. The first floor is a garage, but you can't see it from the way we came in. Lightning rents out space down there and we both use it for storage. Aubrey put his pie down and I went into the kitchen to get him a beer. He followed behind me still looking around.

"The light is incredible. What a fabulous place to paint."

"I can't imagine working anywhere else," I said, handing him his beer. I led him over to my living room, which consisted of Barbara's old black leather sofa, two red-and-white-flowered chintz overstuffed chairs Mother was going to donate to Goodwill, and two black plexiglass cubes I had found at Rich People's Rejects, a consignment shop down the street.

"Nice floors," he said, looking down at oak hardwood. "And nice rug too."

"The floors came with the apartment. This used to be a sewing factory back in the thirties. The rug was a gift from my sister Barbara," I said, flopping down in a chair, "who changes the color scheme of her house every two years."

"The red looks great in here against the black leather." Aubrey looked across the room at my bedroom.

If there was anything I didn't like about the loft it was the fact that my bedroom was open to display. I had taken some plywood and made a privacy screen, which I then placed at the end of my bed. I had painted a jungle scene on one side and a wildflower garden on the other. There wasn't much else I could do about it because I didn't want to cut up the loft by enclosing my bed. My studio was on the other side of the bedroom and took up most of the loft. Aubrey looked in that direction next.

"What are you working on?"

"Picture of the wife of the CEO of Benton Electronics."

"Doris Benton?"

"Don't tell me. You took her to a Helman mixer."

"Actually I did...when her name was Doris Van Cleavington."

"Is there anyone you didn't take to a Helman mixer?"

Aubrey sipped his beer and laughed. "There were quite a few I wished I hadn't."

Aubrey got up and walked over to the studio. He stood in front of the portrait.

"Mind if I look?" he asked.

"Not at all," I said, taking a sip of beer.

He lifted the cover and stepped back. He didn't say anything at first. Then he looked over at me and said, "How do you do that?"

"Do what?"

"Make her look like herself, only better."

I stood up and walked over to the portrait.

"I got her to wear a hat. Actually, it was either that or a wig. Talk about outdated hair. Did she have that beehive when you took her to the dance?"

"Yep. Try running your fingers through that—not that I wanted to." Aubrey made a face and we both laughed. Then he turned to me and said, "What you've done with her is brilliant." He stood back and shook his head.

147

"I can't take all the credit because she actually came up with the idea. I got her to talk about her ancestors one day and she told me her family was originally from Savannah, Georgia. She showed me pictures of her maternal grandmother when she was a debutante, and I said, 'Wouldn't that be a great dress to wear in the painting?' never thinking that it still existed. Well, Doris had the dress and was thrilled at the idea of wearing her grandmother's ball gown. From there it was easy. Her grandmother was wearing a hat in the picture, and I just commented that the dress wouldn't look as good without that hat."

"Clever."

"No, lucky."

"Are you always so lucky when you paint?"

"No," I said, walking away from the painting. "Just last week I had to turn down a big job because I knew there was no way I could make the person look good."

"Anybody I know?" Aubrey asked, following me back to the sofa.

"I feel sorry for you if you do…Frances Lymington."

"Yikes! You turned down Frances Lymington? How on earth did you get out of that?"

"It wasn't easy. I had to plead too busy. Barbara gets so angry at me, but I know I just won't be able to find a way to make her look charitable."

"She wants to look charitable?"

"Yep. She wants her portrait to hang in city hall with a gold plaque underneath that says, 'Frances Lymington – Philanthropist.'"

"Oh my God," Aubrey groaned.

"Exactly."

I settled back on the sofa. Aubrey continued to walk around the loft.

"So, is this the drain?" He leaned over a utility tub that sat out in the open at the back of the studio.

"Yes, that's the one."

"Well, it doesn't look too bad," he said. "Got a plunger?"

"Under the cabinet. The one next to the sink. But I tried that and it didn't work."

Aubrey rolled up his sleeves and leaned on the plunger. I heard a gurgle, a rush of air, and then the swirl of water as it ran down the drain. Aubrey put the plunger back and smiled.

"Oh, stop smirking. I probably loosened the muck when I tried the plunger before. That's why it was so easy."

Aubrey kept smiling as he walked past me and into the kitchen where he washed his hands.

"What?" I said, getting up and following him into the kitchen. "You think I got you here on false pretenses?"

Aubrey dried his hands and looked at me. "False pretenses? Now what would those pretenses be?"

"You know what I mean."

"No, I don't."

I watched him dry his hands on my tea towel, and then he began opening my cabinets.

"Looking for something?"

"Plates."

"For what?"

"Pie."

"You want pie? With beer?"

"Don't you?" He reached up and got down two plates and then rummaged around looking for silverware.

"Wait," I said. "Here." I handed him two forks. Then I got a large knife and cut two pieces of the apple pie.

"This better be good."

"Malqueen's pies are always good."

"Got any whipped cream?"

"I'm telling you, her pies are so good you don't whipped cream."

"I'll be the judge of that."

He opened the refrigerator and looked inside.

"Now let's see," he said. "Ah, yes, the essentials are here...milk, butter, beer, a jar of pickles...an unidentifiable moldy thing..." Aubrey reached in and tossed the green cheese into the trash, "And, voila...the item we've been searching for...a can of Redi Whip."

"I don't know how old that is."

"Is your refrigerator always this bare?"

"Well, I eat out a lot."

"Looks like every night. You probably can't cook either."

"Can too. It's just easier to eat out."

"Sure." Aubrey took out the Redi Whip and gave it a hard shake. He continued to smile at me as he positioned the can over the pie and squirted. Redi Whip exploded in his face, his hair, and even on the cabinets, the floor, and the table. Cursing, I ran for paper towels.

"I'm so sorry," I said. "I tried to tell you it's been in there for ages. I should have known it was clogged. Here, stand still. It's all in your hair."

Aubrey looked down at me as I tried to get it off his face and out of his hair. Then he said, "Hand me the can."

"What?"

"Hand me the can."

I hesitated and then handed him the can of whipped cream.

"He gave it another hard shake and then pointed it at me.

"Oh no you don't," I said, backing out of the room. "Aubrey, stop it! No!" I slipped on wet floor, and Aubrey blasted me in the face with whipped cream.

"You creep!"

"I'm a creep?" he said, aiming the nozzle in my direction again.

"No, you're not a creep." I covered my face. "I didn't mean that. Just stop...don't shoot. I tried to get up but slipped again. Aubrey reached down and pulled me up. My nose ended up in his chest. When I looked up, Aubrey was looking down. He took both hands and pulled my face up to his. We kissed. Then he leaned in again and sampled some of the whipped cream from the side of my neck.

"Is it bad?" I asked.

"No. It's pretty good. You should try some."

I laughed and took my finger and scooped some cream off his forehead and ate it.

"Not bad for old exploding whipped cream," I said, licking my finger.

I started to turn away, but Aubrey reached down and pulled me back. Holding both my hands he said, "No fair using your hands."

I looked down at my hands and up at Aubrey.

"Where would you like me to start?"

He took my right hand and pointed to a spot right below his ear. I ran my tongue down his neck and into the base of this throat and whispered, "Just your neck?"

He groaned and pulled me down on the floor. We kissed again, but I could feel him reaching around the floor for something.

"What are you looking for?"

"Just keep doing what you were doing," he said, rolling over on top of me. "While I look for the damn can."

"More whipped cream?" I said. "We'll probably both get sick...Do you know how old that stuff is? It must be two years old—"

"Shut up," Aubrey said as he unbuttoned my blouse. "Just concentrate on this." His tongue touched my skin and I gasped.

"Still worried about salmonella?" he asked as his tongue continued its journey south.

"...under the table," I mumbled. "Under the table."

"Kinky. You want to do it under the table?"

"The whipped cream is under the table, you idiot."

Aubrey laughed and we rolled under the table.

Chapter Twelve

—————————————— • ——————————————

"And now abideth faith, hope,
charity, these three;
But the greatest of these is charity."
Corinthians 13-9

Aubrey and I got married six months later. We wanted a small intimate wedding and ended up with a three-hundred-guest extravaganza. It was Father's last year as bishop, and Mother was determined to have "a wedding befitting his position."

"But it's my wedding. I don't even know these people," I said to her as I tried on wedding gowns.

"That looks lovely on you, doesn't it, Barbara?" Mother said as she pulled the train out and walked around me.

"That's it as far as I'm concerned," Barbara said, nodding to the saleswoman. "Sara, you have to have a big wedding. Father's position dictates it."

"Don't I have any say in my own wedding? I'm beginning to wish we had just eloped."

"Oh please. That sounds like something Natalie would do," Barbara said. "Miss, we'll take this one, but we need some alterations."

"Wait a minute. I haven't said I even liked this one."

Barbara, Mother, and the saleswoman stood back and waited while I looked at myself in the mirror. The dress was high-necked, long-sleeved, and champagne in color. The bodice was covered in hundreds of tiny pearls. The skirt tapered in sharply at the waist and then hung straight down. It was simple and sophisticated, and when I looked at myself in the mirror, I couldn't help but smile.

"Told you that was the one," Barbara said, nudging Mother.

"Let her make up her own mind," Mother said to Barbara.

"You don't think this train is too long?" I asked.

"Not if you're walking down the aisle of Redeemer," Barbara said.

I stepped down from the platform in front of the mirrors. "Actually, I'm not walking down the aisle of Redeemer."

"What!" Barbara said, looking at Mother.

Mother came over to me and pointed out to the seamstress what needed to be taken in. "That's right, she's not. Sara and Aubrey are being married in Tom Bennet's church."

"In Waverly?"

"Yes," I said. "In Waverly."

"But three hundred people can't fit in that church."

"How do you know? Have you been there?"

"Well, no, but really, Sara...Waverly?"

I saw the saleswoman raise her eyebrows at the seamstress.

"Barbara," Mother said. "Sara and Aubrey want to be married in their own church. Your father agrees. After all, Tom is performing the ceremony. Besides, I checked out the church, and it will hold three hundred people."

"You did?" I said, looking at her.

"Yes, I did."

"Well, if Father thinks it's all right," Barbara said, "then I guess it is. It's just such a blue-collar area."

"Barbara, Aubrey is a construction worker."

"Which is something else I don't understand. He had a perfectly respectable job as a stockbroker and—"

"Barbara?" Mother said sharply.

"Yes, Mother?"

"That's enough."

"Well, I'm only saying—"

"I know what you're saying, Barbara," Mother said as she motioned to the seamstress to take up a little more on the sleeve of my dress. "Your father and I are very proud of Aubrey. He overcame a great tragedy when his parents died. He sold his parents' business, went to college, and built a business in the Caribbean."

"It sunk."

"Yes, dear, we know that. But he came home, found Sara, and is now building another business. I have no doubt that he'll be very successful. He does have Sara to help him. Look at what she's done with her life."

Barbara's face turned red, and I suddenly felt sorry for her. I was used to being criticized; she wasn't.

"By the way," Mother said, breaking the silence, "has anyone heard from Natalie?"

"I did," I said. "She'll be in next week for her fitting."

"Where's she staying?" Barbara asked.

"With me."

"Figures. Probably spend all her time getting drunk at that bar down the street from you...the one with that awful parrot."

"Barbara!" Mother said, turning around to glare at her. "That's a terrible thing to say about your sister."

"Well, every time I call her she's looped. Sometimes she falls asleep in the middle of the conversation. Can you imagine?"

I could. I had fallen asleep one evening while Barbara rambled on about some silly party she had attended. I woke up when I dropped the phone.

"Natalie has a very physical job. She was probably tired that evening."

"Mother, she was drunk. I could tell by the way she slurred her words."

"Barbara, that's enough," Mother said as she pointed to a pearl that hung loosely from the bodice of my gown. "Why don't you go out and wait in the car."

Barbara was stunned. She opened her mouth, closed it, looked over at Mother, and when Mother wouldn't look at her, she grabbed her purse and walked quickly out of the store. I saw the saleswoman raise another eyebrow as the door to the shop banged shut behind Barbara. I turned to Mother, who appeared oblivious to what she had just done to Barbara.

"Don't you think you were a little hard on her?" I said.

"No, I do not," she said as she helped me out of the dress. "And I don't want to talk about it right now."

I got dressed and joined Mother and the saleswoman at the counter.

"I just don't understand why you can't give us a clergy discount," Mother said. "All the major retail stores in Maryland do."

"I'm sorry Mrs. Gorman. But the owner of this particular store doesn't offer discounts."

"Not even for the bishop?"

"No, ma'am. Not even for the bishop."

"Well, I've never heard of such a thing," Mother looked at me, paused, and then said, "What about a discount for a famous painter?"

"Mother!"

"And who would that be?" the saleswoman asked.

Mother leaned on the counter and pointed to me. "That's the famous portrait painter Saralee."

"Mother, can we just pay for the dress?" I said.

"I thought that since you paint such famous people, like senators, and socialites...and the mayor's daughter that—"

"Mother!" I said again as I whipped out my checkbook. "If you won't pay, then I will."

The saleswoman stopped what she was doing and came over to where I stood in front of the counter.

"Did you really paint Angelina D'ellensio's portrait?"

"Yes, I did," I said, filling in the date on the check. "How much do I owe?"

"And it was your idea to do that to her teeth?"

"You mean the braces?" I stopped writing and looked up. "Yes, it was."

Mother began leafing through a catalog on bridal veils.

The saleswoman held out her hand. "I'm very pleased to meet you, Miss Lee, or rather Miss Gorman. My name is Helen Vincenti; I'm Angelina's aunt. My sister married the mayor."

I shook the woman's hand. "How do you do. Your niece is a delightful young lady."

"Thank you. I think so too." She smiled at me and then said, "I'd like to repay the favor you did my niece and my sister. The dress is on me."

"Oh, no...I couldn't possibly...I mean, that's very nice of you," I said, shaking my head. "But I don't want you to get in trouble. I mean, since the owner doesn't give discounts."

The woman looked over at Mother, who still seemed engrossed in the veils, and then said, "I am the owner, and while I normally don't give discounts, in your case, I'd be honored."

"You're very kind," I said. "But I—"

Mother slapped the book shut, grabbed my arm, and pulled me toward the door. "Thank you very much, Mrs. Vincenti. You are most generous.

We appreciate your kind offer. Come, Sara. We still have lots to do." Mother pushed me toward the door.

"My pleasure, Mrs. Gorman. The dress will be ready for a final fitting in two weeks. See you then."

Mother gave me one final push out the door. When we got into the car, Barbara rolled down the window and said, "What were you doing in there?"

"Ask Mother," I said, getting in the backseat. Barbara looked over at Mother.

"I don't know why you're so upset, Sara. I just asked for a clergy discount."

Barbara started the car. "Is that all? She always asks for that discount. You wouldn't believe the number of stores that give them out. It's a great deal. We get them all the time."

"Barbara, there's no such thing as a clergy discount. The reason the stores give you a discount is probably because they feel they have to."

"We do not coerce shopkeepers, Sara."

"Oh really? Then how come Mother insisted on this particular Bridal Shop," I said, leaning over the front seat. "You knew who owned this store, didn't you?"

"I most certainly did not," Mother said. "I was just as surprised as you were."

"Baloney."

"Sara! I will not be talked to like that."

"I know you knew."

"Oh, Sara, so what if she knew? What's wrong with a discount? Nobody pays retail anymore." Barbara pulled out of the parking space and headed for home. I looked out the window and tried to think pleasant thoughts. I heard Barbara say to Mother, "Did they really give you a discount because Sara painted the mayor's daughter?"

Mother smiled and said, "Yes, they did."

"Wow, this could come in handy."

"You two seem to forget that the reason I chose to paint under the name of Saralee was to remain anonymous," I said, sitting forward again. "I don't want people to know who I am."

"Which is the most ridiculous reason in the world," Barbara said. "I mean, if you go to all the trouble of becoming famous, why not be famous under your own name? I just don't understand you sometimes, Sara."

"No, you wouldn't."

"And that awful name. Saralee? Everybody thinks you're Japanese."

"I like the idea that people don't know who I am."

"But Japanese? Where do you get these kooky ideas?"

"Barbara, that's enough," Mother said. "If your sister wants to remain anonymous, that's her business. However," Mother turned around to me, "while you might not appreciate trading on your name, Sara, you could at least think of all the money you're saving your father. Weddings aren't cheap."

I leaned forward and said, "I didn't want a huge wedding. You did."

Mother turned back around and got out her wedding list. "Have you decided on the flowers?"

"Yes," I said, falling back into Barbara's soft leather seats.

"And?"

"And what?"

"What have you decided on and where are you getting them?"

"Roses and gardenias in sprays at the end of every pew…two big bouquets on the altar…and vases with three roses in them on the tables in the church hall."

"Tasteful," Mother agreed. "From where?"

"Roland Park Florist."

"What!" Barbara almost ran off the road, and Mother turned around to stare at me.

"Did you have to pick the most expensive florist in the state?" Mother said.

"Don't worry. You don't have to pay for them."

"Oh? And why not?"

"The flowers are Lettie's and Oscar's wedding present."

"Wittridge money again!" Barbara said, slapped the steering wheel. "Will we ever get away from those people? Really, Sara you can't let them pay for your flowers. It's tacky."

Mother looked at Barbara and then back at me. "Actually, Barbara, I think that's a wonderful gift."

"You what?!" Barbara said.

"It's a very generous offer." Mother crossed off "flowers" from her list.

"But Mother, you can't—"

"Barbara, that's enough." Now pay attention to your driving before you hit that trash can."

Barbara looked up and swerved. But she still clipped the edge of the can. We watched as the lid flew off and rolled lazily down the street. Mother turned back to her list and subtracted an amount from a figure on the list she held in her hand. She smiled.

According to my estimate, my wedding cost my parents nothing. St. David's was so honored to have Father there that Tom Bennet refused to accept any kind of donation. My dress was free, compliments of the mayor's sister-in-law, and my flowers were paid for by "Wittridge money." Mother nixed the idea of a luncheon or sit-down dinner reception, saying, "That type of reception just gives certain people a license to get drunk." When I protested, she said, "Sara, a champagne-and-cake reception is more tasteful and appropriate for the daughter of the bishop."

It was also free. Malqueen's gift was the wedding cake, and Lightning's gift was the champagne. Aubrey and I looked at each other and shrugged. Neither of us wanted to tangle with Mother in her "remember-you're-the-bishop's-daughter" mode. So we agreed to her plans. In all fairness, it wasn't that bad. I was still in shock that my parents were happy I was marrying Aubrey, and Aubrey was still in shock that I would marry him.

"Are you sure?" he would ask me in the middle of Hollywood Squares."

"About what?"

"That you want to get married?"

"Getting cold feet?"

"No. I just need to know that you're sure."

"I'm sure, Aubrey. Are you?"

And Aubrey would look deep into my eyes and say, "I've never been so sure of anything in my life."

We got swept into Mother's plans, and for the first time in my life I enjoyed it. Mother did all the work, and I shook my head yes or no. To my surprise, we agreed more than we disagreed. Our conversations were either about Father, the center of both our worlds, or Barbara, who we both agreed "was much too materialistic and depended on Frances Lymington for too much." Sometimes, Mother would talk about Natalie.

"Why won't she visit, Sara?" Mother said as we drove to the bridal shop for my final fitting. "We tried to be good parents. She was always so difficult...as a baby...as a teenager...even as a young woman." Mother sighed. "She was so beautiful as a child. Your Father and I never quite got used to that."

"I don't think Natalie ever got used to it either. I mean, I don't think she believes she's worth all the attention she gets."

Mother turned around and stared at me.

"And she blames us for that?"

"I'm not sure who she blames or how she really feels. She doesn't confide in me."

Mother shook her head and said, "She will show up, won't she?"

"For my wedding? I hope so, although with Natalie you never can tell."

While I didn't say anything to Mother, Natalie had actually told me she wouldn't miss my wedding for the world. When I told her what Mother had planned, she had almost changed her mind.

"Champagne and cake?" Natalie said. "You've got to be kidding. Can't they spring for dinner and an open bar?"

"Mother says it's more tasteful if we just have champagne and cake."

"Tasteful? It's cheap. You and Aubrey agreed to that?"

"We did. But listen, Aubrey and I have decided that after the rehearsal dinner at Barbara's..."

Natalie groaned out loud.

"...that we'll all head out to the Parrot and do a little celebrating on our own."

"The Parrot?" Natalie said. "Count me in."

The first time I had introduced Natalie to the bar she had stayed until closing. She could talk to anybody about anything, including sailors on shore leave, who were usually reduced to speechlessness by her looks. Lightning loved her and told her, "Yoose adds class to the place." She thought Lightning was a piece of work and liked to make him laugh at her airline stories. Lightning would lean forward and listen in disbelief and say, "Natalie, I don't believe that. You mean people really go to the bathroom up there?" Lightning was afraid to fly. In fact, he was only in an airplane once in his life and he swore he'd never get on one again. His favorite mode of transportation was his Lincoln Town Car, or in special cases, Amtrak.

Besides the atmosphere of the bar, Lightning, and the sailors, Natalie liked the parrot.

"Hey, bird," she'd say when she walked in. "Remember me?"

And the parrot would squawk, "BLONDIE!"

Then Natalie would talk to the bird like he was her long-lost friend.

"So, how's it hanging, bird? Getting any? I bet it gets lonely in that cage. Seen any cute pigeons flying by?"

The parrot would cock its head to one side, jump up and down, and utter something that sounded like, "Heh, heh, heh."

It sounded exactly like the damn parrot was laughing.

"Sara," Mother interrupted my thoughts on Natalie. "Natalie will be there?"

I came back to the car and Mother and said, "Now that I think about it, she did say she wouldn't miss it for the world."

Mother smiled and settled back in the seat. I didn't mention the party at the Parrot or the fact that most of the wedding party might be hung over for the wedding.

Chapter Thirteen

---•---

"Happy is the bride the sunshines on."

Proverbs

It rained on my wedding day. It wasn't a fine mist or even a sporadic rainfall. It was an all-day torrential downpour. Lightning flashed and thunder boomed as the limousine pulled up to the front of the church and the wedding party refused to get out of the car. Tom finally sent out two ushers with umbrellas, and we were escorted into the church one at a time.

"Jesus Christ," Natalie said. "Look at my shoes."

"Natalie! Stop cursing in church," Barbara said. "Shit! Look at my hair!"

"I can't say 'Christ' but you can say 'shit'?"

"Oh, just shut up, Natalie."

Lettie and I looked at each other in the dressing room mirror and went back to trying to repair our own hair. We were lucky we had decided to wear our hair up. Barbara, on the other hand, had gone to one of those "hairdressers of the month" listed in *Baltimore Magazine,* and he had talked her into a style that was as complicated as it was unflattering. To make matters worse, the rain had made her hair frizz and her glamorous "do" now resembled Bozo the clown's wig.

Mother walked in looking perfect and chic in her pale blue silk shantung suit.

"Good heavens, Barbara," she said. "Do something with that hair."

Barbara bowed her head and looked like she was ready to cry. I went over and began brushing her hair back into a knot.

"Lettie, hand me one of the roses from my bouquet," I said.

Lettie handed me the rose and a sprig of baby's breath. We secured the back of Barbara's hair and strategically placed the flowers over the bobby pins. I stood back and Barbara smiled at her reflection. Natalie was still staring at her shoes.

"Natalie, no one will see your shoes," Mother said. "But put some lipstick on."

Natalie rummaged around in her purse and Mother looked at me. I waited for her to comment on my hair or my lips, but all she said before she walked out was, "Sara, you look exquisite."

Natalie pinked her lips and mimicked Mother's "exquisite" line in the mirror. Then she whispered, "Now's the time to call it all off. You can run out that door, and I'll be right behind you. We can hop a train to New York, and nobody will know for hours."

"Do I look like I want to run out that door?" I asked.

Natalie leaned over and whispered again. "He's one of my old rejects. What do you see in him anyway? He looks twenty years older than you."

"He's only ten years older, Natalie. And you only went out with him once...to a dance when you were sixteen. Besides, I happen to love him."

"Yeah, yeah, yeah. Well, let me know if you want to make a break for it."

Natalie smiled and winked at me and then said, "Hey, Red, how come I get to walk down the aisle with Baldy and you get the Wolfman?"

Lettie laughed and said, "Because Mrs. Gorman thought that Randall and Barbara should walk together. And since I'm the matron of honor I have to walk with the Wolfman...er...Aubrey's brother."

I saw Barbara frown. She hadn't been happy when I'd told her Lettie was my matron of honor.

Mother walked back into the room.

"Time to line up, girls. Remember to smile and keep in rhythm with the music," she said. "And Natalie, stand up straight when you walk down the aisle. It isn't attractive when you hunch over."

"I was only trying to make Baldy look taller."

"Stop calling him Baldy, Natalie, and get in line."

We lined up in the hallway outside the entrance to the church. Mother was escorted to her seat and the first strains of the "Wedding March" began.

Natalie and Oscar were the first ones down the aisle. Natalie, looking beautiful and elegant, held her head up and glided down the aisle as if she were walking beside Prince Charles. Mother had known all along that it didn't matter how short and bald Oscar was because no one looked at him anyway. All eyes were on Natalie.

Barbara and Randall followed. They walked down the aisle with the comfortable and easy rhythm of a couple who had been married for over twenty years. Friends smiled as they passed by. Randall looked lovingly at Barbara as Barbara looked out into the pews to see who was there.

Lettie and Edgar (aka the Wolfman), Aubrey's brother, followed. Edgar was six feet four, had a full beard, and was built like a professional wrestler. Alone, Edgar looked like an escaped backwoodsman, but next to Lettie he looked less wild and unkempt and more like the gentle bear of a man he really was. I watched as he timidly took her arm, and I saw him adjust his stride so that she could keep up with him as they walked up the aisle.

I looked over at Father who was nervously fiddling with his boutonniere. "Stop that. It looks fine."

"Does it?" He looked down at the flower.

"We're up next," I said as the music rose and fell.

Father finally looked over at me, and I saw tears in his eyes. He took my hand and said, "I love you very much. Don't ever forget that."

"I won't," I said, trying to hold back my own tears.

"Don't forget if we ever get a real football team…and I'm not talking about those Canadians…I'm buying season tickets and we're going together. Deal?"

"Deal."

"Because you'll never be too old or too married to go to a game with your father now…right?"

I smiled through tears and kissed him, and we took our first steps down the aisle and toward the altar and Aubrey.

Chapter Fourteen

•

"Double double toil and trouble."
Shakespeare

Aubrey and I adjusted easily to married life. There were no arguments about who cooked or cleaned or took out the trash. Aubrey did it all. My life hardly changed except that I now had Aubrey. I never resented the fact that I made more money than he did. And when he finally felt ready to go into business for himself, I gave him the money.

He started with one house. When he had finished the work on that house, he sold it and bought another. Aubrey didn't overcharge on materials like some builders. He wanted people to associate his name with quality work and fair prices. By the time Aubrey bought his sixth house, he and I became partners. He felt that it was important for me to be part owner "in case he keeled over and dropped dead." I didn't see that happening any time soon—he was only forty-five and in good health—but I signed all the business papers he wanted me to. When tax time rolled around, I suggested that we let my old boyfriend, the accordion-playing accountant, do our taxes. Aubrey wouldn't hear of it. He wasn't jealous, he said, and he just thought that paying someone else to do your taxes was a waste of good money. "After all," he said. "Ninety-nine percent of figuring your taxes is getting all the information together. Any idiot can do that."

Not this "idiot" I thought to myself. I had turned the checkbook over to him the day we got married and told him he could handle the money. He didn't rant and rave like the accountant about my lack of bookkeeping skills. Instead he said, "I guess it's boring for you. You do have an artistic temperament." We both knew that my lack of interest in bookkeeping had nothing to do with my artistic temperament. But at the time, I thought it was a nice thing for him to say.

Aubrey's business grew steadily and made a profit for four years. Then the recession hit, and the real estate market dried up. I should have noticed something was wrong but I didn't. My first clue was when I noticed Aubrey spending more and more time at home.

"You're home early," I said as Aubrey walked in the door at three in the afternoon.

"Slow day. Figured I might as well spend some time with you." Aubrey went to get a beer. I stared at the portrait of Mrs. Janet Simms Willey. Mrs. Willey had a nose that put Jimmy Durante's to shame. I had painted her with her head turned so that her nose looked less like the honker it was and more like the nose of her dreams. Aubrey came up behind me and hugged me.

"Stop! Look, I've smeared the paint," I said. "Don't sneak up on me like that when I'm painting."

"Leave the smear," Aubrey said. "With a nose like that, you'll never get her to look normal."

I turned around and watched him walk over to the sofa and pick up the paper.

"Are you all right?"

Aubrey looked up from the paper and said, "Yes, why?"

"Just wondered. You usually aren't that critical."

"Sorry. Didn't mean to be."

I put my brush down and walked over to the sofa.

"What's wrong with you?"

"Nothing."

"Could have fooled me."

"You're the one who doesn't want to be touched."

"Aubrey, that's ridiculous. I just don't want you sneaking up behind me while I'm painting. I get paid a lot of money for these portraits."

Aubrey put the paper down and looked up. "And what's that supposed to mean?"

"Just that it's our bread and butter."

"And what I do doesn't count at all?"

"Yes, it does. I didn't mean that. All I meant was—"

Aubrey threw the paper down and got up. He walked over to the closet, got his coat, and headed for the elevator.

"Aubrey, I said I didn't mean—"

"I know what you meant…and you're probably right too."

"Where are you going?"

"Out," he said as I watched him descend down to the first floor.

After that he didn't come home early anymore. In fact, sometimes he didn't come home for dinner. When that happened I'd go out looking for him. Usually he was at the Parrot or with Tom Bennett.

My first clue that there was trouble in paradise was when Lightning told me he was worried about Aubrey. I had gone to the Parrot. Aubrey wasn't there but Lightning was.

"Hey, Lightning," I said, shaking off my coat. "Aubrey been in today?"

Lightning watched me sit down and said, "No. Don't you know where he is?"

Iron Man slid a Bud down the bar, and I caught it before it went off the other end.

"No, I don't," I said, taking a sip.

"Look," Lightning sighed. "This ain't none of my business, but he should tell you where he is. Especially now that he's not working."

"What do you mean he's not working?" I said, putting the beer down.

Lightning rubbed his crew cut and said, "Yeesh, he ain't told you?"

"Told me what?"

"I shouldn't be the one tellin' you this. Aubrey shoulda told you."

"Told me what, Lightning?"

"OK. But don't tell him you heard it from me." Lightning tapped his glass for a refill and Iron Man sent one flying down the length of the bar. "He owes people."

"What people. What are you talking about?"

"He owes building supply companies, he owes laborers, and he owes the bank."

"Lightning, how can he owe people? We made a profit off that last house."

"You been painting too much. Don't you read the newspaper? Ain't you heard we're in a recession? Look around you, Sara. See all these iron workers in here? They've all been laid off. See all those for sale signs in Fells Point? Some of those signs have been up for a year. Nobody is buying and nobody is selling. And you can believe me when I tell you, nobody is renovating either."

"But he told me we made a profit."

"Did you see anything in writing?"

"No. But then I never see anything in writing."

"Your name on the business?"

"Yes, but what's—"

"Get your name off." Lightning reached into his pocket and pulled out a business card. "Here. Go see this man and he'll help you."

I looked down at a card that read: John Thomas Boone, attorney at law.

"Lightning, Aubrey's my husband. I can't go to a lawyer. We're not getting divorced. If Aubrey has money problems, we'll just have to work it out."

"Look, I like Aubrey. But he never shoulda put your name on those papers."

"He thought he was protecting me. He was afraid he'd drop dead and I wouldn't get any money."

"Sara. That's what wills are for."

I didn't say anything and took another sip of my beer. Finally, I said, "Does everybody know Aubrey's in trouble?"

"Everybody in construction."

I threw money on the bar and got up to leave, but Lightning caught my hand and said, "Sara, I'm sure he thought he was doing the best thing for you, but now it's time to get out before you lose everything. Go see John Boone. He's a good lawyer. He can tell you what to do."

I didn't take Lightning's advice. I went home, and when Aubrey came in, I confronted him.

I had fallen asleep on the sofa. When I heard the elevator, I sat up and turned on the light. The clock on the wall said 2:00 a.m.

"Two things," I said when Aubrey saw me. "Where were you, and why didn't you tell me you were in trouble?"

Aubrey looked visibly shaken, but he recovered quickly and said, "I was at St. David's helping Tom bolt down the new pews." He took off his coat. "And just what kind of trouble do you think I'm in?"

"St. David's? Until 2:00 a.m.?"

"Sara, that's the only time we can do construction at the church... when no one is there."

"Why didn't you call?"

"Call? You take the phone off the hook when you paint. I gave up call-ing you two months after we moved in together."

I had forgotten that. He was right. I did take the phone off the hook.

"But you've never stayed out this late before."

"True. But you know I'm either at the Parrot or I'm with Tom."

He was right again.

He came over and sat beside me on the sofa. I noticed he was carrying a brown paper bag. He sat the bag on the floor and said, "What's this really about?" he asked as he smoothed my hair back and kissed me on the cheek.

"Your work. How's your work?"

He stopped what he was doing and sat back and looked at me.

"What have you heard?"

"I heard you had serious money problems."

"And who did you hear that from?"

"I can't say."

Aubrey sighed and said, "Doesn't matter. I think I know who." He got up and walked into the kitchen, and I heard the refrigerator door open and close. He came back in with a beer. "The truth is, Sara, that business is terrible. But I wouldn't go as far to say that it's in trouble." I watched him swallow his beer.

"How terrible?"

"Slow terrible."

"So you don't owe money all over town?"

"Sara, contractors always owe money to somebody. It's the nature of the business."

"What about the bank?"

"What about the bank."

"Do you owe money to the bank?"

"Of course I do. I just bought a house, remember?"

I did. I had just signed papers for a house on Fleet Street.

"Can we afford the house?"

"Of course we can." Aubrey came back to the sofa and sat down. "Tell you what. I'll go get all the paperwork, and we'll go over all the bills, and you can see what money is coming in and what money is going out. Would that make you feel better?"

"Maybe," I said. But I knew I really didn't want to look at anything.

"Would you like to do that now?" Aubrey started to get up. I stopped him and said, "No, we can do that later."

Aubrey sat back down. "Sara, I'd tell you if I had serious money problems. You do believe me, don't you?" He kissed the top of my head. "I would never lie to you. In fact, I'd never do anything to jeopardize our relationship. It took me a long time to find you, and I'm not about to screw this up, especially over some dumb rumor about money."

I put my arms around him and snuggled closer. I didn't want to lose him either.

"Just tell me the truth about the business. If you need to pay some people, I have money. We can pay them with the money I have in savings."

"Nope." Aubrey said. "That's junior's money."

"Junior?"

"Our son. After all, we'll need money to send him to private school. I'd like him to go to Helman Prep. And then more money for college and—"

"Aubrey, we've never talked about babies before."

"I know," he said, looking down at me. "How do you feel about passing on the Struttgard/Gorman genes?"

I sat up and looked at him. "Are you serious?"

"Of course I'm serious. Why? You think forty-five is too old to be a dad?"

"No. Father was forty-six when I was born and Mother was only a year younger."

"She sure does look great for her age. Obviously, late births didn't detract from her looks."

"No, it just detracted from her parenting skills."

"So you've told me." Aubrey kissed me and again asked, "So what do you say? Are you ready for motherhood?"

"I'm not quite sure. I mean, is anybody ever ready for motherhood?"

"Probably not." Aubrey kissed me again and we fell back onto the sofa. I briefly wondered how we had gone from money woes to making babies, but that thought was quickly erased when Aubrey said, "I have a present for you."

"Is it hard?" I said between kisses.

"Yes, and it's six inches long, tastes great and...oh, and it's red, white, and blue."

"You painted it red, white, and blue?"

"No, it came like that."

"Not the last time I looked."

"You haven't seen it in a couple of years."

"That's ridiculous. It hasn't been that long."

"It has been for this."

And with that Aubrey took a red, white, and blue can out of the brown paper bag and gave it a hard shake.

Chapter Fifteen

"Expectation is the root of all heartache."

Shakespeare

Despite our best efforts I didn't get pregnant. At first I was disappointed. But by the third month, I began to feel relieved. Aubrey was just plain frustrated.

"It's got to be me. I'm forty-five years old. I've got old sperm. That's got to be the problem...old, lifeless sperm."

"Right, Aubrey. They're so old they're senile," I said, looking up at him from the newspaper. "They get lost on their way down my fallopian tubes, and because they're male they refuse to stop and ask directions and end up circling my uterus until they run out of gas."

Aubrey put down his coffee cup and said, "Don't joke about it. This is serious. I think we should talk to someone."

"As in a doctor?" I said. "Aubrey, it's too soon. Let's give it another couple of months."

I gave it three more months and then I had lunch with Lettie.

"We're trying to get pregnant," I blurted out over chicken Caesar salad. Lettie looked up and smiled.

"I was wondering if you two were going to get around to that."

"What do you mean 'if'?"

"Well, I just meant I didn't know if you even wanted children. You never talk about having them. I guess I just assumed it wasn't that important to you." Lettie picked a piece of gristle off a chunk of chicken.

"Why wouldn't I want children?"

Lettie looked up at me and frowned. "Sara, there's nothing wrong with not wanting children."

"Did I ever say I didn't want them?"

"No," Lettie said, staring at me.

"Well, then don't assume so much."

I looked down at my plate. I was angry and I didn't know why. I finally looked up and said, "Were you happy the first time you found out you were pregnant?"

"Over the moon happy," Lettie said. "I tested myself at Hopkins and then ran all the way to Oscar's office to tell him. Then I told everybody in the elevator on my way back to the office. Now that I think about it, I guess I was pretty obnoxious about it."

"You never got scared?"

"No."

"Worried that something might go wrong?"

"No."

"Oh," was all I could think to say.

"Sara, what's this really about? You know how much I wanted a family. It was the most important thing in the world to me."

"I know," I said. And then I laughed. "God, I used to get so tired of playing 'house' with you. You made me feed the baby dolls and diaper them. Then we had to read to them or take them outside for a walk. I couldn't wait to ditch the dolls and hop on my bike..."

Lettie raised an eyebrow and ate a forkful of salad.

"Don't give me that look," I said. "Just because I didn't like to play with dolls doesn't mean I don't want children."

"I never said a word," Lettie said, taking a sip of water.

I ran some of the same questions past Barbara.

"Were you excited when you found out you were pregnant with Randall Jr.?" I asked as I watched Barbara spritz her kitchen window with Windex.

"Excited? No, I couldn't believe it. I had only been married a few months."

"So, you weren't thrilled to be pregnant?"

Barbara stopped wiping and turned around. "Sara, why are you asking me this? You know Randall Jr. was a surprise."

"Well, yes, but you did get excited after you got used to the idea... didn't you?"

Barbara resumed removing imaginary smudge marks from her window. "The only time I ever got excited during my first pregnancy was when Frances

Lymington handed me her credit card and told me to buy whatever I needed for the baby. I did…a Gucci diaper bag."

"That's terrible."

"It's the truth. Remember, I spent the first three months throwing up and getting migraines. The next three months after that I spent watching my ankles swell up to three times their normal size. Excited? Excited is being able to see your feet again after you give birth."

"It couldn't have been all that bad."

"Yes, it was."

"But you always acted like being pregnant was the most natural thing in the world."

Barbara pointed the bottle of spray at me and said, "Natural? There's nothing natural about forcing something the size of a watermelon out of your vagina."

I changed the subject.

When I asked Malqueen about having children, she knew exactly what I was thinking.

"You're trying aren't you?"

"Yes," I confessed right away.

"Well, ain't nothing wrong with that. People have babies all the time."

"I know. But we've been trying for six months."

Malqueen was wiping down the counter at Mrs. M's shop as she talked.

"Well, why haven't you seen a doctor?"

"I don't know. Aubrey did want to talk to one. I told him it was too early." I looked over at Malqueen and said, "But I did talk to Lettie."

"What did Lettie say?"

"I didn't tell her we'd been trying for so long. I just couldn't. All Oscar had to do was look at her and she got pregnant."

Malqueen smiled. "How many in that brood now? Three? Four?"

"They just hit the jackpot on number four. Oscar finally got his son."

"So what did you tell Lettie?"

"I just told her we were trying."

"And?"

"And she seemed surprised."

Malqueen pulled the plexiglass covers over the counter and said, "About what?"

"That we even wanted children."

"Do you?"

"Do I what?"

"Want children?"

"What is this? A conspiracy to keep me childless?"

Malqueen came over and sat down at the table with me.

"Sara, there's nothing wrong with not wanting children. Look at me. I never wanted any."

"Did you ever regret not having any?"

"Never. But then I did have you."

We sat in silence. Then Malqueen said, "You know, lots of people have children for the wrong reasons. They have them because they see their friends having them. They have them so their parents can become grandparents. They have them because they think they can mold them into little carbon copies of themselves. Some people have 'em so they got somebody to take care of them in their old age. But the way I see it is the only reason to have a child is because you really want to be a parent—a parent who believes that they can raise a child into a responsible, independent adult."

Malqueen put her feet up on the chair beside me. "But then most people don't think about all that before they go and do it. And maybe that's a good thing too. If everybody thought about it so much, nobody would be having babies." Malqueen folded her arms and looked at me. "So, you having second thoughts?"

"Malqueen," I said, putting my head down on the table. "I've never been so confused in my life. Aubrey is dying to have a child, and I just don't seem to care one way or the other."

Malqueen leaned forward and put her hand on my forehead. "Don't be so hard on yourself. Maybe you should just tell Aubrey how you feel. Maybe he doesn't care one way or the other either. May he thinks this is something you really want."

"Do you really think so?"

"I think you should talk to him about it."

"Maybe I should," I said as I got up to leave. I hugged Malqueen good-bye and then went back and hugged her again. "What would I do without you?" I said.

Malqueen just smiled and pushed me out the door.

But before I got to talk with Aubrey I got a rare phone call from Natalie.

I could hear the ring as I opened the gate from the elevator. I ran for the phone and was surprised when a voice slurred, "Halloooo, mon petite soeur, how are you?"

"Natalie?"

"Who else calls you 'little sister' in French?"

"Where are you?" I could hear the unmistakable clink of glasses and raucous laughter in the background.

"In my apartment. Where else?"

"Sounds like you're having a party."

"Just a small soiree. Actually it's a bunch of drunk airline pilots. They got stranded in New York, so I'm letting them crash at my apartment tonight. In gratitude they bought champagne. But, true to form, the cheapskates bought domestic. But enough about those cretins. How are you?"

"Fine." I attempted to throw my coat on a hook on the wall. I missed.

"Good. Still married to that reject of mine?"

"Yes, Natalie. I'm still married. Why? What have you heard?"

"I haven't heard anything...but you're a tad touchy. Do I detect trouble in paradise?"

"No, you do not."

"Bingo. Hit a nerve. What's going on?"

I don't know why I decided to confide in Natalie, the sister who always managed to tell me exactly what I didn't want to hear, but I did.

"Do you ever regret not having children?"

There was dead silence on the line. Then I heard a door slam, and I couldn't hear party noise anymore.

"I shut the door," Nat said. "Why would you ask me such a question?"

"Because you never had any. Because you're past the age of having them. I don't know. Maybe I'm asking you this because I'm having so much trouble making this decision." There was more silence. Finally I said, "I don't know what to do, Nat."

Natalie sounded dead sober when she said, "If you have doubts then don't do it."

"You didn't answer my question. Do you regret not having children?"

"It doesn't matter what I do or don't regret. What matters is how you feel about it. Are you willing to take on the responsibility of raising a child? Can you give him unconditional love? Take him to church? Help him with his homework every night? Play with him when you want to paint? Send him to the best schools? Save for his college education? Teach him to be independent? Buy him—"

"Enough. I get the message. You sound just like Malqueen."

"Then listen to Malqueen."

"I never thought I'd hear you say that."

"Why? Just because Malqueen and I have had our differences doesn't mean we both don't care about you."

One of the pilots must have opened Natalie's bedroom door because suddenly I heard laughter and a loud rendition of "Louie Louie."

"Shut that door," Natalie screamed. It became silent again. "Sara, don't let Mother cloud your feelings for a child."

"Mother? What's she got to do with this?"

"If you have to ask that question then you need more therapy than I do."

"Natalie, I would never act like Mother in a million years."

"I'm not saying you would. But sometimes I wonder what Mother's life would have been like if she had been born today—all that pent-up ambition and the only way to get any recognition was through her husband."

An air horn sounded over the phone and a voice that bellowed through what sounded like a megaphone announced, "Ladies and Gentlemen! We're about to crash! Please fasten your seatbelts. Make sure your tray tables are up and your seatbacks are in the upright position. And while you're at it, bend over and kiss your ass good-bye!"

"Oh, for God's sake," Natalie yelled. "Shut up!"

"Listen, Nat, I've got to go. I hear the elevator and it's probably Aubrey. I've got a lot I want to talk to him about."

"OK. But think about what I said."

There was no one on the elevator. I had made that up to get off the phone. I waited for Aubrey to come home from St. David's, but I fell asleep on the coach. I didn't hear Aubrey when he finally came in late that night.

Aubrey woke me up the next morning when he kissed me good-bye.

"Hey, sleepyhead. I'm off early. Got a job hanging drywall. I'll see you tonight."

I raised my head up and managed to mumble, "Huh?"

"I'll see you tonight."

"But I need to talk to you," I managed to get out as he pulled on his coat.

"Tonight. We can talk tonight."

I fell back down on my pillow and went back to sleep.

The phone woke me up.

"Sara?"

"Father?"

"Did I wake you? I'm so sorry. Are you sick?"

"What time is it?" I squinted at the clock. It said 9:00 a.m. "Good heavens, I must have been exhausted."

"I didn't mean to wake you up. But now that you are up I have a favor to ask."

I sat up in bed and pulled the covers up around my neck. "Sure, what?"

"Your mother and I have that terrible flu that's going around, and neither of us can move more than three feet from the couch. It's Mary's day off, and I was wondering if you could get us some cough medicine at Tuxedo Pharmacy."

"When did you get the flu?"

"Well, your mother actually got it a couple of days ago. I just have the sore throat, but I'll probably get the full-blown version in a few days. I know you're busy, but do you think you could run that errand for us?"

"Of course. I'll get dressed and get it right now."

"Actually, it would be better if you came over around two o'clock. We're still trying to get ourselves together."

"Do you need anything else?"

"No, no...just the cough syrup."

"See you then."

I arrived at two o'clock and rang the bell. Father answered the door in his robe.

"You don't look so good," I said, handing him the bag with the cough syrup in it.

"Come into the study. If you think I look bad, you should see your Mother."

Mother was wrapped up like a mummy on the sofa. She had two giant pillows behind her that kept her propped up in a sitting position. Her nose was red, she was shivering, and she sneezed as I entered the room.

"Have you seen a doctor?"

"Your father called in that quack, Doc Barker." Mother reached for a Kleenex. "The man is so undignified. His shirt is always hanging out," she said as she stopped to sneeze again, "...and his hair looks like it's never combed. Really, William, why he has to be our internist, I just don't..." Mother sneezed again.

"Because, Caroline, he's a wonderful physician."

Mother started to cough and Father poured some cough syrup into a shot glass.

"Here you go...bottoms up," he said, handing Mother the glass.

I watched Mother chug the medicine, and then I turned to Father and asked him if I could make tea for them. Father refused but Mother said, "That would be lovely, dear."

I saw Father frown at Mother. Mother sneezed again.

"Why don't you sit down," I said to Father. "I'll go make some tea."

When I returned with the tea, I could tell Mother and Father had been arguing. Father's face was red, and Mother wouldn't look at him.

"Are you two all right?" I asked, setting the tea service down.

"Of course, we're fine. Well, we're not great. This flu thing has knocked the wind out of both of us." Father got up and helped me pour. I couldn't help but notice that he seemed in much better shape than Mother.

"Sara, I'm afraid I have another favor to ask of you," he said, handing Mother her cup.

"Oh?"

"I have some church documents I forgot to give to Tom Bennet. He's working on a homeless shelter for Waverly with the new bishop, and I know he needs them for a meeting tomorrow. Unfortunately, he won't be home until late tonight. He's away on some other church business." Father paused and took a sip of tea.

I looked at Mother who was studying the squares of the afghan she had been wrapped up in. "And?" I asked.

"And I really need to get these documents to him today."

"Why not just call the bishop?"

Mother looked at Father and he said, "Well, I sort of helped Tom, and he doesn't want the bishop to know it was my idea."

"You didn't sort of help him, William. You designed the whole thing."

"Now, Caroline, no one needs to know that."

I knew there was no love between my father and the new bishop. Father had been one of the most popular bishops Maryland had ever had. Everyone felt the new bishop was in over his head. It didn't help that everyone compared him to Father. The new bishop always came up lacking, and, naturally, he resented it.

"So you want me to sneak over to St. David's and leave the plans for Tom so he can go over them tonight and present them to the bishop tomorrow morning?"

"Correct. Except I think it would be safer if you left them in Tom's study at the rectory."

"You want me to leave them in Tom's house? How am I supposed to get in?"

Mother coughed again and said, "Sara, if you feel uncomfortable going into Tom's house, then by all means you don't have to do this. Your father will figure something out." Once again Father looked at Mother.

"I don't mind," I said. "If Tom doesn't mind."

"Of course Tom won't mind. He's getting a chance to impress the new bishop," Father said as he got up and opened his desk drawer. "Here's the key to his front door. Just leave the papers on his desk in the study. Do you remember the layout of the house?"

"It's been a while, but yes, I remember where the study is."

"Good girl. This way I can stay home and take care of your mother." As if on cue, Mother sneezed again.

I sat down to finish my tea, but Father stood over me with an envelope.

"Here are the plans. Try not to bend them."

I put my teacup down, took the envelope, and got up to leave.

"Sara, must you leave so soon?" Mother tried to raise up, but she was bound so tightly into the afghan that she was forced to fall back into her previous position. "I was just telling your father. We hardly see you anymore. Who are you painting these days?"

I started to sit down again, but Father held my coat up and said, "Now, Caroline, give Sara a break. She doesn't want to hang around with two old sickies like us." I put my coat on and let Father escort me out the door. Mother called from the study. "I'd kiss you good-bye, dear, but I don't want to give you any germs. Be careful driving."

Father laughed and said, "I think she's getting sentimental in her old age. She even tells me to be careful when I take out the trash."

I kissed Father good-bye and ran to the car. It was twenty degrees out, and the wind had picked up. I blew on my fingers and turned the key. Surprisingly, my ten-year-old Volkswagen started on the first twist. I waved to Father as I pulled onto Greenway, and as I turned my head, I saw the curtains in the study move and Mother's head peek through the folded opening. She waved, and I waved back, then I headed out in the direction of Waverly.

Chapter Sixteen

•

"O! I am Fortune's Fool."
                    Shakespeare

The Volkswagen sputtered to a stop across the street from St. David's rectory. Tom's house wasn't as big or as impressive as Father's first rectory. If Tom had been married and had a family, the Diocese would have found him bigger and better accommodations. But because he was single, which was unusual in itself for a priest, he had to settle for a modest Cape Cod. It was small by Episcopal standards.

Most rectories sit next to the church. Tom's house, however, was a block away. St. David's had been destined for the Episcopal scrap heap when Tom had asked Father for the parish. Waverly was a neighborhood in transition. The affluent had moved out, and the working class ethnic had moved in. The neighborhood was a mix of Muslims, Baptists, and Catholics. But Tom had convinced Father and the Diocese that he could double the membership at St. David's if they gave him the chance. He kept his word. But then something happened that no one could ever have predicted. The neighborhood changed back. The young professionals, who were just starting their families and careers, began moving in and renovating the forty-year-old houses. The houses began selling for more than they were worth, and the original owners found it difficult not to take the money and move out to the suburbs. Tom now found himself running a parish where the members didn't need before- and after-school care. These new more affluent members wanted a new roof that didn't leak, pews without splinters, and a furnace that worked. Tom was under pressure. That's why Aubrey spent so much time at St. David's. He volunteered his time to help Tom save money on labor.

As I walked down the street toward the rectory, I noticed that every now and then a sad little house still stood in the middle of a row of redesigned and expensive-looking homes. They weren't ugly houses; they just needed some work, and in some cases a coat of paint would have done the job. But the people who lived in these neglected houses seemed to have given up. It was as if they knew they didn't fit in with these new professionals who drove BMWs to work and who sped past Waverly Elementary on their way to private schools.

I climbed Tom's front steps and looked in the round window at the top of the door. The rectory was modest, but Tom had done a lot of renovating in his spare time. I knew that Aubrey had helped him on that too.

I hesitated before I inserted the key. It was strange to be letting myself into someone else's house, even though I knew Tom wouldn't mind. The key turned and the door opened noiselessly. I smelled pine cleaner and decided Tom's cleaning lady must have just finished her duties.

The study was down the hall and off to the right. I found myself tiptoeing down the hallway until I realized what I was doing. I placed the envelope on his desk and turned to leave. On the coat rack next to the door I saw Aubrey's coat and scarf. I knew it was his scarf because I had given it to him for Christmas last year. I looked down and saw that his work boots were placed neatly next to the rack. Without understanding why, I went out into the hallway and climbed the stairs. With each step I told myself to turn around, leave, go home. But I couldn't. I heard music at the end of the upstairs hall, and I followed the strains of *Madame Butterfly* until I stood outside the door from where the music was coming from. I willed my hand not to turn the doorknob, but it did anyway. The door gently swung open, requiring no effort on my part.

At first I didn't understand what I was seeing. I knew there were two nude people in bed, but it didn't register who those two people were. By the time I finally realized that one of them was Aubrey and the other one was Tom, I was already out the door, down the steps, and running down the street. I didn't remember hearing Aubrey cry out, "Oh, dear God, no." Or Tom say, "What are we going to do now?" until much later. The truth was my mind had gone blank.

Chapter Seventeen

———————————— • ————————————

"A merry heart maketh a cheerful
countenance:
But by sorrow of the heart the spirit
is broken."

Proverbs

When I was very young, Father said that his old Chevy could find its
own way home. He would let the wheel go, close his eyes, and I would squeal
in terror. Father would never let go for more than a few seconds, and the car
never swerved, but at that time, I really believed the car was driving itself.

Maybe that's what happened that afternoon. My VW actually steered
itself all the way to Lettie's because I certainly don't remember how I got there.

I left the car running in the circular drive and banged on the front
door. Lindsay, the ten-year-old, answered the door.

"Aunt Sara! What are you doing here? Mummy didn't tell us you were
coming by. How come you left your car running? Are you in a hurry? I'll go tell
Mummy you're here. You sure do look funny. Are you sick?"

I leaned against the wall in the foyer, and I heard Lindsay yell, "Mummy!
Aunt Sara's here! Come quick! She looks like she's about to upchuck!"

Lettie came running down the stairs followed by Oscar. I managed
to throw up into the pot of the ficus tree before they got to me. Oscar put his
arm around me and half-carried and half-dragged me into the library. Lettie
followed behind him and told Lindsay to go upstairs. I heard Lindsay say,
"What's the matter with her? Does she have the flu?" And Lettie saying, "Yes,
darling, she has the flu. Now go up and watch your brother."

I pulled the covers over my head and shook with chills. Then, hot with
fever, I threw the covers off, got out of bed, and stumbled around the room in
a delusional stupor. When Lettie led me back to bed, I fought her.

"Sara." Her voice sounded muffled and faraway, as if she were speaking
through the heating vents in the floor. "Come back to bed. Rest. You need to

sleep and drink plenty of fluids. Come on. Get under the covers. You do want to get well, don't you?"

I didn't. If I shook with chills or burned with fever, I didn't have to think about what I had seen in Tom Bennet's bedroom that afternoon. I didn't have to wonder why I hadn't seen this coming. I didn't have to wonder what kind of man I had married. And I didn't have to think about what I was supposed to do next.

I had been at Lettie's for a week before I finally told her what had happened.

"Sara?" she said, pulling back the draperies. "Look, it's a beautiful morning."

I squinted into the sun and ducked back under the covers.

"Sara, we need to talk." I heard a chair being dragged over to the side of the bed. I pretended I didn't hear her.

"Sara, Aubrey has called twice a day since you've been here. He wants to see you."

"No."

"He sounds desperate, Sara. He really does." Lettie pulled the covers back and I turned my face away from her. "Do you remember the afternoon you came here?"

I kept my face turned away.

"The last thing you said to Oscar and me before you passed out was, 'No Aubrey. Keep him away.'"

I half turned my face toward her.

"We did. He was on the front porch that night. Apparently he'd been all over the place looking for you. Oscar wouldn't let him in. He was crazed. I thought Oscar was going to have to call the police."

I turned my head a little more toward her.

"I'm not trying to talk you into seeing him. I'm just letting you know how desperate he was...and is. He looked terrible."

I turned to her and said, "Good."

"Your fever's gone," she said. "Feel up to some chicken soup? It's the Beast's recipe. It's the only thing she makes that really tastes good. "

"I hate him."

"I know," Lettie said.

"You have no idea."

"You told me a little bit when you were delirious."

I sat up too quickly, got dizzy, and immediately fell back down. "What did I say?"

"Just that you caught Aubrey in bed with someone."

"Did I say who?"

"No, you didn't. Most of the time you rambled on about scarves and boots and the bishop's secret document."

I turned my head away again and fell silent.

"Your mother called too."

"Mother?" This time I did look at Lettie. I noticed she was pale and had dark circles under her eyes.

"Yes, it was very strange." Lettie tilted her head to one side. "She called here the afternoon you showed up sick. She asked if I had heard from you. I told her you were here with a terrible case of the flu."

"A case I probably got from her."

"That's just what she said. She seemed upset that you were ill."

"Are you sure we're talking about my mother?"

"I'm sure. She even thanked me for taking care of you and asked if I needed anything."

"Now I know you're not talking about my mother."

"Oh, it was your mother all right. She said your father was out of town on church business and wouldn't be back for a few days and she just wanted to make sure you were OK. She sounded really concerned."

"Sure." I rolled over again.

There was a knock on the door, and Cerise came in with a tray.

"You can put it on the table, Cerise," Lettie said. "I think Sara can keep down the soup."

Cerise placed the tray on the table and looked at me.

"I can tell you are better by your color today. The flu is gone. I told you the potion would work." Cerise nodded her head to Lettie as she handed her the cup of soup and the spoon.

"You drank one of Cerise's homemade herbal potions last night. She said it builds up the immune system and wards off infections."

I swallowed a spoonful of soup and said, "Got any potions that cure a broken heart?"

Cerise stood at the end of the bed and stretched her hands up to the sky. "I have as many as there are stars in the sky. The bigger the hurt, the more complicated the potion."

"Then this potion would be a doozy."

"I will see what I can do. But I must ask how you feel about the man. Do you still love him? And do you want him back?"

Lettie stopped feeding me, and Cerise leaned forward on the bed.

I frowned into the bright beam of sunlight that poured forth from the open window and thought to myself, "Yes, of course I still love him, and yes, I'll always want him back." But what I said to Cerise was, "I hate him. I wish he was dead."

Two weeks passed and I was still weak but over the flu. I sat in Lettie's pajamas and ate whatever Cerise brought me. Lettie went back to work. I turned the television on at 9:00 a.m. and watched game shows designed to sharpen my wit but which instead dulled my brain. I didn't know how much longer I could impose on Lettie, but it wasn't something I even wanted to think about. I clicked the remote and stared at two fat ladies who were about to mud wrestle for the home of their dreams.

The bedroom door burst open and Malqueen stood in the doorway.

"What do you think you're doing?" she said, walking over and turning off the TV.

"Watching TV?"

"Sitting here for two weeks like a zombie in the same pajamas? They beginning to smell, you know. Eatin' other people's food. Taking advantage of their kindness—"

"I did not! I was sick. I had the flu."

"The key word there is 'had.' You ain't got it no more. It's time for you to get in the shower and get into some regular clothes."

"I don't have any regular clothes."

"You do now," Malqueen said, waving a bag in front of me. "Now get up."

I saw Cerise peek into the room from the hallway.

"Thanks a lot, Cerise. Did you call her?"

"No, I did not. I do not know who called her here. I told her I was taking very good care of you, but she just pushed her way past me and found you all by herself."

"Did Lettie call you?"

"Don't matter who called me," Malqueen said, grabbing my arm. "I'm here now, and you're getting a shower. You'll feel like a new person once you get cleaned up."

I got in the shower, but when I got out, I didn't feel like a new person. All I felt was clean. When I walked out of the bathroom, showered and dressed, Malqueen and Cerise were sitting in front of my recently vacated TV set watching the fat redheaded housewife, who was now covered in mud, as she was presented with the key to her brand new home.

"Used to be a show on years ago called *Queen for a Day*," Malqueen said to Cerise. "A bunch of housewives would tell the audience how hard their life was and why they needed a new dryer or a new washer. They were pitiful stories, I tell you; I cried more than once. In that show you were glad to see one of those women get something, even if it was only a washer or a dryer. But this show is pathetic. Two women mud wrestling for a house? Why do people watch this stuff?"

"Ahem."

Malqueen took her feet off the chair and stood up. "Now you look better, and I bet you feel better too."

I didn't. I just said, "Who called you? Barbara?"

"She's at a convention in Atlanta with that roving-eyed husband of hers. She'll be back tomorrow...which is a good reason to get you out of here. You know how she feels about," Malqueen lowered her voice and whispered, "the Wittridges."

"And just where am I supposed to go?"

"Go? You gotta go home. To the loft."

"Not in a million years." I sat down and folded my arms.

"He ain't there."

That threw me for a few minutes and then I said, "Oh? And where is he?"

"In the hospital."

I wanted to know why, but I didn't want to appear too eager.

"Couldn't happen to a nicer guy," was all I said.

"I came over here to get you," Malqueen said, putting her coat on. "Because we got some important business to take care of. Lightning is meeting us at the loft, along with that nice Polish accountant fella you used to date and a lawyer Lightning knows."

"Why?"

"'Cause you're in big trouble, that's why."

"That's an understatement," I said.

"I ain't foolin', Sara. This is big trouble. We got to get over there, and we got to figure out what to do before they come after you next."

This made me sit up, and Cerise lean forward.

"Why would anyone come after me?"

"'Cause you owe them hundreds of thousands of dollars, that's why."

"I never borrowed any money from anybody."

"No, but Aubrey did."

"He borrowed from the bank, Malqueen."

"Oh, he borrowed from them too...and Lightning...and the people who beat him up three nights ago and put him in the hospital."

"What!"

"Waited for him outside the loft and broke his arm and all the fingers on his right hand. Lightning found him on the pavement outside when he was coming home from The Blue Parrot. Lightning got him to the hospital and called the po-leece...not that the po-leece will ever find the men that did this. Lightning said they were probably from out of town, like Jersey or Philly."

I got up and looked around for my coat. Cerise found it in the closet.

"What does Lightning think I should do?" I asked as I zipped up my parka.

"I'll let him explain," Malqueen said. "I need to call him and let him know we're on the way."

Malqueen dialed the phone, and Cerise moved over next to me and handed me an ugly-looking straw doll. When I looked up at her, she smiled and said, "All you need is some of his hair. You can get it from the bathroom drain or his brush. Then you need some of his sweat. You can get that off of some old dirty underwear. Tuck something personal of his, like a toothbrush, inside the doll. The pins are in the plastic bag. Then puncture the head and he will get a severe headache, but don't put it in too far or it will give him a stroke. If you stick it into the stomach, he could either get a bad case of diarrhea or the gas…or end up writhing on the floor in agony…puncture his—"

"She ain't puncturing nothin'," Malqueen said as she grabbed the doll and threw it on the floor.

"I can't believe you're still practicing that voodoo business anyway. What they teaching you at that St. Mary's of the Sea Cathedral I see you going off to every Sunday? Way I understood it, you Catholics spend all your time 'Hail Mary-ing' and throwing that holy water all over yourself. I never heard of no Catholic sticking pins in Mr. Scarecrow voodoo dolls."

Cerise bent over and picked up the doll. She straightened its hat and said, "I am a good Catholic. I have been a Catholic since I was a child in Jamaica. But that has nothing to do with this," she said, shaking the doll at Malqueen. "This is powerful magic. This is what my mother taught me and what her mother taught her. Besides," Cerise shrugged, "I was only trying to help her get over the unfaithful husband."

"Unfaithful husband?" Malqueen snorted. "That's the least of her problems. Come on, Sara."

I followed Malqueen out the door. But I stared longingly at the doll Cerise held in her hands.

Chapter Eighteen

"When sorrows come they come
not single spies; But in battalions."
Shakespeare

I had to drive home because Malqueen had never learned how. She still preferred buses and when they weren't available, taxis.

I still wasn't feeling all that great either. I had just spent more than two weeks with the flu and another week doing as little as possible. Malqueen had to steady me when we got on the elevator. I turned the key and we lurched upward. When the door opened, I saw Lightning.

"Hey, how ya feelin'?"

"Terrible. What's this about?"

"Let's wait for the accountant and the lawyer. Want a beer?"

"Not unless you want me to throw up."

"I'll pass. Malqueen, how 'bout some coffee?"

"How 'bout it," Malqueen said as she went into the bathroom.

Lightning sighed and went into the kitchen to make coffee. I followed him in.

"She's mad at me," he said.

"Oh?"

"Yeah, she thinks I should have told you about all this sooner."

"Why didn't you?"

"Aubrey kept saying he didn't want you to get involved. He said he was going to get out from under and pay everybody back. I knew how much he loved you. I believed him."

"That a bunch of you-know-what," Malqueen said, coming out of the bathroom. "Didn't want her to get involved. Why did he have her sign all them papers if he didn't want her to get involved?"

"I really think he thought he was protecting her," Lightning said.

"Hogwash! Man knew what he was doing. And that don't excuse you none either," Malqueen said, shaking her finger at me. "Where was your sense? Why did you sign papers that made you liable too?"

The elevator motor whirred as the lift descended and then ascended and deposited my old flame, the accountant, and Lightning's lawyer friend, John Boone.

I listened to the accountant and the lawyer talk. And after it was all over, I realized that I owed a lot of money to a lot of people.

"The bank loan is for one hundred and twenty thousand dollars," the accountant said. "Aubrey also owes approximately thirty thousand dollars to building suppliers. Then there's the loan from Lightning—"

Lightning started waving at the accountant in an attempt to get him to shut up.

"Lightning!" I said. "Why didn't you tell me?"

"Now you know why I'm mad," Malqueen said, looking over at Lightning as he rubbed the gray stubble that passed for hair on his head and looked down.

"I don't want any money," was all Lightning said.

"We'll see about that," I said and turned back to the accountant. "What else?"

"He also owes Randall twenty thousand dollars for his truck—"

"What!" I said. "How did Randall get involved in this?"

"The truck was repossessed three months ago, and it ended up on Randall's used car lot. He must have seen Aubrey's name on the invoice list and called him. He paid the truck loan and gave Aubrey his truck back. Here's the receipt." The accountant held up a piece of paper and said, "Do you want me to continue?"

I looked over at Malqueen, who was still glaring at Lightning.

"The biggest loan—and this information we got from Lightning— was from a shark down on North Avenue for two hundred thousand dollars." The accountant looked over at Lightning. Lightning wrung his hands and looked at me.

"The shark goes by the name of Keno. I think he lives in Jersey, but he does business all up and down the East Coast. Aubrey found him through one of the iron workers who hangs out at the Parrot. I didn't know he was that desperate or I woulda warned him not to go that route. When Aubrey couldn't pay, Keno sent some men down to rough him up." Lightning raised his hands and shrugged. "You know the rest. They put him in the hospital."

I listened to all this, and finally I said, "What's the bottom line?"

"You're in debt to the tune of four hundred thousand dollars."

"No," Lightning broke in. "I said I don't want any money."

"OK," the accountant shrugged. "You're in debt to the tune of three hundred and fifty thousand dollars. Two hundred thousand of it needs to be paid to Keno right away. Otherwise, according to Lightning, you're going to end up in the hospital too."

"And what does my wonderful husband say about all this?"

Everybody avoided my gaze.

"What's going on now?"

"He skipped," Malqueen said. "Lightning went over today to check on him, and he just checked out of the hospital and disappeared."

"How could he disappear? I thought you said the cops were watching his room?"

"They were. But he didn't commit any crime. Remember, they were there to protect him."

"So he just left?"

"The officer said he just told him he was going away and that he'd be fine. He did give the office a note for Lightning."

"Oh. What did the note say?"

"Just that Lightning could find all the paperwork on the business in the garage."

"Did you find it?" I looked over at Lightning.

"Yeah. I turned it over to John."

"Sara, we need to know how much money you have. Do you have joint checking?"

I nodded. I saw the lawyer shake his head.

"Where's your checkbook?" the accountant asked.

"In here." I got up and opened a kitchen drawer. It was gone.

"Don't panic," the accountant said. "What bank?" He got up and went for the phone. "Got any old statements or deposit slips?"

"First Union," I said as I went to my bedroom and pulled out an old statement with my checking and savings accounts numbers on it. I was beginning to feel sick again.

We discovered that the checking account, which, by my last estimate, had around $2,000 in it, was empty. The savings hadn't been touched.

"Thank God for that," Malqueen said.

I looked at the balance and saw that I had $250,000 in the account.

"Well, I can pay the shyster at least."

"What about the bank loan?"

The lawyer stepped in and said, "Sell it. See what you can get for it."

"But it's not finished."

"Doesn't matter. Sell it as a fixer-upper. You might get lucky."

"Not the way my luck's been running."

Lightning took the money to Keno, who agreed to call off the goons now that the debt was paid. The house went on the market and sat there until the following spring, when it went up for auction and a young couple bought it and turned it into a bed and breakfast. I didn't get anything out of the sale, but at least I didn't go to jail.

I paid the building suppliers off and tried to give Lightning what I had left over. He didn't want to take it, but I insisted. I knew that Lightning never wanted me to know that he had loaned Aubrey any money in the first place. The only reason the accountant knew that Aubrey had borrowed $50,000 from Lightning was because of a signed IOU he had found in the box. I also suspected that Aubrey probably borrowed more than $50,000 from Lightning.

I called Randall at work and thanked him for what he had done. He promised me he wouldn't tell Barbara about it.

"This is between you and me," he said. "You're my favorite sister-in-law, and your sister adores you. Besides, you've always been nice to me, even when I was a jerk."

Aubrey remained missing in action. I had no money, no husband, and rent to pay. I had no choice but to go for the big bucks. I signed a contract with the devil.

Chapter Nineteen

—————————————————— • ——————————————————

"Hell is empty and all the devils are
here."

Shakespeare

Barbara was thrilled when I told her that I was finally ready to paint
Frances Lymington.

"Remember to make her look good," Barbara said over the phone.

"It'll be hard. But I'll do my best."

"Sara, please. This is important. Do more than your best."

I arrived at the Lymington estate at nine o'clock sharp. I was to paint
for two hours Monday through Friday, from nine to eleven, until the portrait
was finished. I was told to be prompt because Frances had an exhausting social
schedule and she didn't like to waste time.

I rang the bell and Montrose opened the door.

"Good mornin', Miss Sara. How are you today?"

"Fine, Montrose. And you?"

"Just wonderful. May I take your coat?"

I handed over my coat and marveled at how Frances had managed to
keep Montrose for twenty years. He was mannerly, handsome, and articulate.
The only reason I could think of to put up with the likes of Frances Lymington
was money. She must pay him a fortune.

I dragged my easel and paints and followed him into what Frances
called, The Morning Room.

It actually was a lovely room to paint in. One wall had floor-to-ceiling French doors and faced Frances's animal topiary garden. A baby grand
piano sat in one corner and Frances's Chinese figurine collection sat in a glass
étagère in the opposite corner. There was a traditional fireplace on the wall that
faced the topiary gardens, and a huge picture of Frances's father, Earl Broxton
Lymington Sr., hung over the mantel. It should have been an imposing room,
but Frances's decorator had given it warmth by painting it a pale yellow. I de-

cided that if I had to spend any time with Frances, this was a good room to do it in.

I set up my easel and waited for the very busy Frances to appear. I waited an hour. While France didn't want other people to waste her time, she apparently had no qualms about wasting mine.

I flipped through her magazines and found myself dozing off when she suddenly swept into the room.

"Sara, how perfectly delightful to see you. How's that darling Barbara? Tell her we must have lunch." Frances paused to kiss the air on either side of my head. "Now I must set down some rules before we begin."

I picked up charcoal and began to sketch.

"Now, now, don't start. Let me tell you what I want."

I put down the charcoal and waited.

"First, I want to pose next to the fireplace with Seth's picture behind me. Like this." Seth was Frances's deceased husband.

Frances put one arm up on the mantel and turned her head in profile. It wasn't a pretty sight.

"Ah, very nice Frances. However, I think you should tilt your head the other way…that's it, to the left. That way the light illuminates your features and gives your face an ethereal glow."

"Ethereal? Yes, I like that. But wait. I'm still not ready." With that Frances went over to the intercom and buzzed Montrose.

"Montrose? Would you bring Duchess in please?"

I silently groaned. Duchess was a nineteen-year-old Yorkie who had lost her mind about the same time she had lost control of her bowels. The dog wore doggy diapers and had to be carried around because she couldn't remember where she was.

Montrose held Duchess well out in front of him as he handed her over to Frances. The dog snapped the air around Montrose in an attempt to bite him. I noted that Duchess didn't have her diaper on today. As Frances hugged Duchess to her bosom, two Tootsie Roll-sized poops rolled down the front of her dress.

"Oh, my poor sweetie," Frances said as we watched the little brown drops roll across the floor. "You have such a hard time, don't you, my baby?"

Hard? I thought. This was the luckiest dog alive. All it did was eat, poop, and bite people.

"Now, Sara. I'd like to stand here and hold Duchess like this."

"Tilt your head to the left," I said. "Remember, we're going for ethereal."

"Should I tilt Duchess's head too? We want her to look ethereal as well." Frances leaned over and kissed Duchess on the head. Frances pulled back before Duchess took off a piece of her nose.

There was no way in hell Duchess would ever look ethereal. Her eyes were yellow and stared unseeingly through cataracts. Frances had tried to hide the bare spots on her head where her fur had fallen out by placing two pink bows on top of them. Every time the dog yapped, which she did often, the bows flew up in the air and dangled drunkenly off to the side of the Yorkie's head. When Frances straightened the bows, the dog tried to bite her again. I could almost tolerate the dog's meanness; after all, the dog was old. What made me crazy was the dog's smell. Frances kept an atomizer on the mantel and every few seconds would spray perfume into the air around Duchess. This would send the dog into a snapping frenzy and then into a sneezing fit. There is no way to describe Georgio mixed with old dog smell. I often wished for a gas mask.

I tried to block all this out. This was business I told myself. I needed the money, and therefore I was going to paint Frances Lymington and her foul dog and make them both look just goddamn heavenly.

Of course, it didn't happen. After three weeks of Frances and her odoriferous canine, I snapped.

It started when Frances kept me waiting again. It escalated when Duchess almost took off my ear when I leaned over and tried to tilt the dog's head. And it all fell apart when Frances looked down her nose at me and said, "Isn't this taking rather long? I had heard you were so speedy."

There are rare magical moments in an artist's life when a painting appears in the mind so perfect and vivid that the artist has only to place the brush on the canvas and the picture literally paints itself. That's what happened to me that day. I began to paint faster and faster, throwing colors and mixing paints at breakneck speed. The image went directly from my brain to the canvas. All sound ceased for me. I didn't hear Duchess bark or Frances drone on about how long this was taking. I just visualized the painting. When I stopped, I stood back and looked at what I had done. Until that moment, I had only envisioned it in my mind. On canvas it was brilliant.

"Thank God, you've stopped," Frances said. "My neck is cramped and Duchess is very hungry," Frances lifted Duchess's limp body in the air and kissed her nose. "Aren't you, my precious?" Duchess, who had fallen asleep an hour ago, now awoke at the mention of food. Her yellow rheumy eyes opened wide and she snapped at the air and snarled.

I wiped off my brushes and began to pack up my paints. I saw Frances eyeing me.

"What are you doing?"

"I'm finished."

"What? You can't be," she said, coming around behind me.

I continued to pack up paints while she stared at her portrait.

"This is some kind of joke, isn't it?"

"No joke."

"You can't be serious."

"Sure I can."

"I will not pay for this," she said. "This…is…an…outrage! I should sue you for wasting my time. You call yourself an artist? This is a disgrace—"

"Call it what you will," I said as I lifted the painting off the easel. "But that's exactly how I see you."

I left Frances still sputtering as I carried my supplies out to the car. I arrived home, unplugged the phone, and took a nap.

The buzzer rang not too long after I had fallen asleep.

"Yeah? " I said into the intercom.

"It's me. Lettie."

"Come on up." I buzzed her in.

She stepped off the elevator and I hugged her.

"If it isn't my Florence Nightingale."

"*Doctor* Nightingale to you."

"Oh, that's right. I forgot."

Lettie and I hadn't talked all that much after Malqueen had dragged me back home for that meeting on my financial crisis. I knew she had to know about the debts from Cerise, but she never asked me about them.

"Want some tea? Or something stronger?"

"Tea's fine. What's this?" she said, walking over to my easel.

"Frances Lymington's portrait."

"You're a glutton for punishment."

"Maybe, but I needed the money."

Lettie turned around and looked at me. "Cerise told me. Is it all settled?"

"Well, I've paid back the people who wanted to kill me. I still owe Lightning, although he keeps leaving the money I give him on the table. And every now and then some building supplier sends me an invoice...but I can handle it."

"And you're working."

"Sort of."

"Mind if I look?" she said, lifting the cover.

I waited and watched. She looked at me and then back at the portrait. When she started to laugh, I grinned at her from the kitchen as I made the tea.

"I don't believe you did that," Lettie said, shaking her head and looking at the picture. "Has she seen it?"

"Saw it this very morning...and promptly fired me."

"Oh, Sara. I'm so sorry."

"It was a stupid move on my part. I shouldn't have tried to paint someone I absolutely abhor."

"Does Barbara know?"

I looked at the phone. "I don't know. I unplugged the phone."

"You'd better keep it that way until she calms down."

But Barbara didn't even try the telephone. She just came over and read me the riot act.

I heard the buzzer and didn't answer. Then I heard Barbara's voice scream over the intercom.

"How could you do this to me?"

I didn't answer.

"You humiliated me. She's Randall's aunt. I'm caught in the middle on this."

I still didn't respond.

"I know you're up there. I can see your lights from the outside window...Sara? Answer me. Don't be such a coward."

I reached for the intercom and said, "I'm not a coward. I don't feel like talking about it."

"I can't believe you did this to me."

"You already said that. And I didn't do anything to you."

"Frances Lymington is part of our family, Sara. How could you do this?"

"She's not part of my family. And I think if you check with Randall, he'll tell you he doesn't like her either. You're the only one who talks to her."

"Not true. Mother talks to her."

"Only when Mother needs money for the church."

"Sara, let me in."

"Only if you stop yelling."

There was silence and then Barbara said, "OK. I won't yell."

I buzzed her up. She was yelling as she came out of the elevator.

"I trusted you. You told me you'd do your best."

"I did. It's probably the best portrait I've ever done."

Barbara walked past me over to the painting and lifted the cover.

"Oh my God," she said, holding her head. "It's worse than I thought. How could you do this? How could you do this?" She sank to the floor.

"Once I got inspired, it was easy," I said, helping her off the floor and dragging her over to the sofa. "Look, I didn't set out to humiliate you. All I wanted to do was make a lot of money. But something strange happened. I ended up painting her from a vision I had in my mind."

"Vision-smision. You painted Duchess's head onto Frances Lymington's body and Frances's head onto Duchess's body because you hate her and you wanted to make fun of her."

I sighed. "Does it matter why I painted her that way? I just did."

Neither of us spoke for several minutes. Finally I said, "You know I really screwed myself on this one. She'll never pay me for this."

"She'll also try to ruin your portrait business. Have you thought about that?"

I hadn't and I told Barbara, "She can't. My reputation's too sound for her to hurt me."

Barbara just shook her head. "She's vicious when she's crossed. She'll find a way to get back at you, or me, or someone in the family." Barbara shuddered.

"Barbara, Frances can't hurt me. Frances can only hurt the people who need her."

Barbara looked at the picture then over at me and shook her head in dismay.

"I worry about you, Sara."

"Don't. I'll be fine. Frances Lymington can't hurt me."

I was right. I didn't need Frances to ruin my career. I ended up doing that all by myself.

Chapter Twenty

⸱

"The course of true love never did
run smooth."

Shakespeare

I painted three portraits before I gave up. The first two turned out so-so, and I did get paid for them, but I never finished the third one. The gift of being able to enhance a person's flaws and still make that person look like themselves became something of a mystery for me. I would stand in front of the canvas and know how to do it, but I couldn't make my hand do what my mind wanted it to do. I finally just stopped painting. I slept a lot, and when I was awake, I watched a lot of television. The same programs that had mesmerized me during the time I had the flu kept me a prisoner in my loft. How could I go out when *Hollywood Squares* was on? Did I really need milk? I could drink my coffee black if it meant I wouldn't miss an episode of *As the World Turns*. And did I really need coffee if it meant I might miss *The Price Is Right?* I unplugged the phone and stayed in for weeks at a time. And just as before, Malqueen came to get me.

Malqueen got Lightning to let her into the building. I heard her talking to herself as the elevator rose from the basement.

"Can't believe the child is disappearing from the human race again...don't know what children think nowadays...get in a tough spot you got to keep workin' to get out of that spot...can't be sitting around watching game shows and thinkin' your troubles are just going to melt away...got to fight to set your life right."

The cage opened and Malqueen said, "Get up."

I was spread out on the sofa watching reruns of *GÕligan's Island*.

"Sara? Let's go."

"Where?" I said as the Professor and Gilligan snuck up behind MaryAnn.

"With me."

"To do what?"

"I need help."

"That's a joke. What do you need help with?'

"Rosa quit."

"Sorry," I said as I sat up and tried to see around Malqueen's hips. "Why'd she leave?"

"Got a job at T.Rowe Price as a stockbroker."

"No kidding? Good for her. I didn't even know she had a business degree."

"You don't know a lot of things." Malqueen still stood in front of the television.

"Malqueen, I can't see the TV."

"That's the idea. Get your coat."

"Why?"

"Because you're comin' with me."

"And where would that be?"

"Back to the shop. I told you I need help."

"Wait a minute. You want me to take Rosa's place?"

"Yep."

"Malqueen, I'd be happy to help out for a while, but putting pies in boxes and cookies in bags is not exactly my first career choice."

"And what exactly is your career choice?"

"I'm a portrait painter."

Malqueen looked around the loft. "That's funny. I don't see no portraits being painted...do you?"

"I'm in a slump. I'll be painting in no time."

"Well, until 'no time' gets here, you can get your coat and come help me...just until you decide to start paintin' again."

Malqueen turned off the TV and handed me my coat. I followed her out the door, down the street, and into my new place of employment.

Working the counter at Mrs. M's Homemade Pies and Desserts kept me from thinking about my missing husband and also about my inability to paint. Malqueen gave me my choice of the morning shift or the evening shift. I chose the morning, not because I enjoyed getting up at the crack of dawn, but because at that hour everyone, not just me, was miserable.

I got up at 5:30 a.m. to open the shop at 6:00 a.m. From 6:00 a.m. to 9:00 a.m. Rhonda and I worked the counter. Then from 10:00 a.m. to noon I was by myself. My day ended at noon. Malqueen paid me minimum wage, which was five dollars an hour back then. I usually went home and took a nap for a couple of hours, and then I spent my evenings in the Blue Parrot. It took me a while before it finally dawned on me that Malqueen watched me during the day and Lightning kept an eye on me at night.

During the three months I worked for Malqueen, I still hadn't heard from Aubrey. But I did hear rumors...especially when I was in the Parrot.

One night a merchant marine came into the bar and wanted to know where Aubrey was. When Iron Man told him he had disappeared, the sailor said, "Well, maybe that was him." When Iron Man asked him what he meant, the merchant marine said, "I thought I saw Aubrey on a boat in Grenada."

But then another sailor would come in and ask for Aubrey, and he would tell us he saw Aubrey on a boat docked in Antiqua. Aubrey sightings became common whenever a new ship came into port. If all the rumors were true, Aubrey was sailing into a different port every night.

I finally learned where Aubrey really was when Edgar, his brother, called me from Australia one night.

"Sara," a familiar voice said.

"Aubrey?"

"No, it's Edgar. Sorry to bother you at this hour...the time difference and all...but Aubrey asked me to call you."

"Oh?"

"He said he's sorry, Sara. He never meant for any of this to happen."

"Do you even know what happened?"

There was a long silence and finally Edgar said, "Yes, he said it was a repeat of something that happened in his senior year at Helman Prep."

"And what happened during his senior year?"

"He was caught with another student in the gym."

I didn't say anything.

"...and it wasn't a female student."

I still didn't say anything.

"Father was devastated. Aubrey was the heir apparent. All his dreams of future generations went down the drain...Mother always thought it was a phase he was going through. She kept insisting if he found the right girl he would change. And Sara he did with you. I've never seen him so happy. I really thought the two of you could make it work. I never thought he would risk his relationship with you to—"

"You knew he was gay?"

"He's not gay. He's bisexual."

"Is that supposed to make me feel better?"

"I just wanted you to know that he's never been gay. He's always had relationships with women."

"Good for him. Gives him more dating options. But it still doesn't make me feel any better about it."

"Sara, I just wanted you to know, I mean, Aubrey just wants you to know that he did love you. He made some terrible mistakes, but he never wanted to hurt you."

"I guess he never wanted to steal from me either."

"What?"

"Steal from me. As in wiping out my checking account? Or didn't he tell you that?"

"He took your money?"

"Two thousand dollars. But then I guess it got him to wherever he is now."

"He's in Mexico. He's working on a boat. Sara, let me send you a check for the two grand. I'm so sorry. I didn't know—"

"Edgar, keep your money. After all, you aren't your brother's keeper."

I hung up, poured myself a glass of wine, and stared out the window into the street. I didn't want Edgar's money. I just wanted my old life back.

Chapter Twenty One

"Having nothing, nothing can he lose."

Shakespeare

Two things occurred that changed my life again. The first event happened while I was behind the counter at Mrs. M's serving up a dozen bagels with low-fat cream cheese, along with two dozen low-fat multi-berry muffins.

"Must be a weight-conscience office," I said as I handed the bags to a well-dressed male thirtysomething.

"It's not an office. But the people I work with are very concerned about their appearance."

I had to ask. "Where do you work?"

"Landstrom."

Rhonda stopped pouring coffee for two electricians who were talking to Malqueen. She leaned over and said, "I was in there once, you know... saw a dress hanging on one of the racks by the front door...beautiful red velour dress...you know red's my color. Anyway, it woulda been perfect for New Year's." Rhonda resumed her pouring. "Then I looked at the price tag."

"And?" I said, taking the thirtysomething's money.

"It was four hundred dollars. Can you imagine? Four...hundred...dollars. That's a down payment on a car, for Pete's sake." Rhonda stopped pouring again and pointed the coffeepot in my direction. "Who'd pay four hundred dollars for one dress?"

My customer chuckled. "You'd be surprised. Some of the dresses in The Boutique sell for thousands of dollars."

"Oh, good Lord," Rhonda said. "What person in Baltimore can afford a thousand-dollar dress?"

Malqueen and I exchanged looks and I said, "Obviously nobody behind this counter."

I handed the man his change and said, "I've been in Landstrom...It's a lovely store. Must be a terrific place to work...I mean, listening to that piano music all day, surrounded by beautiful clothes, the smell of Starbucks wafting up from the first floor—"

"Why don't you apply?" he said, looking at me.

"Who me? I don't know anything about selling clothes."

"They actually prefer that. They like to start with a clean slate."

"Are you serious?"

"Look at me," he said. "I have a degree in communications...They got me right out of college, and I'm working toward a buyer's job in men's shoes."

"Really." I looked over at Malqueen, who had stopped talking.

"Really. You ought to come over and fill out an application. You seem bright, and you're very friendly. They like that."

"They don't care if you have no sales experience?"

"I didn't," he said as he turned and started to walk away. "And they hired me."

Something made me walk around the counter and stop him.

"I should introduce myself, "I said, holding out my hand. "My name's Sara...Sara Gorman."

"Jonathon," he said, shaking my hand. "I'm serious about the job... Come over and see my boss. His name's Dan Quinter...Tell him I told you to come in."

I watched him leave the shop, and then I went back to the counter.

"So, you going over to that Landstrom's and applying for a position?" Malqueen said from behind me.

"Well, I don't know," I stuttered. "I mean, I don't want to leave you in the lurch right now...I mean—"

"You're not leavin' me nowhere," Malqueen said. "Rhonda?"

"Yes ma'am?"

"Tell your sister the job is hers."

"Wow, will she be thrilled! When can she start?"

Malqueen smiled at me and said, "As soon as Landstrom hires Sara."

Landstrom hired me the day I applied. I gave Malqueen my notice and began my training with Landstrom the following Monday. Landstrom never did tell me how to sell. They just said to think of my department as if it were my own business. They promised me that if I knew my merchandise and believed it was a good product that it would sell itself..

At first, I wasn't even sure I could sell anything. After all, I was an introvert in an extrovert's job. Management placed me in Men's Shoes. Since I knew nothing about what I was supposed to be selling, I listened to Jonathon and some of the more experienced salesmen. I did learn. And the more I learned about shoes, the more sales I made. It also helped that I was selling to men.

Jonathon told me that men hate to shop. They only go to the store when they really need something. That's why all the men's departments in stores are located on the ground floor near the exit. Men want to get in, buy something, and get out. Jonathon also explained that, unlike women, who think trying on shoes is fun, men would rather spend a day being stuck with pins. And unless they are the rare GQ type, most men have only two thoughts when they come in to buy dress shoes: brown or black.

"All you have to do," Jonathon said, "is get them to look at the shoes. Most of them won't even bother to try them on. If you can do that, you've got a sale."

Jonathon was right. If I got them in the chair and got them to tell me their size, I usually could sell them something. Sometimes it was too easy.

"But wouldn't you like to try them on?" I'd urge. "Just to make sure they'll fit?"

"No, no. They're my size. They'll fit. How much are they?"

"Eighty dollars. How about some shoe polish and some shoe trees?"

"Sure. Whatever."

"You really should try them on. Sometimes the sizing's different."

"Can I bring them back?"

"Absolutely."

"Good. Then I'll take them and try them on at home."

After two months I discovered I liked working in Landstrom. When Dan, the buyer of Men's Shoes, discovered I had an art background, he encouraged me to arrange the shoe displays. The rest of the selling staff liked the way I displayed the shoes because I was a salesperson just like them, so I understood they needed the shoes to be grouped together in a way that made sense to them.

"I like the way you did this," Jonathon said, looking around the department. "You've got all the sports shoes on the right side of the store, the middle-of-the-road-priced numbers in the middle of the department, and the high-end shoes over on the left. Makes a lot of sense."

"Yeah," Cecil said as he flew by carrying six boxes of stacked shoes. "Remember that wacko from New York? He hung shoes from the ceiling. He told us that shoes dangling down from the ceiling would create drama and create more sales. It created drama all right. If a tall person walked into the department, he'd hit his head on one of the suspended shoes and send it into motion. Then that shoe would hit the shoe next to it, setting off a chain reaction. In a matter of minutes, the whole ceiling was in motion. I used to look up sometimes and think I was going down on the *Titanic*." Cecil gracefully dropped the boxes next to his customer. "Not to mention all the headaches I used to get trying to look up at the bottom of soles all day trying to read the price."

"Whatever happened to him?" I asked.

"Oh, I think he got a job at IKEA," Jonathon said.

I kept my career change a secret. The only person who knew was Malqueen.

"You tell anybody yet?" Malqueen asked as I picked up the muffin and bagel order for my department. Jonathon, who worked in the same department, had passed that job onto to me.

"No, and I don't plan to."

"Why not?"

"They'll never understand."

"Someone's going to find out," Malqueen said, shaking her head. "Don't you think it's better if you just tell them?"

"No, I do not."

I should have known Barbara would be the first one in the family to discover my secret. After all, a large part of her day was spent cruising shopping malls in search of pink golf pants for Randall and checking out the sales at Talbots and Eddie Bauer for herself. I heard her before I saw her.

"Sara! Yoo-hoo! Over here," she called to me from the cosmetic counter. I waved to her but stayed in my department. I watched as she continued to wave me over. When she realized that I wasn't coming, she picked up her bags and marched over to Men's Shoes.

"Why didn't you come over when I called? I wanted to show you this new lipstick. It's called 'Cardinal Red.' Do you think they mean the bird or the color of His Eminence's robe? It sort of looks like the color of the bird, but it could—" She stared at my chest.

"Why are you wearing a name tag?"

"Because I work here."

"Randall would love these Cole Haans." Barbara picked up a loafer on display. "Feel the leather. He's on his feet so much he says these feel just like bedroom slippers, and sturdy too. But you know how Randall is about spending money on shoes...DID YOU SAY YOU WORK HERE?"

"Yes. And I have a customer. Excuse me." I left her standing there with a loafer swinging off her index finger as I headed for the stockroom. She came after me.

"Wait. You can't be serious. You work here? In this store?"

"Yes."

"But where do you work? I'm in here at least twice a week. This is the first time I've seen you."

Barbara, I work here...in this department...Men's Shoes. I've been here for three months."

Barbara clutched the shoe to her chest and fell back into one of the leather chairs. Sidney, one of our salesmen, rushed over to find out what was going on.

"Madame, are you ill?"

"I'm sick, just sick. I can't believe what I'm hearing. My baby sister sells shoes? To men!" Barbara threw the shoe in the air, which ricocheted off Sidney's knee and rolled onto the floor and under a chair. "Tell me this is a joke," Barbara said, sitting up again.

"No joke, Barbara. I work here."

Sid rubbed his knee, picked up the shoe, and placed it back on its polished podium. He began eyeing my customer.

"Barbara, there's nothing wrong with working in a department store."

"Sara, be reasonable. Selling shoes is a far cry from painting society portraits. Why on earth would you do such a thing?"

"To eat and pay rent are two pretty good reasons." I watched as Sidney sidled up to my customer and engaged him in conversation.

"Look, Barbara, I'm working. Can we talk about this later? I tried to steer her out of the department. She would have none of it. Using her shopping bags, she pinned me against the Johnson and Murphy shoe display.

"NO! We will NOT discuss this later. I told you that if you ever needed money to come to me. Why didn't you tell me you were in trouble?"

I glanced over at Sid, who now had my customer stroking the leather of a $300 pair of Ferragamo loafers. This was the same customer who had asked me if we had Florsheims on sale. Sidney looked up with dollar signs in his eyes. I tried to push Barbara away, but the more I struggled, the more entangled I became with her shopping paraphernalia. The nylon handles of her bags had somehow gotten wrapped around my wrists, and I now found myself handcuffed to my sister.

"I'm not in trouble. I'm fine," I said as I struggled with the handles. "And I certainly wouldn't ask you for money."

"But I want you to. You're my sister."

"Being your sister doesn't entitle me to your money. Just as your being my sister doesn't entitle you to tell me what to do."

"Well!" Barbara said and stepped back. The bags untangled, and my handcuffs fell to the floor. We glared at each other. I looked away first.

"Look, Barbara, I'm sorry. I appreciate your offer. But can't you just let it be? I'm fine. I'm working…It's a change—"

"Change! Sara, you used to paint important people. You made lots of money. Why would you want to lower yourself and sell shoes in a department store? What happened?" It was as if a lightbulb went off over Barbara's head. She pushed me further back into the shoe display and said, "Oh my God…He took it all, didn't he?"

I looked away.

"I can't believe it. He took it all?"

"Barbara, I don't want to talk about it."

"That gigolo! That common construction worker. How dare he steal your hard-earned money? I know a lawyer. You can get it out of him—"

"No, Barbara, I can't. He's in Mexico.

"So? The lawyer can go to Mexico."

"I don't want any money. I want to divorce him."

I hadn't mentioned the dreaded "D" word until that very moment.

Barbara stood very still. Then she said, "Are you sure?"

"Positive."

I don't know why I expected Barbara to try and talk me out of it. I guess because she had stayed married to Randall despite all his infidelities. But she didn't. Instead she said, "I'll get you a lawyer."

"I already have one."

"Oh," she said sadly still staring at me. I watched Sidney who was practically skipping out of the stockroom, his arms filled with Ferragamo shoe boxes.

"You can't give it up." I saw her eyes fill up.

I knew she meant painting, but I didn't say anything.

"You just can't."

"Barbara, I didn't give it up. It gave me up."

Barbara looked puzzled. "What are you talking about?"

"I haven't been able to paint since Frances Lymington...No, don't look like that. It's not your fault...It's not anyone's fault. I've just lost interest, and along with the interest, I've lost the knack."

"But, surely you can—"

"No. I can't. Anyway, I have another job right now. And while I know you won't believe me when I tell you this...I really like this job."

Barbara sniffled and whacked me in the leg with her Ann Taylor bag.

"Sara, I just want you to be happy. If you like it here..." Barbara said as she glanced around the department in disbelief, "...then that's great. Who knows? Maybe you'll decide to paint again and—"

"I don't think so."

"Well, like I said. I just want you to be happy. Why do you think I do the things I do?"

I had often wondered why she did many of the things she did, especially when it came to me. But, of course, I didn't say that. I did believe that she wanted me to be happy. She just didn't have a clue as to how to make that happen. But then she wasn't alone in that department, because at this point in my life, I had no idea what would make me happy either.

"Barbara, go home. I'm working. I'll talk to you later." I took her arm and led her away from my department. "Besides," I said, "there is an advantage to me working here."

"Oh, Sara, please! What advantage could there possibly be…fooling around with men's feet…" Barbara wrinkled her nose. "Wasting your education…ignoring you talent—"

"Thirty percent," I said.

"Thirty percent, what?"

"I get a thirty percent discount on all the merchandise in the store."

"Really?" Barbara's face brightened. I watched as she struggled to control her excitement.

"Just tell me what you want and I can get it for you."

Barbara's eyes darted around the store.

"On anything?"

"Anything."

"Coach bags?"

"Yep."

"Versace suits?"

"Sure."

Barbara's eyes glittered, but then she remembered she wasn't supposed to be excited about my new place of employment. She stuck her chin in the air and said, "Well, it still doesn't make me feel any better about you working here. If you wanted to sell something, you could have gone to work for Randall and sold Cadillacs. Randall would have—"

"Good-bye, Barbara," I said, giving her a friendly shove toward the door. She reluctantly headed out. I watched her various shopping bags swing from her side and smiled as she spied the cashmere coats by the mall door. She ran her hands up and down the fabric and then discreetly flipped over the price tag. Her brow wrinkled, and then she looked up with delight. My sister, who for years claimed to be no good at math, could figure 30 percent off a designer coat faster than a Sharp calculator.

I turned to check out the shoe department and saw my customer hand his Visa to Sidney. I tried not to think about how much commission I had just lost. Sid was singing, "Oh what a beautiful morning," as he rang up three pairs of Ferragamo shoes, three shoe trees, and various jars of shoe polish. In shoe sales talk, I had just been "snaked." I decided to ignore Sid and find another sale. I struck up a conversation with a young guy looking for a pair of Docksiders. But I wasn't really concentrating. I kept wondering just how long it would take before Barbara told Mother and Father I was now selling men's shoes for a living—and, of course, the even more astounding revelation that I was getting divorced.

As a parish priest, Father had spent a great deal of his time counseling couples out of divorce. And Mother had spent a great deal of her time gossiping about the people who actually went through with it. For them, as for most of their friends, marriage was a lifetime sentence. They took their marriage vows seriously—for richer or for poorer, in sickness and in health, and of course, the unspoken but always present, in love and in hate.

I hadn't known I wanted a divorce until I had spoken those words to Barbara. But now that I had, I understood that I couldn't forgive or forget what Aubrey had done. But preaching forgiveness was Father's life's work, and I didn't know what reason I was going to give for divorcing Aubrey. I just knew I couldn't tell them the truth.

I was summoned to the new rectory for tea the following Saturday after my run-in with Barbara.

"Sara," Father began, "I know how difficult this must be for you. Barbara told us what happened." I gave them both my best blank look. I wondered to myself what Barbara had told them.

"I can't believe Aubrey would do this," Mother said. "Steal all your money...money you made from your lovely portraits...He came from such a good family...I am appalled at what a cad he turned out to be...If I ever see his face again I'll—"

"I don't think you will. He went back to Mexico."

"So, he's a coward too. Runs off to a foreign country to hide. How could he do this? Just how could he embarrass our family like this? I just—"

"Caroline," Father said, "I'm more concerned about Sara than any embarrassment to the family."

"Why, of course, dear. What kind of mother do you think I am?"

That question hung in the air for several seconds before Father finally said to me, "Barbara also told us you have a new job."

Barbara must have been burning up the telephone wires.

"Yes, I'm selling shoes at Landstrom." I cringed and glanced over at Mother. But she smiled and said, "She told us you get a 30 percent discount. How absolutely divine."

I began to feel like I had entered the Twilight Zone. I had expected histrionics from Mother and disappointment from Father. I got neither.

"Do you enjoy your new job?" Father asked.

"Yes, I do."

"Good. That's important. You should always enjoy what you do for a living."

I looked at both of them and wondered if I had stumbled into someone else's house. They actually didn't seem to mind the fact that I sold shoes. They didn't ask me why I had stopped painting, and it looked as if Aubrey's stealing was going to be an acceptable reason for divorce.

I decided that now was probably a good time to give them the presents I had picked out for them. Mother opened her box first.

"My...what an expensive-looking pair of shoes," Mother said. "Sara, these are lovely. William, aren't they lovely?" Mother held her foot up for Father to see.

"They certainly are. And look what I have. Loafers! I haven't worn loafers in years. And with tassels too; let me see how they fit." Father slipped his feet into the shoes and walked around the study. "These feel wonderful!"

"European leather," I said. "It's softer than American leather."

"Caroline, are yours unbelievably comfortable? I feel like I'm walking on a pillow." Mother took two steps and said, "Yes they are—" But before she could finish her thought, Father grabbed her and waltzed her around the living room. When Father finally released Mother, and they both flopped down on the sofa, I asked, "So...you two don't mind if I sell shoes for a living?"

"Mind? Of course we don't mind. Not if that's what you want to do," Father said. I turned to Mother.

"And it doesn't embarrass you?"

"Why should it embarrass me, dear? After all, the good Lord bathed the feet of the poor."

Father smiled at her, put his arm around her shoulders, and kissed her on the forehead.

I ate a whole plate of gingersnaps and drank three cups of Darjeeling as Father and Mother asked me about working at Landstrom. Aubrey and my impending divorce weren't mentioned again. It was one of the most perplexing, yet pleasant, visits I had ever had with my parents. Apparently, Barbara was the only one who was mortified by my career change. My parents didn't seem to care. In fact, they were dancing when I left. Mother had slipped off her new pumps, while Father, still in his new Italian loafers, waved good-bye, as he and mother fox-trotted out of the living room and disappeared down the hall.

The second important thing that happened to me after Aubrey left was much more insidious. I spent almost every night at the Parrot. I'd wait while Lightning locked up and then we'd walk home. One night, about six months after Aubrey had left, I said good night to Lightning in the foyer as usual and got on the elevator. As soon as the lift lurched upward, my heart began to pound. I felt like I was suffocating, and I couldn't get a deep breath. I managed to push the down button as my heart raced and images of dying filled my head. But as soon as I got to the lobby, I felt fine. Lightning, having heard the lift come back down, had stuck his head out of his door and said, "Yoose OK?" I said I was fine and pushed the up button again. I got to the second floor, and my heart started to race again. I was savvy enough to put two and two together. Obviously, my strange symptoms were tied to going back to the loft. I told myself that this was all in my head. I willed myself to the third floor, and once I was in the loft, I was fine.

The heart-racing and the breathlessness didn't occur every evening. Sometimes I could go a whole month and feel fine. But then I noticed something else. I began checking the locks on the elevator and the windows three and four times a night. I put double window locks on the skylights. And when the phone rang at night, I jumped. Before Aubrey left, when I couldn't sleep, I used to spend hours on the sofa, staring up at the moon as it made its journey from one side of the loft to the other. I had found the moonlight enchanting then. Now, when I watched the moon glide overhead, all I saw were distorted shadows on the wall—shadows that made me turn on lights and watch infomercials until 4:00 a.m.

It took a conversation with Lettie to make me understand what was happening.

"So I'm probably not having a heart attack when my heart races like that?"

"Do your hands tingle and are your palms sweaty?" she asked.

"Sometimes."

"Do you feel like something terrible is about to happen?"

"Yes. But I don't know what it is."

"Well, if you're worried come in for a checkup. But it sounds like an anxiety attack to me."

"About what?"

I don't know, Sara. Could be anything. You've had a rough year."

"Thanks, Doc."

"Want to come in and talk with someone?"

"As in a shrink? No, thanks."

"Well, then you might want to think about moving. Maybe there are just too many bad memories in the loft for you to deal with right now."

"Leave the loft? I can't do that. I've been here for twenty years! It's the best deal in Fells Point."

"I know. But you do have a new job. Why not a new place to live?"

"I couldn't. What would I tell Lightning?"

"The truth. He'd be sad but he'd understand."

"Where would I go?"

"Wherever you wanted to go."

"No, Lettie. I just can't do it."

It took me several more months and three more panic attacks before I finally decided to move. I began to read the real estate section. And I also began to drop hints to both Malqueen and Lightning.

"What do you think of Roland Park?" I asked them one day as we all had coffee in Mrs. M's.

"What are we supposed to think?" Malqueen said. "That's where you grew up. The old rectory is there. I have good memories of that place."

I looked at Lightning.

"Don't look at me. I never lived there. I was born and raised in Fells Point. I'll die here."

I held up the paper in front of my face and said, "What if I moved there?"

Malqueen smacked the paper down.

"Why?" she said.

Lightning looked like I had smacked him.

"I don't know. Change?"

Malqueen leaned over and said, "What's wrong?"

"I'm not sure. I just know I'm not happy there anymore."

"I knew this was going to happen," Lightning said to Malqueen. "He ruined the place for her. Left her with all kinds of bad memories. Didn't I tell you about her going up and down and up and down in that elevator sometimes?"

"You knew?"

"Well, it was pretty easy to see. You'd come down on the elevator and act like nothin' was wrong, all the while you're holding your heart and breathing funny. And then, just when I was ready to call the ambulance, you suddenly looked fine again. Wasn't hard to figure you was havin' trouble going in there."

"Look, you two, the last thing I want to do is move away from you. But maybe it is time to find a new place. You can help...Look around and we'll see if I can stay in the neighborhood."

When I said that, I really did believe I was going to stay in Fells Point. But then I got an offer I couldn't refuse.

Chapter Twenty-Two

"My kingdom for a horse."
Shakespeare

Lettie called me one day while I was getting ready for work.

"What are your days off this week?" she said as I buttered toast and listened.

"Tuesday and Wednesday, why?"

"Good. You have an appointment to see Snookie Carmichal on Tuesday."

"Are you talking about THE Snookie Carmichal?"

"Yes, the horse breeder. She has three or four cottages on her estate. I know she rents them out. Remember Ursula the witch?"

"How could I forget?" Ursula had been in our class at BrownWood. In tenth grade she had fallen into the occult section of the library. She had never escaped.

"Well, Ursula rented one of Snookie's cottages last year. But they had some kind of misunderstanding, and Snookie kicked her out. The cottage is for rent."

"I don't know, Lettie. Isn't she way up York Road? I mean, that's so far."

"It's only a twenty-minute drive to Landstrom. Thirty minutes into the city. It would be a real change for you, Sara."

"I don't even know Snookie Carmichal. How can I—"

"Not to worry. It's all set. All you have to do is show up for the appointment."

"I don't know."

"Sara, just go and talk to her. But promise me one thing."

"What?"

"Don't tell her you're afraid of horses."

"Can't I just tell her I was thrown as a child and I'm still a little gun-shy around them?" That was the truth.

"NO! Not if you want that cottage. Horses are Snookie's life."

And so on Tuesday, I drove north up York Road, the road Father called "the scenic route to Pennsylvania," and headed for Snookie's horse farm. I picked up the farm's white fences just past Hereford and followed them for two miles until I came to a sign that read, "Carmichal Stud Farm." Turning off York Road, I bumped up the dirt road and found myself surrounded on both sides by thoroughbreds galloping past me, snorting their frosty greeting in the cold morning air as they glided by and continued on along inside the fence. I stopped the car and watched them race toward the other side of the pasture— truly beautiful creatures when they ran, and truly terrifying beasts when I had to get close to them. While we had all taken riding lessons as children, Natalie had been the real horsewoman of the family.

"Come on, Sara. You can do it. Give me your foot and I'll get you up. Dish is gentle. He won't hurt you."

I eyed Dish and he eyed me.

"I'm scared."

"There's nothing to it. Just do what I do."

I watched as Natalie swung up easily into the saddle.

"See?" she said, hopping off Dish. "Now you try."

"I'm still scared."

"I promise I won't let anything happen to you. Now, don't be a baby... come on." Natalie gave me a leg up onto Dish's back. From where I sat, I might as well have been hanging out of the top window of the Empire State Building.

"Now, hold the reins firmly in your hands, give him a gentle kick, and remember your posture!"

I took a deep breath and circled the ring as Natalie shouted, "Posture, Sara, posture! Sit up." But it wasn't too long before "old Dish" sensed who was really in control. One minute I was trotting by a smiling Natalie, and the next minute, "gentle" Dish had thrown me off to the ground. I landed on my back under Dish. Natalie quickly rolled under the horse, grabbed me, and rolled out from the other side before Dish could even move. But the memory of staring up at the underbelly of a thousand-pound horse was enough to keep me from ever wanting to ride again.

A horn honked behind me, and I realized that a pickup truck had been waiting to get by. I waved an apology and continued on, coming to a fork in the road. There were two signs: one said "Stables" with an arrow to the left, and the other simply said "Snookie's Place," with an arrow to the right. The pickup turned left, and I turned right onto a tree-lined road that snaked through what seemed like miles of forest. Just when I thought the road would never end, the woods thinned, and I came into a clearing. What I saw made me slam on the brakes. Snookie's "place" was a castle.

It was just like Lettie not to warn me that Snookie lived in a castle, I thought, as I eased the VW down the narrow road. "Snookie's Place" sat in a secluded valley the size of several football fields. The dirt road led right up to an actual drawbridge, passed over a water-filled moat, and then curved under a stone arch. The road became cobblestone under the arch, circled in front of the castle, and disappeared around the back of the building. I bounced over the wood-planked bridge and followed the cobblestone around to the back, parking between an old white Mercedes station wagon and a brand new black 250 SL. A chestnut thoroughbred with white stockings was tied to a hitching post on the other side of the sports car. I gave him a wide berth, keeping close to the trash-can size blocks of gray stone that made up the exterior of "Snookie's Place."

There was no doorbell, only a rope hanging in front of the main entrance. I pulled it and was treated to the sound of trumpets announcing the "Call to the Post."

The door opened and Peter Lorre in white gloves and an ill-fitting white serving jacket said, "Good day, madam. May I help you?"

"Uh...I'm...ah...here to see...uh...Mrs. Carmichal," I said, trying not to stare at the scars on his face. I have an appointment. My name's Sara Gorman."

Very good, madam," said the butler. "I'll tell Mrs. Carmichal you have arrived. Please follow me."

I did and walked smack into the fifteenth century.

As the daughter of the bishop of Maryland, I have been in some pretty impressive houses. (the most impressive being the Wittridge estate with Frances Lymington's mansion coming in a close second), but nothing could compare to this. Twenty-foot high arched ceilings loomed above me. The walls were crammed with ancestral paintings and medieval-looking tapestries. Armor and ancient weaponry filled the hall. I was no expert on the fifteenth century, but my gut feeling told me that what I was seeing was authentic. I tiptoed behind Snookie's butler through a maze of stone hallways and into a room filled with leather-bound books neatly lined up on massive mahogany bookshelves. A roaring fire provided what seemed to be the only heat in the room. When the butler left, I moved closer to the fire. Either Snookie was a purist or cheap; it was freezing in this place. But before I could even get warm, the jangling of spurs on stone announced Snookie's arrival.

"Sara Gorman?" Snookie offered me her hand.

"How do you do, Mrs. Carmichal."

"Call me Snookie. Everybody does...even the stable lads...They just put a Mrs. in front of it...sometimes."

"You have a lovely...uh...estate."

"Isn't it grand? I designed it after Stirling Castle. Have you heard of it?"

I hadn't, but I knew from the Society pages that Snookie's maiden name had been McKenzie.

"Scottish?"

"Right! They called it the gateway to the Highlands. Great view from the castle. James the Third was born at Stirling and Mary Queen of Scots lived there as well...quite a gory past it had too," she said, rubbing her hands together.

"How interesting," I shivered.

"How rude of me...It is a tad chilly in here. Would you care for some coffee or tea?"

"Coffee would be lovely."

Snookie got up, pressed a buzzer, turned her back to me, and talked for some length into a grate in a stone in the wall. She was dressed to ride: skin-tight tan breeches, black turtleneck, and black boots. My eyes were drawn to the spurs on the boots. Horse people in this part of the country don't wear them. Cowboys use spurs, breeders don't. It takes an expert horse person to use them properly, because if used carelessly, they can cut a horse to ribbons.

"So," Snookie said, pivoting quickly and catching me staring at the spurs.

"Ah...you're wondering why I have spurs on."

"Oh, no...not really."

"Nonsense! Of course you are. Very observant of you. No one wears spurs around here...except Cowboy Bob down the road, and he's a fool...Man should be shot...wears stupid ten-gallon hats and western shirts...thinks he's Roy Rogers...acts more like trigger's ass. Anyway, one of my trainers suggested I try them on a difficult stallion I just bought. Can't seem to make the bastard understand who's the boss. You know how stubborn some horses can be." She looked at me expectantly.

"Oh, yes...uh...about the cottage?"

"Cottage? Oh, right. Doc Wittridge tells me you'd like to rent one."

I suppressed the urge to laugh. It was difficult for me to think of Lettie as "Doc." And I knew it was difficult for Lettie as well. She still introduced herself, even to her patients, as just plain old Lettie.

"Do you even have a cottage for rent?"

"Just so happens I do. I have three of them, you know. But I only rent one of them out. Your father's the bishop, right?"

"Yes, he is."

"Can't ask for better references that that, I suppose. Although I'm not all that religious myself...all that singing and praying...rather tedious... Well...to each his own, I say. Does the Bishop ride?"

"Yes, in fact you've probably seen him at Hunt Cup. He usually rides one of Austin Benedict's Irish thoroughbreds—"

"Now I remember him! Fine jumper...Didn't he deliver the prayer at the start of last year's Hunt?"

"Yes, I believe he did."

"Well done. Short and sweet. Can't stand when the prayer lasts longer than two minutes. Makes the horses nervous." Snookie paused to pluck a hair off her shoulder. "And your mother?" she asked, looking over at me.

"What about her?"

"Does she ride?"

"Yes, she was at Hunt Cup with Father." (Mother actually rode better than Father, but I didn't volunteer that information.)

"Hmmmmm...well...and what's the story with your husband?" Snookie put one black boot up on the coffee table and leaned toward me.

"There is no story, other than we're getting divorced."

"Oh, never mind…none of my business. I've not had much use for husbands myself…been married three times." Snookie stood up and stretched. "First one tried to spend all my money, and the second one was a skirt-chaser…got rid of them both. Third one was a charm, though…dropped dead at forty and left me stinking rich…I still toast him at New Year's…"

"Uh…Mrs. Carmichal…Mrs. Snookie…I mean, Snookie, about the cottage?"

Snookie stood up and re-tucked her turtleneck into her pants. I knew she had to be at least fifty, but she could have passed for my age. And I wondered if her youthful appearance was the result of the tightness of her ponytail or the skilled knife of a plastic surgeon. She picked up a hunting crop that had been lying on top of the mantle and absentmindedly began slapping the palm of her hand.

"Well, I don't know why I shouldn't rent the cottage to you. I've known the Wittridges for years." She shrugged. "And, after all, your father is the goddamn bishop…Oh, sorry, guess I shouldn't have put it quite like that. Anyway…the rent for the cottage is three hundred dollars a month."

I forced myself to keep my jaw from dropping. But Snookie must have seen my expression.

"You're wondering why it's so cheap?"

"No," I said a little too quickly.

"Well, it is cheap. But I expect you to do other things in return."

"Like what?" I asked suspiciously.

"I'll expect you to maintain the grounds around the cottage…mow the lawn…prune…plant geraniums or whatever it is people plant in those window things…just make it look better than it does now. The inside you can do what you want. It's just been painted white, so don't paint it neon orange or black for God's sake. Had a woman in that cottage last year who painted the inside black—thought she was a witch or something. Name was Irma. No…that's not right, name was Ursula. You don't know her, do you?"

"Never heard of her."

"Addled woman ran around chanting to spirits or some such nonsense and scaring the hell out of the lads…took four coats of white to cover the frigging black paint…so I can't have any of that…And, of course, there are five stalls not too far from your cottage. When they're filled, which they aren't at the moment, I'll expect you to help muck them out. You can clear that with Ian, the farm manager. Any questions?"

"No."

Snookie slapped the whip against her thigh and looked out a bay window that overlooked her racing track. She turned abruptly and said, "You do ride, don't you?"

"Uh. Sure."

"Uh? Sure? Not a lot of enthusiasm there."

"I took lessons as a child...with Mr. Granger."

"We all did. What about now?"

"Well, I don't really have the time now."

"But would you if you had the time?"

"Well, maybe...but I really don't have the time."

"Nonsense! You make time. I'll let you ride any horse in my stable provided you're competent...How about now?"

"Now?" I gulped. "I don't think so. I'm very rusty, and I'd probably spook the poor horse...Besides, I have to get to work—"

"I can have Old Greta saddled and ready in a matter of minutes. Come. We can ride by the cottage and—"

"No!"

Snookie turned slowly from the window, the tip of her whip peeking up from behind her shoulder.

"No?" she said softly.

"I said I don't care to ride."

"Today? Tomorrow? Or never?" The side of her mouth began to twitch. I fidgeted on the divan and fixed my gaze on Snookie's spurs.

"Oh, all right. I confess. I was thrown as a child, and I haven't been on a horse since I was eight. If you want me to muck out a few stalls, I'd be happy to. But I won't be riding...ever." After several seconds of silence, I finally looked up. Snookie's nostrils flared as she raised her arm to the ceiling and cracked the whip on the stone floor.

"I knew it!" she shouted. "A horse-hater! I can smell a horse-hater a mile away."

"I'm not a horse-hater," I said, jumping up and moving behind the divan. "I just don't like to ride."

"How can you possibly like horses," Snookie said, snapping the whip in the air and knocking over a lamp, "and not want to ride?"

"Some people just appreciate them from a distance. You can like horses from a distance."

"Horse manure!" Snookie's upper lip curled revealing too many big yellow teeth as she whipped the arm of the wing chair. The butler got halfway into the room with the coffee, took one look at Snookie and the whip, dropped the tray, and sprinted out of the room.

"Well…" I said, looking wildly around the room.

"Well, what?" said Snookie as she slowly crept around the chair toward me, the whip held tightly in her hand, her spurs jingling with each deliberate step.

As Malqueen would say, "The Lawd, he works in mysterious ways," and he certainly did that day. My eyes fell on a bookcase filled with Dick Francis novels.

"Well, for one thing…I love Dick Francis novels," I said, pointing to the bookcase. "I've read every novel he's ever written."

The spurs stopped jangling.

"Oh? Is that so? And what was the title of the first book he ever wrote?"

"The Sport of Queens."

"What's your favorite novel?"

"Actually, I like the earlier books better like *Dead Cert and Whip Hand*. I like when the story revolves around the jockey or life on the farm or at the race course." Snookie lowered the whip.

"Me too. I didn't like that one novel where he's supposed to be a computer whiz…"

"Hmmm…or the pilot…"

"Bor-ring. He should just stick to racing."

"I thought *For Kicks* was good, the book about the stud farm. But then you'd know more about that than me."

"It was quite accurate," Snookie said, tossing the whip on the table as she sat down on the divan, crossed her legs, and patted the cushion for me to sit. I eyed the whip as I perched on the edge of the cushion beside her.

"Do you know what he did before he became a writer?" she asked, leaning back into the cushions and putting her hands behind her head.

I shook my head and said, "Rode for Queen Elizabeth. He's a former steeplechase jockey. When he retired at thirty-six, he became a sports writer, which eventually led to the racing books."

Snookie studied me for a few minutes more, then she leaned forward and yelled, "Horst!"

There was silence.

"Horst!"

Still no answer.

"Horst! Goddamn it!" said Snookie, getting up and walking over to the doorway. "Now the dumb shit's deaf! I only hired him because he looks like that gangster actor...What's his name..." Snookie snapped her fingers trying to remember.

"Peter Lorre?"

"That's the one. I thought all those scars would intimidate people. Unfortunately, the man's afraid of his own shadow. Horst!"

Horst finally minced into the room.

Yes, madam?"

"Clear this mess away," Snookie said, kicking the tray and sending it spinning down the hall, "and bring us fresh coffee."

"Certainly, madame." Horst started to bend over in front of Snookie, changed his mind, and instead began picking up bits of broken cups and saucers as he backed out of the room. Snookie flopped back down on the divan next to me.

"You do know Dick Francis, don't you?" she said. "Oh hell, I supposed anyone who can read twenty or so horse novels can't be a complete horse-hater...although we'll have to work on that riding problem of yours," she said, leaning over and brushing an errant wisp of hair out of my face. "Perhaps a few private lessons would restore your confidence...eh?" I sat perfectly still and forced myself to smile.

"Well, we'll see," she said, patting my thigh. "Now tell me what you thought of his latest novel."

I told her and she rented me the cottage.

Later I told Lettie what had happened.

"Did you get it?"

"Yeah. Thanks for not telling me she lived in a castle."

"What? And spoil the surprise? Isn't she a character?"

"That's an understatement. You won't believe what she did when she found out I didn't ride."

"I told you not to tell her that!"

"She knew, Lettie, she knew. I think she can smell a horse-hater from a mile away. God knows she spends enough time with them. She even looks like one."

"How much rent is she charging?"

"Three hundred a month. Do you believe it?"

"What's the place look like?"

"Beats me."

"You didn't look at it? What if it's a dump?"

"It will be an affordable dump. Besides, she scared the hell out of me. It was bad enough I had to stay another hour and talk about books with her. All I wanted was to get out of there and away from that whip."

"She had a whip?"

"And spurs...wait'll I tell you..."

It didn't take me long to pack my belongings and move. Lightning borrowed a truck, and Malqueen and I packed boxes as two friends from the Blue Parrot carried my furniture to the truck.

"You sure about this?" Lightning asked for the hundredth time.

"I think it's best for now, Lightning. It's a change. And everybody seems to feel that's what I need right now." Lightning looked down at the floor.

"Well, if you change your mind..."

"I know I can come back. Thank you." I leaned over and kissed him on the cheek.

"Stop kissin' that Pollock and get over here and help me pack some boxes," Malqueen yelled from the other side of the loft.

"I think she's jealous," Lightning whispered.

"In your dreams, Sausage Man," Malqueen said.

Lightning looked sheepish as I laughed and grabbed an empty box.

We arrived at the cottage at noon. Malqueen, Lightning, and I got out and stood in front of what was to be my new home.

"Boy, the Lawd was lookin' out for you," Malqueen said. "You didn't even know this was what you were getting, did you?"

"Nope."

The three of us stared at the small whitewashed cottage that sat on the edge of one of Snookie's pastures. It had a porch that wrapped around the entire house with several rocking chairs lined up in front. Window boxes held dirt but no flowers. And there was a neatly stacked cord of wood on the porch.

"I must have a fireplace."

"Looks like a retirement home with all them rocking chairs," Lightning said. "And a small one at that."

Malqueen and I exchanged glances. I hooked my arm in Lightning's and said, "You're right. The loft was much bigger. This looks more like Snow White's cottage." I pulled his arm. "Come on, Grumpy, let's see what the inside looks like."

"You mean Dopey, don't you?" Malqueen said as she followed behind.

Even though it was small, I wasn't disappointed. It had oak floors and a brand new kitchen. The living room area did indeed have a fireplace with two small windows on either side of the chimney. My cottage backed up to one of Snookie's six horse pastures. Lightning and I looked out one of the windows and found ourselves staring at a huge black horse with a white star on his forehead who shook his head and stamped his foot as if demanding to know who we were.

"Good thing there's a fence," Lightning said. "He don't look too happy to see you."

"Well, that makes two of us. As long as he stays on his side of the fence and I stay on my side of the fence, we'll both be fine."

"Looks like you got two fireplaces," Malqueen said from the other room. "You got one in the bedroom."

"How romantic," was all I said as I opened and closed cupboards in the kitchen.

"What are you lookin' at the kitchen for?" Malqueen asked.

"Just checking it out."

"It ain't a room you spend too much time in."

"Now what's that supposed to mean?"

"Just what I said."

"I eat out a lot."

"No. You eat at other people's houses a lot."

"Gee, you never complained before."

"Ain't complaining now. Just wondering why you headed for the kitchen first instead of the bedroom."

I waited until Malqueen and Lightning went outside to the truck. Then I walked into the bedroom. It wasn't much bigger than a large walk-in closet. It would be a tight squeeze, but I thought my double bed would fit, and maybe even my dresser if I jammed it into the corner. The bathroom was small too. But it had an old claw-footed tub. It also had a shower with an old-fashioned circular shower curtain. It was all very charming, and when I walked out of the bedroom I found I was smiling.

"Thought you'd like that," Malqueen said as she threw a box on the counter.

"I think, Malqueen, that this is just what the doctor ordered."

"Speaking of the doctor," Lightning said, trying to push one of my chairs through the front door. "She just pulled up."

"Stop that! Let the iron workers bring that stuff in," I told him. "You'll get a hernia."

"From this chair? This hardly weighs anything."

Malqueen shook her head and rolled her eyes. I helped Lightning get the chair through the doorway and into the living room, then I went out to meet Lettie.

"Did you know how great this place was when you suggested it?" I asked.

"Nope. I think you lucked out again."

"No, I have you to thank, not luck."

We both stood out front looking at the cottage and the surrounding fields.

"It is rather far out, though, isn't it?" Lettie said.

"It's just what you said. Thirty minutes to the city...twenty to Landstrom."

"Well, what I meant was, it's remote. Aren't you nervous about being out here all alone?"

"Lettie," I said, looking at her, "are you trying to talk me out of this?"

"No, no...I'm just thinking of your security—"

"Ah-oooooooo."

"What was that?" I said.

"I didn't hear anything."

"You didn't hear that howl?"

"No, I—"

"Ah-ooooooooo!"

Malqueen stuck her head out the door and said, "You got wolves out here?"

"That's what I'd like to know. Lettie, that howl was coming from your car."

"Oh, that howl."

"So now there is a howl."

"I completely forgot he was in the car."

"Lettie?"

"What?"

"No dogs."

"But Gretchen just had her puppies eight weeks ago and they are so adorable, and now that you're in the country and you could use some protection—"

"No dogs, Lettie."

"But Ludwig's your housewarming present."

"Ludwig?"

"Let me get him," Lettie said, running back to the car and returning with a Boxer puppy whose legs dangled down well past her knees.

"Lettie, how am I supposed to take care of a dog? You know what kind of hours I work."

"You could get one of those electric fences."

"Are you going to ask Snookie? Because I sure don't want to."

"Actually, I already did," Lettie said as she juggled the squirming puppy. "She thought it was a great idea. She even said one of the stable lads...does she always call them lads?...could look in on Ludwig when you have to work late."

I looked up and saw Malqueen and Lightning looking out the window at us.

"Lettie, I said no dogs."

"Oh, Sara, just pet him," she said holding him up. "Isn't he cute?"

"No…he's really pretty ugly." At that comment, Ludwig looked up at me with his big brown eyes and protruding lower canines and wagged his stub of a tail. I had a dog.

I also had Barbara and Mother knocking on my door the next day.

"Surprise!"

"No kidding," I said, pecking them both on the cheek. "What brings you two all the way out here?"

We were in the neighborhood."

"Barbara, there is no neighborhood out here…try again."

"We were at Graul's and decided to stop by?"

"You have a Graul's in Ruxton."

"Oh, all right. We wanted to see where you lived…and we have fresh pastrami and that rye bread you like from Eddie's."

"Why didn't you say so? Come on in."

Mother walked over to the window and looked out at the pasture.

"What a lovely view," she said.

Barbara walked around the cottage opening drawers and peeking in closets.

"Now tell me who this Snookie person is."

"She's a horse breeder…Snookie Carmichal…She's quite famous in racing circles.

"Is she local?"

"If you mean was she born in Baltimore, I believe she was. She did say she took lessons from Mr. Granger."

"Then she's socially connected. What's her maiden name?"

For some reason her maiden name escaped me. "Something Scottish… MacIntosh, MacDonald, something like that."

Barbara looked puzzled. "How old is she?"

"Hard to tell. I think around fifty."

"Well, I should know her then. But I don't remember anyone by the name of Snookie. Where does she live?"

"In a castle."

Mother turned from the window. "In a castle?"

"I'll explain later…Come out and look at the view."

Mother went outside. Barbara stopped me from joining her.

"She's acting funny."

"Who?"

"Mother."

"She seems fine to me."

"Well, she's not. And I can't find Father."

"What do you mean you can't find him?"

"I mean, every time I go over there he's gone."

"Well, he does still work for the Diocese."

"I know. But he's gone all the time. I asked Mother where he was today, and do you know what she said?"

"What?"

"Bye-bye."

I stared at Barbara.

"Not that he was at a meeting, or having lunch with someone, or even running errands. She just said, 'bye-bye'."

I looked out on the porch. Mother was gone.

"That's weird."

"You're telling me? When has she ever said, bye-bye?"

"I don't mean that, although that's strange too. I mean...Mother's not on the porch."

We both moved around to the other window. From there we could see that Mother was standing next to the white fence that separated my backyard from Snookie's pasture. The black horse was pressing its massive chest against the fence boards toward Mother. I held my breath and Barbara shrieked, "Oh my God!" We watched as the horse reached over and very gently took something from Mother's hand. Then the horse tilted his head and nuzzled Mother on the shoulder, almost knocking her off-balance. Mother laughed and reached up and stroked the star on his forehead. Then she turned around and headed back to the house. I pulled Barbara away from the window and back into the kitchen. When Mother came in, we pretended we hadn't seen anything.

"Mother, how about a sandwich?" I asked.

"Yes, dear. That would be nice."

"Barbara?"

Barbara was staring at Mother.

"Barbara? Sandwich?"

"Oh, sure. I think I'll visit the little girl's room. Where—"

"Through the bedroom," I told her as I unwrapped the bread.

Mother was strangely quiet as she sat down at the table. She looked all around the cottage and then over at me.

"It's very cozy."

"I think so too."

"I like it."

"So do I."

"I like that horse."

She rearranged the silverware and refolded the napkin on her place mat. Then she picked up the fork and looked at it as if she didn't know what it was for. Barbara called from the bedroom.

"Sara, you only have one bedroom?"

"What would I need more for? Planning on moving in?"

"Very funny. Just seems so small, especially after the loft."

"Well, I don't need a loft anymore."

"But there's no room to paint in here."

I didn't answer.

"Sara? You can't just stop painting…all that talent and schooling—"

"And all that money?"

"I didn't say that."

"No, you didn't have to."

Mother looked up at me and said, "Why aren't you painting anymore, Sara?"

I looked down at her and just said, "Because I don't seem to do it very well anymore."

"Well, that's a good reason." Mother put the fork down and picked up the spoon. I was beginning to see what Barbara meant about Mother's strange behavior.

"Are you all right?" I asked her.

"I'm fine, dear. Just a little tired."

"Barbara," I yelled to her, "did you fall in?"

"No, I'm just looking at your 'quaint' bedroom, and I can't believe that—"

"Arf, ack ack ack ack, growllllll..."

"What in heaven's name is that? Oh, stop it, you beast. Sara! What's this thing under the bed?" Barbara came running out of the bedroom. Ludwig was right on her heels. He slid around the corner, fell on his side, and spun into the wall. He recovered immediately and eagerly began sniffing Barbara's shoes.

"That's Ludwig. A present from Lettie. He's one of Gretchen's puppies."

"What's wrong with his teeth?"

"Severe case of underbite. Lettie can't breed him because of it."

"I should think not. He looks like a warthog! Get away from my shoes, you ugly beast! Shoo...stop that! Sara, he's biting my shoes! Get him away from me. Sara, he's drooling!"

Mother and I laughed as Ludwig chased Barbara around the living room.

I settled into life in the country. Ludwig and I took long walks in the woods. On one of those walks, we discovered the stable that Snookie had told me I might have to muck out. As we approached the building, the door flew open and Snookie burst out of the stables on the horse with the white stockings, the one that had been tied up next to the Mercedes that first day I had met her. Ludwig and I watched her fly down the path and were startled when Hannibal, one of the "lads," stumbled out of the stable trying to get his pants up and zipped.

"Eeez not what you theenk..." he stammered as he ran back into the barn.

"Well, well," I said to Ludwig, who was off in the bushes taking care of his own business. "Looks like the horses aren't the only ones being serviced on Snookie's Farm."

•

"Death and love are the two wings
that bear the good man to heaven."
Michelangelo

The only cloud on the horizon after my move to the cottage was Barbara's suspicion that something wasn't right between Mother and Father.

"What do you mean?"

"I mean he's never there."

"So you've said. Did you ask him?"

"Yes."

"Well, what did he say?"

"He says it's church business."

"Barbara, then that's what he's doing. Father doesn't lie."

"Then how come Mother doesn't even know what he's doing?"

"What do you mean?"

"Whenever I ask her where he is, she says she doesn't know."

"Well, maybe it's church business she's not involved with."

"When has Mother not been involved with his church business?"

"I don't know. I just think you're overreacting."

"Do me a favor. Go over and talk to him. Ask him what he's doing."

"Barbara, this is ridiculous."

"I have this feeling...Just humor me."

I went over on a Saturday afternoon and found them both in the study doing a crossword puzzle together.

"Sara," Father said. "What a pleasant surprise. Look who's here, Caroline...Sara."

Mother looked up from the paper, squinted at me, and then said, "Sara? Oh, Sara...how good of you to stop by."

"Nice to see you too," I said, handing my coat to Father.

"She's just preoccupied with that puzzle. Been driving her crazy for the last two hours."

Mother looked up me. "What's a seven-letter word for suspicious?"

I sat down, thought for a moment, and then said, "Dubious?"

"That's it!" Mother cried, filling in the blanks. "William, I swear I'm losing my mind. I should have known that!"

"Well, then we're both losing our minds. I couldn't think of the word either."

Mother put down the puzzle, sighed, and said that she would go make us some tea. I turned to Father and asked him what he was doing with himself these days.

"Just helping the Diocese out when I can."

"That's not what I hear."

"Oh?"

"Barbara tells me you're never home.

"Barbara's exaggerating," Father said, standing up and walking over to the bookcase. Then he turned and looked at me rather sheepishly and said, "Well, actually I am gone a lot...but I'd really rather not tell your mother."

"Not tell her what?"

He held up an autographed baseball. "...This might explain some of it."

"A baseball?"

"Caught it at the game last week. We creamed the Blue Jays."

"Is that where you've been disappearing to? Baseball games?"

Father sat down on the sofa beside me. "You know how your mother feels about baseball. I just tell her I'm on church business, and I sneak off to a game. I know someone in the Orioles front office, and he gives me free tickets."

"Lucky you. But why not just tell Barbara that?"

"Because, unlike you, Barbara thinks I should spend all my time with your mother...when the truth is, it's nice to get away every now and then."

I could understand that. Barbara did have a tendency to romanticize my parents' relationship.

We both looked up as Mother came back in without the tea.

"Where's the tea, dear?" Father asked.

"Oh my goodness. There I go again," Mother said, sinking down on the sofa. "You know I just read that after age fifty we lose millions of brain cells every year. That must be why I forget everything these days."

Father slid over beside her and said, "I think you try to do too much. You still serve on three hospital committees, volunteer, and chair that Ladies Luncheon Prayer Meeting. Maybe you should just drop some of the committee work."

"William! What am I supposed to do? Sit at home and do crossword puzzles all week? Especially now that you're gone so much working for the Diocese."

Father winked at me and said, "Well, I have a feeling that the work I'm doing for the Diocese is almost finished. I expect I'll be home more in the fall."

Mother smiled at him and said, "That would be nice, dear."

I left knowing that I had done my duty. Father was sneaking off to Orioles games, and Mother was preoccupied because she was overextending herself trying to keep busy because Father was gone so much. Once the baseball season ended, Father would be home more. It seemed perfectly reasonable to me, and I told Barbara so after my visit with my parents. Too bad it was a lie.

I discovered the truth about a month later while I was visiting Lettie at Hopkins.

"Are you sure you can't get away and have a decent lunch? Someplace fun like Café Hon?"

"I'm swamped. I'd love to get away. But today all I can manage is Le Cafeteria Hopkins."

"Well, then it's the cafeteria."

As we stood in line, I saw Lettie looking behind me. I turned around and thought I saw my father walk out of the cafeteria.

"Was that my father?"

"I think so," Lettie said, looking puzzled, "Although I don't think he saw us."

"He must be visiting someone," I said. "What are you having? Pizza or a burger?"

"I'm having a salad. The baby's almost two years old, and I still have ten pounds to lose." I saw her look longingly at the pepperoni pizza.

Lettie and I were halfway through our lunch when her beeper went off. "Oh drat! I thought I could at least squeeze some time for lunch," she said, staring at the number on her beeper. "Listen, I'll talk to you later. I'm afraid this doesn't look good. I've got a kid in trouble."

"Go. Save the kid. I'll talk to you later," I said as I continued to eat my french fries.

When I was finished, I left the cafeteria and headed for the parking garage. But because I was in Hopkins, the world's most confusing hospital, I ended up going in the wrong direction. I finally realized my mistake, stopped where I was, and looked around to get my bearings. When I looked up, I saw Father walking down the hall in front of me. I hurried to catch up with him, but he turned the corner and disappeared. When I rounded the corner, I caught a glimpse of him as he pushed a red button on the wall and walked through a gray double door with a yellow sign on it. When I got to the door, I stopped. The sign read: Patients Only – Radiation Therapy. I only hesitated for a moment. Then I pushed the button, marched into Radiation Therapy, and discovered that my father was being treated for advanced pancreatic cancer. He died four months later.

Chapter Twenty-Four

"Cheer up! The worst is yet to come."

Philander Chase Johnson

We discovered Mother's illness after Father died. We had been so preoccupied with Father's diagnosis and treatment that we assumed Mother's odd behavior was caused by these events as well. Mother's confusion and indecision seemed almost normal then, considering what she was facing. It was only after he was gone that I began to notice how erratic her behavior had become. Mother began telephoning me at all hours of the night.

"Sara?"

"Mother?"

"Do you have my reading glasses?"

"What? Glasses?" I sat up and looked at my alarm clock. "Mother, it's 3:00 a.m."

"I saw you take them."

"Mother, what would I want with your glasses?" I was trying to clear my head and wake up.

"Sara, I need my glasses. I can't read without them. I saw you take them."

"Mother, I didn't take your glasses. Did you check your purse?"

"My purse?" Mother hung up. A few minutes later the phone rang again.

"Barbara?"

"No, Mother, it's Sara."

"Who?"

"Sara. Did you find your glasses?"

"What glasses? Just who is this?"

"Mother, you just called me five minutes ago because you couldn't find your glasses."

"Don't be ridiculous. I'm wearing my glasses. Anyway, I'm looking for Barbara, not you!"

Mother never remembered the phone calls the next morning. Barbara was convinced Mother was dreaming.

"She's asleep. That's why she can't remember."

"Can people be asleep and dial numbers and carry on conversations?" I asked.

"Don't you remember Aunt Biddy?"

"Barbara, Aunt Biddy wasn't right to start with. (Aunt Biddy had fallen off the roof of a three-story house when she was ten and had landed on her head.)

"Aunt Biddy always made perfect sense to me," Barbara said. "She was just slow."

"Slow? Aunt Biddy was more than slow, Barbara. Don't you remember how she wore tents on her head?"

At some point in Aunt Biddy's childhood she had been told to cover her head when she went to church. Aunt Biddy decided she'd design a permanent contraption that sat on her shoulders and covered her head, much like an army pup tent. When Aunt Biddy didn't feel like being social, she'd pull the flaps down and disappear behind a canvas wall.

"Oh, that. Well, sometimes she did overdo things."

"Barbara, Mother is not Aunt Biddy. I think Mother's in trouble."

"She's still grieving. She's still in shock. Father was her whole life. She needs time."

"It's more than that. Half the time she doesn't even know who I am. Besides, you were the one who suspected something was wrong with her months ago."

"I suspected something was wrong with Father."

"Don't you remember that day when you visited me at the cottage? When we watched her with the horse?"

"Oh, that wasn't so odd. She always did like horses."

"But the way she spoke? I like the horse? I like the cottage? What was that all about?

"It was about nothing. Once she gets back to her charity work and her luncheons she'll snap right out of it. In fact," Barbara said, catching me off guard, "what are you doing next Monday?"

"Working."

"But you can switch."

"Why do you assume I can change my days off at the drop of a hat? I have a schedule, you know."

"But you can switch."

"What if I don't want to switch?"

"Sara, this is very important. Let's help Mother out, OK?"

"What are you talking about?"

"She's decided she feels well enough to host the Ladies Luncheon Prayer Meeting—"

"Oh no, I'm not helping out with that fiend fest. You can just—"

"Sara, I need your help. Please. Mother needs your help. And don't you think Father would have wanted you to help Mother right now?

The mention of Father is what made me finally say, "Yes."

I arrived late and I expected Barbara to be furious with me. I was surprised when she wasn't.

"There you are. We were wondering what had happened to you. Weren't we, Mother?"

"Hello, dear. My, don't you look nice."

"You certainly do," Barbara added, approving of my below-the-knee skirt and low-heeled pumps. I wanted to tell her I had bought the skirt for five dollars at Clothes Rich People Don't Want Anymore, the place where all her tony friends dropped off their discards, but I didn't. I was trying to behave myself.

"Hello, Mother." I leaned down and gave her a peck on the cheek.

"Mother, Sara and I are going to the kitchen to check on the sandwiches and cakes. Why don't you look over your notes on the table before the ladies get here."

"Good idea." Mother put on her reading glasses. She began to scan the papers in front of her.

Barbara pulled me out into the foyer.

"How does she look?"

"Fabulous. She's dressed, her hair's done, how did you do it?"

"Well, I think she might be finally snapping out of it. I got here at eight and she was up, had her clothes all laid out, and was even discussing what kind of sandwiches she wanted Mary to make. She seems her old self."

"I hope so. What time are the barracudas arriving?"

"Sara, they're not barracudas. They're Mother's friends."

"Hardly. They're a bunch of social sharks that devour people with their gossip."

"Sara, I can't deal with both you and Mother today. Just try to be nice, OK? Please? For me?"

The doorbell rang.

"Will you get the door while I check on Mother?"

"Oh, thanks. I get to greet and meet the barracudas?"

Barbara gave me her "act your age" look and then her face softened and she said, "By the way, Frances will be here today...I've convinced her you were under a lot of pressure when you painted her...you know, with the divorce and all. Anyway, she's forgiven you."

"Just what I've always wanted...Frances Lymington's forgiveness."

The doorbell rang again. I took a deep breath and opened the door. Three barracudas filled the doorway.

"Good afternoon, ladies," I said as Frances Lymington swept into the hallway.

"Afternoon," Frances said barely looking at me as she threw her coat at me.

"I assume the meeting will be held in the sitting room?"

"Yes, it is. Go right in."

Frances marched down the hall.

"Good to see you, Sara," said Mrs. Eleanor Thomas.

"Good to see you too. My, what a lovely hat," I lied.

"Oh, thank you, dear. You don't think it's too much, do you?" she whispered.

"Too much for what?"

"You know...too much color since your mother is still in mourning."

I looked at the red and orange roses that cascaded over the side of the brim of Mrs. Thomas's black hat and lied again.

"Not to worry, Mrs. Thomas. Mother doesn't care about that."

"I thought not."

"Afternoon," said Mrs. Carolyn Brown.

"Afternoon, Mrs. Brown. May I take your coat?"

Mrs. Brown waited until Mrs. Thomas had left the foyer and then in a rush said, "Isn't that the ugliest hat you've ever seen? I told her not to wear that hat. She looks like she has a flowerpot on her head. But no, she thinks she looks good in it. She needs new glasses and just won't admit it. I don't know what she sees when she looks at herself in the mirror. Don't you think she looks like she has a flowerpot on her head?"

"Uh…it is different."

"Different! How kind you are. The damn flowers don't even look real. Different!" Mrs. Brown propelled herself forward with her walker, mumbling about "flowerpots" and "inappropriate colors" as she disappeared into the sitting room. I turned around just in time to see the second wave of white-haired barracudas swim up the walkway.

When I finally had all the coats hung and got back to the sitting room, the meeting had started. Mother was leading the prayer.

"To our prayers, O Lord, we join our unfeigned thanks for all they mercies; for our being, our reason, and all other endowments and faculties of soul and body; for our health, and friends…"

I looked up to see Frances Lymington staring at Mrs. Thomas's hat.

"…food, and raiment," Mother continued to pray. "…and all the other comforts and conveniences of life. Above all, we adore thy mercy in sending thy only son into the world, to redeem us from sin and eternal death, and in giving us the knowledge and sense of our duty…"

Mrs. Thomas looked up and glared back at Frances.

"…toward thee. We bless thee for thy patience with us, notwithstanding our many and great provocations; for all the direction, assistances, and comforts of thy Holy Spirit; for…"

Mrs. Brown whispered something to Frances. The three of them stared at Mrs. Thomas's hat.

Mother continued to pray, and I saw Frances mouth the word "cheap" to Mrs. Brown. When Mother said, "Amen," she looked up and smiled. "Frances, I understand you would like to be the first to address the group today?"

Mrs. Lymington stood up and attempted to pull the back of her navy coatdress over her ample derriere. She wasn't successful. It crept even further up the back of her legs as she walked to the center of the room and began to speak.

"Our society is filled with loose morals and corrupt souls. It is our duty as Christian ladies..."

Mrs. Van Meter smiled at Mrs. Thomas and Mrs. Westlake and waved her ring finger at them. Both ladies leaned over to get a closer look.

"...to help those less fortunate than ourselves—those who are not born into the privileged life and must beg for their next morsel of food. But these unfortunate souls need another kind of nourishment. The nourishment of the spirit..."

Mrs. Thomas tried on Mrs. Van Meter's new ring and held it up for the rest of the ladies to admire. I looked over at Barbara and mouthed the word "kitchen." She nodded back. We backed out of the room and into the kitchen.

"Did you see what was going on while Mother was praying?" I unwrapped sandwiches as Barbara got the tea ready.

"It was hard not to. I don't know who's worse, Frances or that Mrs. Van Meter flashing around that three-carat rock on her finger."

"I told you they're barracudas. Why does Mother put up with it? Why are they even in a prayer meeting? Malqueen's right. All they do is talk about each other."

"Maybe Mother feels she's setting an example or something. I really don't know...but she's put up with them for over thirty years. Can you carry that tea service in for me?"

I picked up the silver tray, bumped open the swinging door with my hips, and staggered back into the hallway. "No problem," I said to Barbara who was behind me with the sandwiches. "Let's go feed the fish."

"You're awful."

Frances was still holding court. I passed out tuna on toast points and ham salad on white bread squares as she droned on about the poor. Information she could only have gleaned from her many servants.

"...and as responsible citizens we must lead the poor..."

A flying tuna toast point smacked Frances right in the face.

"What the..." she sputtered, "...is this?"

I looked at Barbara and we both turned to Mother.

Mother had her hands folded in her lap and was smiling at Frances. "Do go on, Frances. I believe you left off with leading the poor?"

"Go on? Caroline, someone in this room just threw a tuna sandwich at me! How can I go on? I have tuna fish on my face. Who's responsible for this?" she demanded. I took a quick inventory and realized that the only member of the group without a sandwich was Mother.

"Nonsense, Frances. I'm sure it just slipped out of someone's hand. No one meant to throw anything at you. Sara, give Frances a napkin."

I ran over and tried to wipe tuna off of Frances's navy silk dress. She grabbed the napkin from me and rubbed her face, taking not only the tuna off but all the crimson rouge she had haphazardly smeared on her left cheek. Mrs. Thomas giggled and played with one of the flowers that now hung limply down in her face. Barbara continued to stare at Mother.

"It was you, Eleanor, wasn't it?" Frances said, pointing her finger at Mrs. Thomas.

"Me? I think not. I would never throw a sandwich at anyone...even you," she added under her breath.

"Oh, admit it! You're just angry because we were making fun of your stupid hat during the prayer."

"What? My hat? What's wrong with my hat?" Mrs. Thomas stood up and straightened the red and orange roses that sprouted from her head.

"It's damn ugly! That's what wrong with it. And if you weren't so stubborn you'd get new glasses and be able to see just how UGLY that hat really is!"

"Ladies, please!" Mother stood up.

"Glasses? You think I need glasses? When was the last time you had your prescription checked, Frances?" Mrs. Thomas yelled. "Put that rouge on with a paint roller?"

"Well! At least I try to maintain my appearance," Frances screamed. "And I have the good sense not to run around with a flowerpot perched on my head!"

"Enough!" Mother yelled. "Eleanor, Frances, sit down."

"But..." sputtered Frances.

"No buts. Sit down." Mother repeated.

"But she..." began Mrs. Thomas.

"You too, Eleanor. Sit down."

They both sat.

"Ladies," Mother looked at both Eleanor and Frances, "since you are both good Christians and we are in the middle of a prayer meeting, I know you will apologize to each other for your behavior." Frances and Eleanor refused to look at each other. "However, I'm afraid I must apologize too...to all of you. I should never have called this meeting so soon after..." At this, Mother stopped, stood up, and calmly walked out of the room. Barbara ran after her. That left me alone with the barracudas.

"Ladies," I said, moving to the center of the room, "if you'll just bear with us for a few minutes...finish your sandwiches? Have more tea? Please stay and..."

But no one did. Frances stormed out first, followed by a sea of white hair and navy coatdresses. To my face they were understanding.

"I'm so sorry, dear. Make sure she calls me."

"Not to worry, dear. It's a difficult time."

"Time heals all wounds."

"Anything you need...just call."

But as they drifted down the walkway, I heard whispered fragments of different sentiments.

"Can you believe she..."

"Whatever possessed her to..."

"Didn't you think it odd..."

Mrs. Thomas was the last to leave. She had taken off the hat and now twirled it around in her hands.

"Dear, I didn't say anything in front of the group, but you do know your mother threw that sandwich at Frances...don't you?"

I just looked at her.

"I'm sure quite a few of the other ladies noticed it too. I'll try my best to get them to keep their mouths shut, but I can't guarantee it. I certainly won't ever admit I saw what Caroline did. Your Mother was always kind to me. She was such a help when Mr. Thomas passed on. Besides, Frances had it coming... such a pompous ass...giving a speech on poverty. Well, I don't have to tell you about Frances." Mrs. Thomas stopped and looked down at her hat. "The point is, dear, I think your mother is depressed. Several of my friends are on that

Prozac drug and it's made a tremendous difference in their lives. Perhaps a little dose of that would help her."

I leaned against the open door as Mrs. Thomas slowly made her way down the path, pausing only once to lift the lid on Mother's trash can and gently place her hat inside.

Even though I hadn't seen Mother toss the tuna at Frances, I was sure Barbara had. Because it was after "that unfortunate luncheon incident" that Barbara finally agreed to take Mother for a checkup. I thought that perhaps Mrs. Thomas was right. Maybe Mother did need some kind of antidepressant. But instead of prescribing Prozac, Mother's internist referred her to a neurologist.

"Will you go with us?" Barbara asked me.

"I have to work."

"You can switch."

"Barbara, I have a job."

"I know you can switch."

"What day?"

"Next Tuesday."

"Dan's not going to like it."

"He'll let you switch."

"Oh, all right!"

On Tuesday we guided Mother through the maze of corridors that functioned as Johns Hopkins Hospital.

"I hate this hospital," I said to no one in particular.

"It's world renowned," Barbara answered, turning down yet another corridor.

"But that's what bothers me. If it's 'world renowned' how come they couldn't do a better job designing the place? They employ some of the best doctors in the world and make them work in a maze...like rats. The doctors must spend all day trying to find their patients."

"You just don't like this hospital because it's where Father...well...you know..." Barbara trailed off.

She was right, but I didn't like to think about that.

"Come on," Barbara said. "Try and keep up."

"Who is this doc anyway?"

"Name's Hever...supposed to be the best in his field. Let's see, I think this is the elevator we're supposed to take."

Barbara nudged Mother inside and pushed four. I looked over at Mother. She hadn't said a word since we had left the house. I saw her edge closer to the control panel and squint at the buttons.

"Now, the directions say turn left at the elevator, right at the next corner, and right again past the swinging doors."

We did and ended up where we started.

"Oh dear." Barbara looked down at her notes again.

"Are we lost?" Mother asked.

"We're at Hopkins. Of course we're lost. They ought to pass out maps and a canteen when they hand you your visitor's badge," I said.

Mother tapped me on the shoulder and pointed in the opposite direction. Then she started walking.

"Wait! Mother!" Barbara said. "I know where we are. I just have to..." But Mother kept on walking the other way. We caught up with her just as she entered an office halfway down the hall.

"Is this Dr. Hever's office?" Mother asked a young lady in white who was seated behind a glass partition.

"Yes, it is. Do you have an appointment?"

"Yes, we do," Barbara answered before Mother could respond. I mean, my mother is the one with the appointment...Mrs. William Gorman."

"Just fill out this insurance form, Mrs. Gorman, and Dr. Hever will be right with you."

Mother looked at the form. Barbara took it from her and led her to a chair in the waiting area.

It only took Barbara five minutes to fill out the form, but Dr. Hever wasn't with us for another hour. Barbara read an outdated copy of *House Beautiful*. I leafed through every *People Magazine* I could find. And Mother stared at a copy of *Your Brain!* Finally, the door to Dr. Hever's office opened.

"Mrs. Gorman?"

We all stood up. Mother offered her hand. "Caroline Gorman. And this is my daughter Barbara and my other daughter...uh..."

"Sara," I finished for her.

"Well, ladies come in and have a seat while I look over your mother's medical file."

Mother walked past me and gave me a puzzled look.

"Let's see." Dr. Hever slowly read Mother's medical file from her internist. He looked up at us and smiled. "Heart of a thirty-year-old. Well, Mrs. Gorman, that's a pretty young heart."

Barbara and I smiled.

When Dr. Hever finally finished reading, he looked at Mother and said, "Mrs. Gorman, I'd like to ask you some questions. Nothing earth-shattering. Just take your time answering and remember this isn't a test. Ready?"

Mother didn't answer.

"Mrs. Gorman?"

"Oh, questions."

"Good. Who is the current president of the United States?"

Mother didn't answer.

"Mrs. Gorman?" Dr. Hever raised his voice. "Did you hear me?"

"What?"

"I asked you who is the current president of the United States."

Mother looked down into her lap and then looked at Barbara who mouthed "Clinton."

"Clinton," Mother said.

"Now, Mrs. Gorman. What day of the week is it?"

Mother began opening and closing the catch on her purse.

"Mrs. Gorman?"

Mother looked at me, and I mouthed "Tuesday."

"Tuesday," Mother said.

Dr. Hever scribbled more notes.

"Mrs. Gorman, can you tell me what year it is?"

Mother began playing with the catch on her purse again. Barbara leaned back in her chair, hiding behind a plant on the doctor's desk, trying to catch Mother's eye. Mother studied a picture of a golden retriever on Dr. Hever's desk. I looked over at the picture and noted the dog only had one eye.

"Mrs. Gorman. Do you know what year this is?" Dr. Hever repeated gently.

Barbara was now so far back in the chair I was afraid she'd topple over. She was frantically mouthing "ninety-nine." Mother finally looked over at her and said, "1899."

Barbara shook her head and mouthed "nineteen." Mother looked puzzled and then said, "But Barbara, how could it be ninety-nine nineteen? That doesn't make sense."

Dr. Hever took off his glasses, got up from his chair, and motioned for us to follow him. We turned around as he shut the door in our faces.

"Ladies, have a seat," the nurse offered. "Dr. Hever wants to talk to your mother alone."

Barbara glared at me and said, "He saw you."

"Saw me?"

"You were too obvious about it."

"Barbara, we shouldn't have had to tell her any of those answers. She should be able to remember what day and year it is. Besides, if he saw anybody it was you!"

Barbara folded her arms across her chest and sighed. After several minutes she poked me in the side and said, "Go listen at the door. See if you can hear anything."

I moved two chairs over and leaned toward the door. I couldn't hear a thing. I looked over to see the nurse watching me.

"Well?"

"Couldn't hear a thing. Besides, Old Nurse Ratchett over there is keeping tabs on us."

Barbara looked over at the nurse and frowned. The nurse frowned back. Barbara got out her datebook and began checking events off. I fell asleep reading "Synapses: The connections you want to make." When the door finally opened, Barbara jerked me to me feet.

"Mrs. Gorman, why don't you wait out here with Nurse Reynolds while I chat with your daughters." Dr. Hever motioned us to follow him.

"Yes…well…thank you." Mother sat down and picked up my discarded article on synapses. Barbara shoved me back into Dr. Hever's office.

"Ladies, have a seat. I just have to make a few more notes."

Barbara and I watched him scribble mysteriously into his notebook. After five minutes, Barbara began fidgeting in her chair. Unable to contain herself any longer, she finally blurted out, "Dr. Hever, just what's wrong with our mother?"

The doctor stopped writing and pushed his glasses on top his head. Then he looked directly at Barbara and said, "At the moment I don't have an absolute diagnosis. All I can give you is an educated guess."

"Which is?" I asked.

"Alzheimer's disease. Now, remember, I've still got more tests to run. I'd like your mother to see another specialist. I—"

"She's here to get Prozac," Barbara interrupted. "What do you mean... Alzheimer's?"

"I mean that there's a pretty good chance that your mother is suffering from Alzheimer's disease. Now, I'd like to set up another appointment tomorrow with Dr. Poole. He's a specialist in this field and he's right here at the hospital and then—"

"NO!" Barbara stood up. "Mother does not have that horrible disease. Our Father just died. She's depressed. I thought you understood that! That information should have been in her medical records. How could—"

"It was," Dr. Hever said. "I'm terribly sorry about your father. But your mother is suffering from some kind of dementia...not depression."

"I will not sit here and listen to some quack tell me my mother's demented! We'll get a second opinion. We'll find out what's really wrong with her!" Barbara flew out of the room, slamming the door behind her.

I looked over at Dr. Hever.

"How sure are you?"

"As sure as anyone can be with Alzheimer's." He rubbed his eyes. "I'm sorry. I obviously didn't handle that as well as I could have."

We were both silent for a few moments. Then he said, "You need information to deal with this." He opened a file and pulled out a booklet and handed it to me.

"What about your sister?" he asked. "Would you like me to talk to her again?"

"I'll talk to her. In time she'll listen."

"In time she'll see. You'll need support," he said, leaning back in his chair. "This is a devastating illness. You'll need to get your mother back in here to see the specialist as soon as possible. There are some new drugs that might help her…at least for a while. And there are several good support groups listed in that book." He began writing again, but he stopped halfway through a sentence, looked up at me, and said, "And you'll have to decide where you want her to go."

"Go?"

"Unless you have nurses around the clock, there's no way you'll be able to care for your mother, especially in the later stages of the illness. My suggestion to you is to scout out good care facilities now. Then, when your mother needs it, you'll be ready."

I clutched the book to my chest as I slowly walked out of Hopkins. I didn't know where I was going. I just began to walk: out the main entrance past the construction for the new subway system that was three years behind schedule, down Orleans Street and St. Paul Street, and finally stopping when I reached the murky water of the Inner Harbor. I sat down on a bench in front of a sightseeing boat called the *Bay Lady* and began to read about the different stages of Alzheimer's. And when I was finished reading, I got up and called Barbara.

"Where have you been?" she asked me.

"Like you were really worried. When did you realize I wasn't behind you?"

"Mother was upset. I thought it best to get her home. Are you still at the hospital?"

"I'm at the Inner Harbor in front of the *Bay Lady*."

"The Bay what?"

"Never mind. I'll catch a cab to Mother's house. We need to talk."

But Barbara wouldn't let me talk. She had decided that what Mother really needed was constant supervision and care—care only Barbara was capable of giving. And so, Barbara moved Mother into her house.

The drugs Dr. Hever thought might help Mother didn't. She quickly went from forgetting where her glasses were to forgetting what her glasses were for. After six months with Barbara, Mother had lost just about all of her short-term memory. She had no idea how to do simple things, like tie her shoes or fix a sandwich. She screamed when the phone rang and went around turning lights on and off all day long. The strain of caring for Mother showed on Barbara's face. For the first time in her life, she looked her age. But every time I suggested a nursing care facility, my sister refused.

"How about Broadmoor?" I asked, waving a brochure at her.

"Too far out."

"Roland Lake Place?"

"Too far in."

"Lightwood?"

"Oh, God no. Frances Lymington has a reservation there."

"Georgetown?"

"Too blue-collar."

"How about that Catholic place...Our Lady of I-Don't-Want-to-Deal-With-This?"

"Very funny."

But Barbara did admit that she needed help with Mother. She asked me to locate an agency that supplied families with home care professionals. Every day an aide would come in to wash, feed, and babysit Mother. But there was a problem: none of the aides suited Barbara. I lost count of how many Barbara had fired in the last six months—aides that I felt were more than adequate but that Barbara let go because they were "too bossy," or "too timid," or her favorite excuse, "too tacky."

"Why did you fire Eliza?" I asked Barbara.

"Too tacky," she had replied.

"Tacky? What does 'tacky' have to do with being an aide?"

"You know," my sister whispered, "those shoes she wears."

"Her shoes?"

"They had holes cut out over her big toes. Her bunions showed. It was embarrassing when anyone came to visit. And she shuffled when she walked."

"You fired someone because they had a few holes in their shoes and they shuffled?"

"Wasn't just the shoes."

"What else then?"

"She kept saying, 'A-Kay.'"

"So?"

"Well, Mother started saying 'A-Kay.'"

"Barbara, Mother says worse things than 'A-Kay.'"

"Well, all the more reason to get someone in here who can speak properly."

I could have pointed out that, thanks to Alzheimer's, Mother was now happily cursing like a stevedore. But I didn't. It was Barbara's house and she had to deal with the ever-changing aides. If I was surprised by anything, it was Randall's reaction to Mother's illness. He still continued to talk to Mother as if she were sane.

"Well, Caroline," he would say, "I see that the new bishop can't get the funds together for the new church school. That wouldn't have happened in your day...would it?"

Mother would look up from the table and say, "I should think not," and then fling her toast through the air like a Frisbee, hitting Barbara or the aide-for-the-day on the head.

"Nice shot," Randall would say.

"Randall, stop that." Barbara would get up and retrieve the toast. "You're encouraging her."

"No, I'm not. It was a good shot."

But Randall's nonchalant attitude toward Mother's more bizarre behavior made Barbara furious.

"Why does he encourage her to do these things?" she would ask me.

"He doesn't. He's just trying to remain calm and not get excited about it."

"But she's got to learn that she can't behave like this."

"Barbara, she has Alzheimer's. She doesn't know what she's doing."

"I just can't believe he would act like this."

"I think you should be grateful for the way he acts. Most husbands don't even want to see their mother-in-law when they're sane. Randall sits down and carries on a conversation with a demented one. What's the matter with you? Can't you see he's trying to help?"

"All I see is he's encouraging her to act weird...That's all I see."

"Barbara," I said, shaking my head, "you're blind."

"I'm not blind. I can see what he's doing. She doesn't need to be egged on."

"Are you listening to me? Mother is not going to get any better...and the sooner you accept it, the better it will be for all of us."

"She'll be fine if I can just find the right aide...someone qualified... someone who can guide her—"

"I give up. You're not only blind, but you're deaf too."

I tried to help Barbara with Mother, stopping by after work and on my days off. But I also knew that if I had been an aide instead of her sister...she would have fired me too.

Chapter Twenty-Five

"Choose a job you love, and you will
never have to work a day of yor life."
Confucius

Steady, monotonous work did help me forget what I didn't want to remember. Months went by when I didn't even think of Aubrey. Then, out of the blue, the door to the Parrot would fly open, and I'd turn, expecting him to be standing there in his torn blue jeans and his old red flannel shirt, grinning at me as he leaned down and kissed me on the mouth. But every time I turned around, there was always someone else who stood in the doorway. One day the door blew open and I didn't turn around. And that was when I realized that I was finally letting Aubrey go.

As for my previous life as a portrait painter, that began to fade too. Word got around that I wasn't painting anymore, and my phone stopped ringing. When I wasn't selling shoes, I took long walks with Ludwig and read books I never seemed to have time to read when I was painting. But there were still times when I got the urge to draw. At sunset, when the horses galloped across the field on their way to the barn, my right hand would begin to trace the scene on the kitchen counter. But when I realized what I was doing, I would stuff my hand in my pocket and wait a few minutes. I found that the desire to paint would pass.

Father was more difficult because I saw him everywhere. I saw him in crowds at the mall. I saw him in the grocery store. I saw him in church. He was even in my dreams. He would sit on the edge of my bed and smile at me. But he never said anything. He just smiled. I would try to talk to him, but nothing would come out of my mouth. I'd wake up in a cold sweat, gasping for air, and unable to speak. And then I'd spend the rest of the night awake and frightened, wondering why these vivid dreams about him left me feeling so lonely and afraid.

Those sleepless nights got me into trouble at work. Before Father died I had always arrived at work on time. But after his death, I'd been late more than I'd been on time. Dan, my manager, had already given me two warnings.

I heard a ringing from far off, and I rolled over and stuck my head under the pillow. But the ringing wouldn't stop, and finally I realized it was the phone.

I reached over Ludwig's head and picked up the receiver.

"Hello?"

"Good thing I called. You have one hour to get your butt to work."

I sat up in bed, looked at the clock, and said, "Oh my God. Jonathon?"

"No, Mickey Mouse. Come on, girl…move."

I leaped out of bed and ran for the shower. I hit the coffee maker button and opened the door for Ludwig. Thirty minutes later, I was dressed and Ludwig and I were in my VW heading down the farm road. When I got to the fork in the road, I saw Ian, the farm manager, standing in front of the old red barn. I opened the car door, and Ludwig bounded over to Ian.

Snookie hired and fired "lads" with almost as much frequency as Barbara hired and fired aides for Mother. The "lads" were really men in their twenties and thirties. Most of them were from Puerto Rico, Mexico, or South America, but a few were from Ireland and Australia. Ian was the only one from Scotland; he was in his fifties and had been around the longest, only because he was Snookie's cousin twice removed.

I waved to Ian as Ludwig leaped in the air around him. I was lucky the "lads," and especially Ian, found Ludwig so endearing.

I floored the VW and managed to hit the rooftop parking lot of Towsontowne with three minutes to spare. I skipped the elevator—it was always slow—and ran down three flights of stairs and threw open the Employee Only entrance door.

"Hiya, Jack," I yelled to the security guard as I ran down the hall and headed for the time clock. I skidded to a stop. Monique was trying to punch in.

"Come on, Monique. I'm late."

"Hold your ponies. I'll be finished in a minute."

"It's hold your horses, and I don't have a minute."

I watched as Monique put her time card in backward.

"Oh Drat! Like, what did I do wrong?"

"Damnit, Monique! The card's in backward. Gimmee that!" I yanked the card out of her hand and shoved it into the machine.

"Now quick, enter your password." Monique stuck her tongue out, thought for a moment, and punched in six numbers. The computer screen above the time clock blinked "Incorrect identification...Incorrect identification...Incorrect identification."

"Oops...Now what did I do wrong?" Monique squinted at the computer screen and scratched her black roots with a recently manicured purple talon.

"Just punch in the numbers again!

Monique did and got the same response.

"Monique! For God's sake! Think! What's your password?"

"I can't tell you that. The company said never to tell anyone our passwords."

Monique turned her back to me and slowly began punching in her code again. I cursed, ran back down the hall where the company had wisely placed another time clock, and punched in with two seconds to spare. I leaned against the wall and exhaled.

"Aren't you glad I remembered to call you this morning?" Jonathon said as he walked by.

"I'm indebted. However, I'm sure you'll think of some way I can repay you."

"As a matter of fact, I have stock work I never got to yesterday..."

"Not the running shoes..."

"Yep."

"Oh, all right."

We passed Monique, who was still trying to punch in. Jonathon looked over at me, and I shook my head "no." He ignored me and said to Monique, "You having trouble with that?"

"Oh, Jonathon...I just can't get this thing to work! I don't know what I'm doing wrong." Monique batted her brand new Maybellines at him. Jonathon reached over and hit a button that cleared the computer. He told her to try again. This time her code worked.

"Cool. Like, exactly what did you do?" Monique leaned into Jonathon.

"He punched clear, Monique. Try it sometime." I pulled Jonathon away by his tie and led him down the hall.

"Don't you think that was a little rude?"

"No, I don't. Monique's a dim bulb. You should see her work the register. The customers are covered in cobwebs by the time they finally get their purchases rung up."

"Oh, she's not that bad."

Oh, yes, she is. Just because she makes your testosterone level rise doesn't mean she's capable of anything else."

"Too bad. She's got a great set of—"

"Yeah, yeah, yeah...I can't wait until they put her in Men's Shoes during the Big Sale. I want to see those so-called 'assets' ring up sales for you."

"Now that's an image that'll hold me till lunch."

"Come on, pervert," I said. "There's B.J. and Jim. Let's go get jacked up."

The four of us fixed our coffee and headed in the direction of the escalator when the PA system crackled on. Everyone in the store instinctively put their fingers in their ears.

"GOOD MORNING, SALES REPRESENTATIVES! WELCOME TO ANOTHER PRODUCTIVE DAY AT LANDSTROM. THE MAGIC SALES NUMBER TODAY IS FIFTY THOUSAND TWO HUNDRED AND TWELVE DOLLARS AND TWO CENTS...THAT'S FIFTY THOUSAND TWO HUNDRED AND TWELVE DOLLARS AND TWO CENTS! DON'T FORGET...FIFTY THOUSAND TWO HUNDRED AND TWELVE DOLLARS AND TWO CENTS. THE DOORS OPEN IN TEN MINUTES...HAVE A NICE DAY." We heard a few more seconds of static and then blessed silence.

"Why does she have to yell every morning? I said, removing my fingers from my ears.

"Everybody in management yells," Jonathon said, hitting the side of his head with his hand. "I think it's part of their training. They think that if they yell loud enough and repeat themselves, then maybe the moronic sales staff will understand. Then again, maybe it's a Scandinavian thing. Did you get the number?"

"Yeah."

"What is it?"

"Uh…fifty thousand two hundred and…uh…something."

"Sara! It's fifty thousand two hundred and twelve dollars and TWO cents. Why can't you ever remember the magic number?"

"Because it's ridiculous, that's why. Who figures out that number anyway? And why is two cents so important? Who cares?"

"You do…if you want to keep your job," Jonathon said.

I looked at him and sighed. "Oh, all right. What's the number again?"

The magic number had almost gotten me fired on my first day at Landstrom. I was minding my own business trying to remember how to ring up a sale when the phone rang. I picked up the receiver and held it under my chin as I stuffed two pairs of New Balance walking shoes into a shopping bag.

"Good morning…Men's Shoes. Sara Gorman speaking…May I help you?"

"GOOD MORNING, SARA GORMAN!" I held the phone at arm's length. "THIS IS SUSAN WELCH, THE SALES MANAGER AT LANDSTROM. WHAT IS THE MAGIC NUMBER?"

"Uh…just a moment, Susan," I said as I handed my customer his package. I looked over the department store floor and waved to my manger, Dan. I held up the phone and mouthed the words "magic number?" to him and shrugged. He did wind sprints across the sales floor and frantically wrote down $30,250.10.

"Oh, that magic number," I said into the receiver. "That's thirty-thousand two hundred and fifty dollars and ten cents."

"MAKE SURE YOU KNOW IT THE NEXT TIME, SARA GORMAN! WE DON'T WANT DAN TO HAVE A HEART ATTACK ON THE SALES FLOOR. PUT HIM ON THE PHONE. HAVE A NICE DAY!"

Dan blanched when I handed him the phone.

"Good morning, Susan. Yes, I understand. Yes…yes…yes. Of course. Yes. Absolutely. You have a NICE DAY too!" Dan looked up at the ceiling above the cash registers. "Goddamn cameras," he muttered as he pulled me out of the department over to the elevators. I looked up at the ceiling as the cameras in the shoe department rotated in their mounts over to where Dan I were now standing.

"Never EVER forget the magic number. It's one of management's pet peeves. Didn't they explain that to you in training?"

"Dan, I'm sure they did. But they covered so much in three days...I guess I just forgot."

"Well, don't forget again. Because they'll fire you for it...And my sorry ass will be right behind yours."

From that day on, I wrote the magic number (which turned out to be the projected sales goal for the entire store on any given day) on my wrist.

As I finished writing the number, the PA system sputtered on again. Our fingers automatically went back into our ears. But this time, instead of a screaming store manager, we heard the instrumental open for the Pointer Sisters' hit song "Jump."

"Pointer Sisters!" B.J. and Jonathon yelled. I moved to the side as Jonathon, B.J., and two of the MAC makeup artists from cosmetics danced at the foot of the up escalator. Pretty soon, Monique and four of the store display coordinators joined them. Jonathon led the group onto the escalator.

"Are you ready to jump for your love?" Jonathon yelled.

"YES!"

"All right then. Here we go."

The song began. Jonathon hopped up one step and they followed his lead. The line continued to hop up one step to the beat of the music. Jonathon pointed his finger down and they marched down the up escalator. When they got to the bottom of the up escalator, they turned around and began dancing back up again.

I sipped my Starbucks and followed their up and down antics as I walked up the steps that paralleled the escalators. When I got to the top, they were on their way back down again. I caught Jonathon's eye and saluted him with my coffee cup. He saluted back. I left the twentysomethings to their gyrations and made my way back to Men's Shoes. By the time I reached my department, the Pointer Sisters had been abruptly silenced and replaced by the soothing rhythms of a baby grand piano playing "Tea for Two." I hummed along with the piano, picked up one of the feather dusters behind the counter, and began dusting off the display shoes. The phone rang and I soft-shoed over to answer it.

"Men's Shoes. Sara Gorman speaking."

"Best get over here now...We got trouble."

"Malqueen? Where? What's wrong?"

"The old rectory."

"Why?"

"Uh-oh. The local TV news truck just pulled up."

"Malqueen, are you going to tell me what's going on?"

"It's your mama."

"Mother? What happened? Is she all right?

"She's all right for a person who's sick in the head...Oh, no...your sister just saw the TV truck."

"Malqueen, would you please just tell me what's going on?"

"Your mama ran away."

"When?"

"This morning...but we found her. That ain't the problem."

"Then what is?"

"It's where we found her."

"At the old rectory?"

"Yes...but that's still not the problem."

"Then what is?"

"She's on the roof...and she's threatening to jump."

"Oh my God. I'll be right there," I said as I threw the duster behind the counter and ran out of the store.

Chapter Twenty-Six

---•---

"Instead of weeping when a tragedy
occurs in a songbird's life,
it sings away its grief."

Shakespeare

I pulled up in front of my childhood home behind two police cars and the TV News truck. A crowd had gathered in front of the house. I saw Malqueen and Lightning standing off to the side.

"How did she get up there?"

"Barbara said the new girl...poor thing already been fired...thought your Mama was takin' a nap. Well, she wasn't. She sneaked out of Barbara's house and walked all the way over here and climbed up on that ladder."

I looked at a ladder that rested against the front of the house.

"The cops are afraid to go up after her," Lightning added. "She keeps threatening to jump."

I looked over at the patrol car. The cops were inside their heated car laughing and drinking coffee. A reporter was interviewing our old neighbors.

"Where's Barbara?" I asked Malqueen.

"Down front."

Barbara stood directly below Mother. I joined her.

"Mother, please get down," she pleaded.

Mother stopped pacing, sat down, and crab-walked over to the edge of the roof.

"Who are you?" she asked, peering down at Barbara.

"I've told you, Mother. I'm your daughter, Barbara. Please come down before you hurt yourself."

Barbara eyed the ladder that leaned against the side of the house. I nudged her and she turned around. "Thank God you came. Can you believe they sent a TV crew out here? What are we going to do? I've never been so embarrassed in my whole life!"

"Calm down. There's nothing to do. We just have to figure out a way to get her to come down."

"You're right. I'll try again. Mother? You've got to come down or you'll—"

Barbara was interrupted by the roar of a motorcycle revving its engine and honking its horn at the neighbors who had come out to watch this fiasco. Mother waved wildly at the black leather blur, and Barbara managed four rungs up the ladder before Mother stopped her.

"Take one more step and I jump!" Mother said, leaping to her feet, legs bent at the knees, arms flung straight out behind her, and body leaning dangerously forward over the edge of the roof. Defeated, Barbara stepped down from the ladder and backed away. I stepped forward.

"Mother, just calm down. No one's going to make you come down if you don't want to. Aren't you getting cold up there? Wouldn't you like a nice cup of hot cocoa?"

Mother relaxed her ski-jump pose and looked down at me.

"Why are you up on the roof anyway?" I asked.

"Well, for heaven's sake, girl. Where else could I find a bird's-eye view like this?" Mother said and then, putting her hands back on her hips, she leaned over the edge and asked, "And who the hell are you?"

"I'm your daughter, Sara."

"I thought what's-her-name over there was my daughter," she said, pointing to Barbara, who was deep in conversation with Reverend Dobb, the new occupant of our old home.

"We both are. You know you can have more than one."

"More than one what?"

"More than one daughter."

"You the one that wants to send me away?" Mother asked. "Because if you are, I'm not going to any funny farm and that's that."

"Mother, no one's trying to send you anywhere.

"I wasn't born yesterday! I saw that paper in the hall. You can't fool me."

"Mother, it was just a brochure for a care center."

I heard a reporter behind me ask one of the neighbors if Mother was going to be committed. I turned around and said, "No. She's not crazy. She's just demented. Now leave us alone."

Barbara looked like she was going to faint. She grabbed my arm and pulled me away. "Sara, don't make these news people angry."

"Well, they're making me angry."

"I won't go to any loony bin," Mother repeated.

"Mother, it's not the loony bin. It's a place where older people go when they're tired of mowing the lawn. They don't have to fix dinner anymore, and they can play gin rummy all day if they like. They learn new crafts and visit with people their own age...people your age—"

"Hah!" Mother scoffed. "People my age die! And as for that basket weaving jazz...well, that's just what they do in the loony bin! Mother shaded her eyes with her hand and glared at the neighbors, who had huddled together at the end of the driveway trying to keep warm as the sun began to set.

"What did you say your name was?" Mother asked again.

"Sara."

Mother scratched her head.

"How do you spell that?"

"S-a-r-a."

"That's the damnedest thing," Mother muttered to herself, again pacing across the roof, pulling her skimpy sweater around her. She dragged her feet, slapping her boots across the roof tiles.

I looked over and saw the TV camera pan with her.

"I mean, I can see naming a kid Barbara...but Sara?" Mother frowned and paced. After a few minutes she stopped and came back to where I was standing.

"I know why I can't remember you. I didn't give you that name, did I?"

"No, you didn't. Father did."

"Where's William anyway?" Mother asked, scanning the crowd on the lawn.

"Father died last year," I said gently.

"WHAT! William is dead? Why didn't anybody tell me?"

"We did." I looked over at Malqueen, who was staring up at Mother and shaking her head.

"You did not! This is the first I've heard of it."

"Mother, you were at the funeral."

Mother threw her hands up in the air and said, "Well, thank heavens for small favors. Can you imagine what the congregation would have said if I hadn't been there?" Mother dropped to all fours and scooted herself to the edge of the roof directly in front of me. In a lowered voice she asked, "Was it a nice funeral? How'd he look?"

I resisted the urge to say that he looked quite dead and instead said, "He looked fine. He wore that blue suit you gave him for his birthday."

Mother stared off into the distance, and I looked across the lawn and saw Lightning talking to Barbara and Reverend Dobb. They seemed to be arguing about something.

Mother sat down, dangled her legs over the edge of the roof, smacked her heels together, and began humming a tune I didn't recognize.

Shivering I pulled my down coat around me and again looked over at the pow-wow between Lightning, Barbara, and the Reverend. Lightning shook his head and walked back to Malqueen. He leaned over and whispered something in her ear. She shook her head too. Reverend Dobb disappeared around the back of the house. I walked over to Barbara.

"What's going on?"

"There's an extension ladder in the basement. Reverend Dobb thinks he can climb up the back of the house and sneak up behind her."

"Barbara…are you nuts? He'll scare her to death. Didn't the police tell you not to do that?"

"The police just don't want to get involved. They've already told me she'll come down when she gets cold. They obviously don't know Mother. Sometimes I think she's bionic. Besides, I want her off the roof and away from those TV cameras."

"Why? She's already made the six o'clock news."

"Oh, God help us," Barbara wailed. "I just want her down from there. I'm tired of standing out here in subzero weather watching my mother make a fool of herself in front of the entire neighborhood." Barbara looked over at the news crew and said, "Make that the entire state! Look at her, Sara. She looks like a New York City bag lady. Where did she even find those hideous clothes anyway?"

I smiled and held Barbara by the arm to stop her from pacing. "Surely you remember that sweater."

Barbara looked up at Mother.

"That's your old BrownWood sweater she has on," I said. "And the green vinyl miniskirt and white go-go boots were mine. Imagine. She kept all that stuff."

"It's disgusting. No eighty-three-year-old woman in her right mind would parade around on a roof in the dead of winter dressed like a reject from *Hullabaloo.*"

"But Barbara, she isn't."

"Isn't what?" Barbara asked absently.

"In her right mind."

Barbara yanked her arm away from me and walked quickly across the lawn. I saw her talking to the cameraman. The reporter had left and was now sitting in the police car drinking coffee with the cops.

I sighed and stared up at Mother. I was tired of explaining Mother's illness to Barbara. I was even sick of listening to myself. No matter what I said, or how bizarre Mother behaved, Barbara would always believe that one day Mother would wake up and suddenly start acting like the Caroline Rebecca Gorman of old, wife of the Right Reverend William Allen Gorman, Episcopal bishop of Maryland, the mother of our childhood.

Malqueen tapped me on the shoulder. "Barbara tell you about that hairbrained scheme she and that Reverend fella cooked up?"

"Unfortunately, yes. Somebody's bound to get hurt."

"That's what Lightning said. They wanted him to go up but he refused."

"Good for him. At least somebody has some sense."

"Don't know 'bout that. He's afraid of heights. But he said he'd hold the ladder."

"Oh great."

Malqueen nudged me and I looked up. Reverend Dobb's head appeared just above the roof peak and directly behind Mother. In a flash, Mother stood up and looked down at us.

"Is that you, Malqueen?"

"Yessam."

"What's for dinner?"

"Pot roast with mashed taters and gravy with green beans and home-made biscuits. Why don't you come down and have some?"

"I don't believe a word of it. You always change the menu on me!"

"Of all the things to remember..." Malqueen said.

"Did you hear that?" Mother asked.

Malqueen and I looked at Reverend Dobb, shook our heads, and held our breath.

"You've got to hear that. Listen! It's that song your father sang to you before he took you to the Orioles games."

"'Take Me Out to the Ballgame'?"

"Yes, that's the one! Listen to that organ play." Mother stood at the edge of the roof and began playing an imaginary keyboard. "Listen to William sing," she cackled. "He never could carry a tune, but boy could he dance." Mother twirled around. Malqueen grabbed my arm and closed her eyes. The Reverend ducked behind the chimney just in time to avoid detection.

"It's OK," I whispered to Malqueen. "You can look. He's behind the chimney."

Malqueen opened one eye and looked up. "This is pitiful...I don't think I can watch this."

Barbara came up behind us and said excitedly, "We got a bit of luck. The camera crew is leaving."

"Oh?" Malqueen said.

"Five-alarm fire on Cold Spring Lane. Lots of excitement. People jumping out of windows and stuff."

Malqueen shook her head and said, "What's the matter with you? You call that luck? Some poor people being burnt outta their homes? I'm beginning to think you is the one with the demented brain instead of your mama."

"I only meant—"

"I know what you meant. I'm going 'round back and check on Lightning."

We watched as Malqueen stomped toward the backyard.

"Heh! You two...what's-your-names. You're not singing!"

I looked up at Mother and saw the Reverend emerge from his hiding place again. He began to inch his way toward Mother.

"Come on," Mother yelled. "Sing!"

I began to sing "Buy me some peanuts and Cracker Jacks," as I watched Mother belt out the song and encourage the neighbors to keep singing. The mother of my childhood would have been mortified at this spectacle singing her heart out on the roof. I, however, was torn. Unlike Barbara, I actually liked this new, funny, free-spirited woman singing on the roof better than the woman I remembered from my childhood.

"I don't care if I never get back..." Mother screeched.

"What's Reverend Dobb going to do once he grabs her?" I whispered to Barbara.

"I don't know. We didn't get that far," she shrugged.

"Oh great," I thought. The Reverend now loomed directly above my oblivious Mother. I looked at Reverend Dobb's Santa Claus waistline and decided that if Mother didn't kill him, his cholesterol would. Arms outstretched, the Reverend was in perfect position to pounce on her. As he reached out for her, however, she suddenly turned, jumped to the side, and screamed, "Reverend Dobb! What are you doing up on this roof?" The last thing the Reverend expected from Mother was coherence. He lost his balance, fell flat on his back, and torpedoed off the roof. He didn't land well.

"Is he dead?" Mother asked, leaning over the roof's edge.

"Well, it's your fault if he is!" screamed Barbara as she shook her fist in the air. "The poor man was only trying to help you! Now look at what you did!"

"Is he dead?"

I too was afraid he was dead and was very relieved when I heard him groan.

Luckily, the Reverend's fall had been broken by a huge grouping of bushes in front of the house. Unfortunately, they were holly bushes.

"Get those do-nothin' po-lice men to call for an ambulance," Malqueen screamed, coming around from the back of the house.

Barbara ran over to the cops, and I ran over to the Reverend. His legs were sticking straight up out of a mound of crumpled greenery. I couldn't help but think that if we added some red velvet bows to the greens and set his shoes on fire, he'd look just like one of my sister's Christmas centerpieces.

The Reverend began to move.

"Don't move, Reverend," I warned. "You'll just keep sticking yourself on the holly."

Reverend Dobb's only response was, "OUCH, Goddamn it! OUCH! OUCH! OUCH!"

"Is he dead?" Mother squawked again.

"No, Mother. He's not dead. Now...just...shut...up!"

Mother stuck her tongue out at me and began to pace back and forth across the roof.

She was still pacing as the ambulance pulled into the driveway ten minutes later. The paramedics, not seeing the Reverend in the bushes, spotted Mother up on the roof.

"How long's she been up there?"

"Anybody tried to talk her down?"

"She on any medication?"

I looked at them as if they were idiots.

"Of course we've tried to talk her down," I snapped. "But she's stubborn! She's been up there for hours...doesn't seem to mind the cold at all while the rest of us freeze to death...has had the neighbors singing in the driveway for over an hour...and has caused that man over there," I said, pointing to the Reverend, "to fall off the roof!"

They slowly turned their heads in the direction of the Reverend's legs, grabbed their medical kits, and quickly made their way over to the quivering holly bushes.

I sat down in the middle of the frozen lawn and watched Malqueen, Lightning, and Barbara talk to the paramedics about the Reverend. When I looked up, Mother was "shaking her booty" to music that only she could hear. When I looked back down, I found myself staring at a pair of Timberland Hikers.

"Nice boots," I said, looking up at the man who wore them.

"Thanks, they're Timberland."

"I know. Gortex-lined, waterproof, and insulated for warmth. Best made boots in the country. Those must have set you back plenty, unless, of course, you were smart enough to catch them on sale."

"I am and I did."

The fact that he was smart enough to wait for the Timberland sale intrigued me. I wanted to get a better look at his face, but at the moment it was obscured by a cloud of cigarette smoke.

"Who's the old lady on the roof," he exhaled, giving me a better look at a nose that looked like it had lost too many fights.

"My mother."

"Nice outfit…1965? No, wait, probably more like 1968. Day-Glo was hot in the late sixties."

"Actually, midsixties to the late sixties…then tie-dye took over."

We both stared up at Mother who was now engrossed in performing the gyrations of the Monkey.

"Do you want me to try to get her down?"

"How?" I asked. "With a tranquilizer gun?"

"No, that only works on lions and tigers and bears. Not on the Wicked Witch of the West."

I should have been offended, if not for myself, then for my mother. But as I watched Mother jerk up and down and hop around the roof, I realized that she did indeed look like Margaret Hamilton.

"Just how are you going to get her down? Give her a broom and tell her she can fly?"

For the first time, I saw something of a smile behind the smoke. And he didn't look half bad when he smiled.

"What's wrong with her?"

"Alzheimer's…they think. Of course, they can't be certain until she dies and they can dissect her brain."

"That's a lovely image."

"It's a lovely disease," I said as I stood up and found myself staring at the word "Paramedic." "How come you aren't helping with the Reverend? Aren't you part of the team?"

"I'm the designated driver today. If they need me…they'll yell."

As if on cue, Reverend Dobb let loose with another litany of "OUCH! OUCH! OUCH! Stop pulling on me, will you? OUCH!" as two paramedics dragged him from the bushes.

"Looks like they're doing just fine. Come on, let's go see if we can get Margaret down from there." I followed him back to the house.

"Hey," the driver waved to Mother.

"Who are you?" Mother asked from the roof.

"Who are you?"

"I asked you first."

"Doesn't matter because you don't know me."

"Why don't I know you?"

"Because I'm new."

Mother thought about that for a while.

"So what do you want, Mr. New?"

"I don't want anything. But this lady here wants you off the roof." The driver smiled at her.

Mother folded her arms over her chest and said, "I'm not getting down, and you can't make me!"

"That's just what I told her." He shrugged and lit another cigarette.

Mother eyed him suspiciously and said, "You did?"

"Absolutely...I told her you wouldn't get down. In fact, I bet her ten bucks you wouldn't get off that roof."

The mention of money had an immediate effect on Mother, and suddenly she perked up.

"Ten bucks? You bet ten bucks?"

"Yep, and it looks like I win, doesn't it? You're not about to get down from there...are you?"

Mother shifted her weight from foot to foot.

"Would you bet me ten bucks?" she asked.

"Sure, but why would I do that? You thinking of coming down from there?"

"Certainly not!" Mother folded her arms across her chest. Then she leaned forward and whispered, "But you could bet me anyway."

"I don't know," the driver took a puff and considered this.

"Oh, come on, Mr. Whatever-Your-Name-Is. Be a sport. You chicken?"

"All right," he said, tossing his cigarette butt into the Reverend's garden. "I bet you ten dollars you won't come down from the roof." He turned his back to Mother and winked a hazel eye at me. I watched as he walked away from Mother and back toward the ambulance. Barbara came around the house in time to see Mother agilely climb down the ladder, run behind the driver, and tap him on the shoulder.

"Hand over the dough, sucker," Mother squealed.

"Well, did you ever fool me," he laughed and peeled off ten ones for her. "You better count that and make sure I didn't cheat you."

"Hah! Cheat!" Mother grabbed the money from his hand and stuffed it down the front of her sweater and then waved both hands above her head in a victory salute. The neighbors cheered, but Mother's victory was short-lived. Her smile faded when she realized that Barbara and Malqueen had book-ended her, each grabbing an arm as they propelled her over to the car.

"HELP! I'm being abducted!" she screamed. "I don't want to go to the funny farm! Please, someone help me!"

"You are not going to the funny farm," Barbara said between clenched teeth."You're going to get in the car, and we're going to drive you home."

I watched as Malqueen and Barbara tried to push Mother into the car. Mother wedged herself inside the door by putting one white go-go boot on one side of the door frame and the other go-go boot on the other side of the frame. No matter how hard Malqueen and Barbara pushed, they still couldn't get her into the car.

I turned to the man who had finally gotten Mother off the roof.

"I can't thank you enough, Mr....?" I offered my hand.

"Zack." My hand disappeared into his. It was a hand I recognized—a hand that had thrown many touchdowns for a football team that no longer existed for Baltimore.

"Zack? As in Zacharowsky?"

"Busted. And you are?"

"Sara," I said faintly, "Gorman. You know, my Father thought you were the best quarterback in the National League. He even said that you should have—"

"That was another life," he cut me off. "I'm glad your mother's safe."

I still held his hand. He looked down, and I finally let go. I stepped back and said, "How did you know she'd go for the bet?"

"I didn't. Just went on a hunch."

"Well, thanks again." I watched him as he made his way across the lawn. And I saw something I hadn't noticed before. He limped.

It was only after he was in the ambulance that I remembered the ten dollars.

"We owe you ten dollars," I yelled.

"You can give it to me the next time you see me," he yelled back.

"What next time?" I asked, walking alongside the ambulance as it backed down the driveway.

But he just smiled as the ambulance pulled away, lights flashing, siren blaring, speeding the injured, but not dying, Reverend Dobb off to the hospital.

"Are you through flirting with that man?" Barbara asked out of breath as she continued to push and pull on Mother.

"Flirting? Me? I was just thanking him for getting Mother off the roof."

"Whatever," Barbara said. "We need your help. She's stuck."

I walked over to Barbara's Cadillac. Malqueen and Lightning were standing next to the car. Mother was still wedged in the door.

"Mother," I said.

"Who are you?"

"I'm the one who lives next to the horse."

Mother's eyes lit up and she stopped fighting.

"Would you like to go see the horse? In my car?"

Mother looked around.

I pointed to the VW.

"OK," she said and walked over to my car. As she got in the backseat, she stuck her hand into a split in the upholstery and said, "How come that one..." Mother pointed to Barbara, "...has a big new car and you drive this?"

"Her husband's a Cadillac dealer."

"The Randy fella?"

I tried not to laugh. Malqueen covered her mouth. I turned to Barbara. "Malqueen will go with me and make sure she doesn't jump out." Then I turned back to Malqueen. "I'll drive you home."

"Fine by me," Malqueen said. "But Lightning, you gotta close the store for me tonight."

"No problem," Lightning said. "Is the key still in the same place?"

"Yes," Malqueen said and then turned to me. "We better do this real quick before she changes her mind."

I ran around and started the car as Malqueen jumped in the backseat with Mother.

"Malqueen?" Mother squinted into Malqueen's face.

"Yessam."

"What's for dinner?"

"Roast pork and sauerkraut. Butter biscuits and fresh peas."

"I don't believe a word of it," Mother said, looking out the window.

"No, somehow I didn't think you would."

Barbara started her car, and we all pulled out for Barbara's house. When we got there, Randall met us at the door.

"Caroline...do you want to see yourself on television?"

Mother said, "TV? Me?"

"I taped the six o'clock news. Come on."

Mother followed Randall into the living room.

Barbara threw her keys on the table and sat down. "I wish he'd stop encouraging her. The last thing she needs to see is herself on the news. It'll give her more ideas."

"I think what he's trying to do," Malqueen said as she sat down next to Barbara, "is give you a rest. Look at her. Look at how quiet she is."

Mother was sitting on the sofa with her hands folded. Her eyes never left the television screen.

I got up and opened the refrigerator. "Who are you expecting for dinner?" I said. "The Maryland National Guard?" I pulled out a whole honey ham.

"I cook when I get stressed," Barbara said.

"No, you buy when you get stressed," Malqueen said. "That ain't home cooked; that's one of those designer hams they sell at Eddie's."

"I don't care who cooked it. I'm hungry," I said. "Anybody want a sandwich?"

Everybody did. So Malqueen and I fixed honey ham sandwiches on rye with hot spicy mustard and red onion. I found gallon tubs of potato and macaroni salad in the refrigerator, and I put those on the table too. Randall and Mother joined us, although Mother didn't eat. Instead, she put her head on the table and fell asleep.

"Have you given any thought to the new Episcopal place," I said between bites.

"No."

"Why not?"

"Because."

"Barbara, you've run out of aides."

"I've got a new one coming in tomorrow."

I looked over at Randall. "Is that true?"

"Yes, it is. She called to confirm while Caroline was on the roof. Hopefully, she didn't see the news."

"I know a lady who goes to my church that might be interested," Malqueen said. "She's a big woman, must weigh 'bout two-fifty...used to be in the army...some kind of weapons expert...real nice lady."

Barbara choked on her sandwich.

"Why don't we go out and look at the Episcopal place?" I tried again. "Old Reverend Bancroft is out there, and I know Mrs. Kanaby and Dr. Wills are—"

"No. I will not let them see Mother like this."

"Like how, Barbara?"

"In her present condition."

"Her present condition? Barbara, her present condition is demented! People in great shape don't go into care facilities."

"I don't want people to see her like this."

"What people? The patients? They don't know who they are...How will they know who she is?"

"She wouldn't want people to see her like this."

"That's just it. She doesn't know. She doesn't know who you are, she doesn't know who I am, she doesn't even know who she is!"

"That's not true. Just yesterday she asked me to read her Proverbs chapter 8...said it was one of her favorite parts of the Bible." Barbara presented this news to me like she was declaring Gin! in a card game.

Malqueen put her hand on my arm, and I held my tongue. One of the more startling things about Mother's dementia was her moments of lucidity. It was like watching a full-rigged sailboat break out of dense fog into clear skies. In those moments, Barbara saw great hope, waiting for and treasuring each clear moment, enduring the chaos for a slice of sanity. I, unfortunately, knew that the ship would eventually disappear back into the fog again. And, even in Mother's most lucid moments, she still did not recognize me.

Mother woke up and began stealing pieces of ham from Randall's sandwich. Barbara got up to make tea. Outside, a dog barked and headlights shone into the kitchen as a car pulled into the driveway. Barbara leaned against the sink and said, "Randall, are you expecting someone?"

"No," Randall said as he fed Mother a piece of his ham sandwich.

Barbara leaned closer to the window, gasped, and pulled back from the sink.

"What?" we all said at the same time.

"Come over here...QUICK!" She waved us over to the window. I stood behind Barbara, Malqueen stood behind me, and Randall stood behind Malqueen. The passenger door opened, and a French twist in three-inch pumps got out and stood looking up at the house.

"It can't be," Barbara whispered.

"I think it is," I said.

"Lordy, Lordy," Malqueen murmured.

Randall said nothing.

The cab pulled away, and its passenger gracefully glided up the sidewalk toward the door to the kitchen.

"What's she doing here?" Barbara glared at me.

"Don't look at me. I haven't heard from her in ages. Well...I did get a postcard from her about a month ago...but that's all."

"Well, that's more than I get! I never hear from her. Of all the nerve. Quick, get away from the window. If she doesn't see us, maybe she'll go away."

This made no sense at all since every light in the house was on. Still, we all backed away from the window and jumped as three sharp knocks shook the door. No one moved, except Mother, who jumped up from the table and flung the kitchen door open. I saw the ship come out of the fog as Mother said in a clear voice, "Natalie...darling...how nice of you to come."

"Hello, Mother," Natalie replied, looking sideways at the three of us huddled on the other side of the kitchen. "How are you?"

"BITCH!" squealed Mother, as she charged through the open door and ran past Natalie into the night.

Chapter Twenty-Seven

—————————————— • ——————————————

"Pray you now, forget and forgive.
Shakespeare

Malqueen whipped past Natalie with Barbara and me right on her heels, but Mother hadn't gone far.

"I'm lost!" she cried from the end of the driveway. "I want to go home!"

"We're right here," Miz Gorman," Malqueen said, taking her arm.

"Is that you, Malqueen?"

"Yessam."

"What's for dinner?"

"Ham and potato salad and macaronis."

"I don't believe you."

"Didn't expect you to. Watch your step now. That's good. Almost there."

Barbara and Malqueen led Mother back into the house. I sat down on the curb and hugged myself against the December cold. House lights snapped on in succession up and down the block, each house strung with identical miniature white lights. The same Eddie Bauer wreath hung on each door.

"Looks like Tavern on the Green," Natalie said from behind me.

"How's Mother?" I asked.

"Barbara and Malqueen dragged her off to bed." Natalie sat down next to me on the curb, lit a Virginia Slim, and handed it to me.

"I gave that up."

"Oh?" Natalie said, still holding the cigarette.

I reached over, took a drag, and passed it back.

"She's in bad shape. I didn't think it would happen this fast."

"I told you. I also sent you all the information."

Natalie sat back and raised an eyebrow.

"Well? Did you read any of it?"

"Oh, yes. I read it." She handed me the cigarette again, and I took another drag.

Barbara stuck her head out the door and yelled, "Sara!"

"Looks like you're being paged."

"I'm supposed to take Malqueen home. It's getting late." I got up and Natalie got up with me.

"I guess there's no chance I can stay with you?"

"I only have one bedroom."

"By design, I think."

I looked down at my shoes and didn't answer.

"It's OK, kid. I can survive here for a few days...I think."

I wanted to ask Natalie why she was even here, especially after what had happened at the funeral. But as I followed her tall, trim figure up the walk, I decided to let Barbara have that honor.

I hadn't even closed the door when Barbara looked at Natalie and yelled, "Just why are you here?"

Natalie smiled and Barbara blinked. Father used to say Natalie could do great things with that smile, called it her one hundred-watt GE Special. Nat smiled and people smiled back, forgetting in the process what they were saying or doing or even thinking. Mother said it was a gift from God to be able to light up a room with a smile. But, of course, Malqueen disagreed.

"Lights up nothin'."

"But Malqueen," Barbara argued, "she's beautiful when she smiles."

"There you go defending her again. That smile ain't nothin' but a black hole."

"Black hole?"

"Seen it on the TV. That science show. These black holes swirl 'round in outer space, and they got something like a vacuum cleaner in the center of them...sucks everything inside...sorta like a drain. They so powerful, nothin' can escape them."

"And?"

"And thats what your sister does. She sucks in everybody 'round her with that smile...whether they want to be sucked in or not."

Natalie's smile did buy her some time with Barbara.

"Got any vodka?" she asked.

"I'll get it," I volunteered, escaping into the library in search of my sister's Absolut. I discovered Randall behind the door.

"What are you doing?" I asked him.

"Shhhh. I'm hiding. If she finds out...I'm dead."

"Finds out what?"

"That I called Natalie."

"What on earth possessed you to do that?"

"I just thought she ought to see how much work your mother is for your sister. Natalie's done nothing since this whole thing started."

"Randall, this is Natalie we're talking about, the daughter who wouldn't even come home to visit. What made you think she'd come home to help with Mother?"

"I just thought maybe if she saw how bad she was..." Randall shrugged. "OK, it was a dumb idea."

"You just better hope Natalie doesn't tell Barbara that it was you who called her."

"I know."

We heard raised voices and I cracked open the door.

"I don't think you should drink, Natalie."

"I don't see why I shouldn't."

"You know what it does to you."

"I really don't care what it does to me."

"Well, I do. And I don't want my household upset by your drinking."

"Your household is already upset. Besides, I'm not going to get drunk."

"That's what you said before the funeral."

The dreaded "F" word had finally been uttered. I leaned against the door and lost my balance. Randall tried to pull me back, but he lost his grip, and I fell into the kitchen clutching the Absolut bottle.

"Oh look," Natalie said. "It's the Vodka bunny."

Barbara briefly looked at me and then turned her attention back to Natalie.

"I can't believe you had the nerve to come back here."

"I know you're still upset about the funeral."

"UPSET! I'm not upset. I'm LIVID! You show up drunker than a skunk at Father's funeral. Our father, the bishop of Maryland, in front of God and all those important people...the new bishop, his wife, the governor, the mayor—"

Oh, baloney...Those people didn't even know I was there. I sat in the last pew."

"That's even worse. Think of the gossip. The bishop's daughter didn't show for his funeral!"

"Barbara, make up your mind. Are you angry with me because I was drunk and I sat in the back, which, in fact, made me present at Father's funeral and, therefore, a dutiful daughter...or are you angry at me because I sat in the back and not with the family and people assumed I wasn't there, thus stirring up gossip and making YOU look bad?"

"It made the family look bad, and I'm angry with you on all counts. Why couldn't you just show up sober and sit with the family...period?"

"It's a much better service when you're drunk. Besides, you handled everything beautifully, just like you always do. You didn't need me."

"Mother needed you."

"No, Barbara, don't lay that guilt on me. That may work with Sara, but you and I know that Mother has never needed anyone but Father." Natalie looked over at me and said, "Hey, kid. Stop gawking and pour us some vodka before your sister pops a blood vessel."

I poured two drinks, looked at Barbara who shook her head no, and sat down at the kitchen table. I saw the white of Randall's eye peering through the crack in the door. I slouched down in my seat, sipped vodka, and tried to blend in with the furniture.

"Why, Natalie, why why why would you embarrass us like that?"

"You, Barbara, just you you you. I didn't embarrass anyone but you! Sara didn't care, did you, Sara?"

"Uh..." I tried to remember that day. I had popped two Valiums with a mug of Father's Johnny Walker Black before getting in the limo with Mother and Barbara. I didn't want to go to his funeral. I wanted him back in his study, with me sitting in his worn black leather chair, listening to him practice his sermons and speeches, and invariably going off on his favorite subject: sports. I wanted to sit in that chair and never leave. And I probably would have if Barbara hadn't come and gotten me...gently removing the mug from my hand, pulling me up, and guiding me toward the car. But while I'd like to forget everything about that day, flashes do come back. Mother and Barbara in black standing side by side and looking up the steps to the church...the long, dark aisle of the Church of the Redeemer and me thinking, "Dear God, can I walk that far?" Hundreds of faces in church, some familiar, some not, with an odd thought that I didn't want to write all those thank-you notes. And the coffin... the squeak in one wheel as the ushers rolled it down the aisle and out the door as the congregation sang "Onward Christian Soldiers."

"Uh...well...uh...I...really don't know that I cared then," I said, looking up at Barbara. "And I don't really know if I care now...I was upset... am still upset, and I just don't remember."

"Not remember? How could you not remember your sister sprawled out facedown on the last pew with a hymnal over her head in plain view of the entire congregation?"

Ah, that. After the coffin went by and the ushers motioned for the family to leave the church, Mother, Barbara, and I walked down the aisle behind it, the squeaky wheel keeping time with "marching off to war..." as the rest of the singing mourners followed behind, emptying out into the main aisle row by row. At the last pew Barbara paused, glanced to the right, and then hurried Mother out the door. I glanced over in time to see Natalie roll off the pew and fall to the floor. In my Valium-induced daze, I watched as a caramel arm reached over the pew and dropped a coat over Natalie's disheveled body. Malqueen moved around to the end of Natalie's pew, looked straight ahead, and, with tears streaming down her face, continued to sing "with the cross of Jesus..." And then I was back in the limo with Mother and Barbara moving toward the cemetery. We hadn't heard from Natalie since then.

"Maybe people just thought she passed out because she was so stricken with grief...nobody knew she was drunk...thanks to Malqueen," I added.

Nat raised her vodka in a salute to me and winked.

"I don't believe you! Are you defending her behavior? How can you side with her on this? Father was the bishop! He deserved more respect than that... Mother deserved more respect than that...and I think I deserved more respect than that!"

Natalie, who had dragged me into this fight, now got me out of it.

"Lay off the kid, Barbara. This is between you and me."

Nat took a gulp of vodka and looked directly at Barbara. "Actually, I came home to apologize to you. You're right. I did a despicable thing. I'm sorry. Can you forgive me?"

It was said with such sincerity that even I almost believed her. Barbara continued to stare at her, but I saw the angry lines around her mouth soften just a bit.

"Barbara, he was my father too. I did want to be there…I just couldn't do it…sober."

"But when you called from New York," Barbara said, leaning forward, "you sounded fine. What happened between there and here?"

"I don't know. I was on the airplane. I knew the crew. They offered me free drinks. We landed and I went to the airport bar and I drank some more. I finally told the bartender I was going to a funeral, and he called me a cab. You can thank the bartender for getting me to the church at all—"

"So you could sit in the last pew and pass out? Natalie, you need help."

"Oh, come on. Forgive me?"

"No!"

"Truce?"

"Maybe."

"Can I stay here tonight?"

"Do I have a choice?" Natalie and Barbara stared at each other.

"I'm ready," Malqueen said as she came through the library door. "She's finally asleep." I wondered where Randall had gone.

"Malqueen," I said. "Thanks for helping today."

"No problem…terrible thing that disease done to her brain." Malqueen shook her head and then looked over at Natalie. "You lookin' better than the last time I saw you."

"I think I was green the last time you saw me, Malqueen."

"More like the color of bile."

"Did I thank you?"

"No."

"Thank you, Malqueen."

"Never thought I'd hear that."

"Never thought I'd say it."

I saw the corner of Malqueen's mouth turn up as I helped her on with her coat.

"Natalie, I think you need professional help," Barbara said as Malqueen and I headed out the door.

"Just what the hell do you think I've been doing for the past twenty years?"

I closed the door.

Malqueen and I were silent for the first fifteen minutes of the drive home. Then I said, "Did you see Randall in the library?"

"Old swivel-head was sneakin' out the other way when I came down."

"He was the one who called Natalie."

"Lord, he won't have a home if Barbara finds out."

"Well, maybe Natalie won't tell Barbara."

"As Lightning would say, I wouldn't want to bet on those odds."

I started to turn down Broadway, but Malqueen said, "No, go down Fleet."

"What's down there?"

"I need to check somethin' out."

I was halfway down Fleet when Malqueen told me to slow down.

"OK, it should be right about…there." She pointed to a house with some kind of display out front.

"What is it?"

"Lightning told me about it. Watch this."

It was dark and still when we pulled up in front of the white formstone row house. Malqueen opened the car door and waved her arm up and down. Within seconds, spotlights illuminated Mary and Joseph, the baby Jesus, two sheep, a cow, and a horse. "Away in a Manger" blared out from hidden speakers as Mary and Joseph twisted and turned over the Manger, while the baby Jesus waved his arms and hiccupped. The animals were cardboard, but this lack of flexibility didn't hinder them from emitting an occasional "moo" or "baaaa." The immobile horse, lacking voice, instead sported two riders. Someone had placed Barney and Tinky Winky on its back.

"Isn't that somethin'?" Malqueen said. "Lightning said it unbelievable."

"Truly amazing. An animatronic nativity scene."

"I got to get over to Caldor tomorrow," Malqueen said, rolling up the window. "Lightning said they're on sale for $59.95...and they're goin' fast."

I dropped Malqueen off and watched as she let herself in. As I pulled away from the curb, I thought about stopping at the Parrot but decided it was too late. I had to get up early for work tomorrow anyway...that is, if I still had a job.

I could hear Ludwig howling as I drove down the road to the cottage. I let him out, turned on lights, and before I got through my mail, Ludwig was snorting at the back door. I let him back in, made the coffee for the morning, and turned off the same lights I had just turned on. When I got into bed, Ludwig was beside me, under the covers with his head on the pillow snoring loudly.

"Good night, sweet prince," I whispered.

"Snorzzoff," Ludwig snorted and rolled on his back.

I awoke to the early morning sun and dog breath in my face. This is a sad existence I thought as I trudged out to the kitchen to get coffee. The only man who's been in my bed for the past year has hair all over him, bad breath, and fleas. I was about to step into the shower when the sound of thundering hooves stopped me. A loud crash on the porch sent me running outside. Ludwig dived under the bed.

"What the heck—" I said as I pulled my robe around me and hung out the front door.

"Mornin', lassie. Sorry for the noise. Snookie sent me 'round to deliver the annual Christmas Eve party invitations."

"Ian, don't you find it odd that Snookie would send you out on Medalia Del Oro at the crack of dawn to toss rocks onto people's porches?"

"Aye...but that's our Snookie." Ian nudged the horse closer to the porch, but Medalia reared up.

"God, I hate that horse. He's such a show-off," I said, backing inside.

"He can afford to show off...a champion he is...and where is the fine lad this mornin'?" Ian looked around the yard.

"Under the bed, where else? He got scared when he heard the bang on the porch."

Ian whistled for "the fine lad," and Ludwig head-butted the door open and came leaping out of the house. Ian calmed Medalia as Ludwig ran circles around the horse. I offered Ian some coffee.

"Sorry, lass. Much as I'd like to, I've still to deliver these invites for Snookie. Will ye be late this evenin'?"

"Yes, getting ready for the Big Sale."

"Dinna worry...Byron will keep an eye on Ludie for ye. I'll drop him off at the stables on my way back. Are ye ready, boy?"

Ludwig and Medalia stood side by side. Ian nodded to me.

"On your mark..." I yelled.

Ludwig crept ahead of Medalia. The horse threw back his head in protest and pranced forward two steps.

"Get set!" Ian pulled Medalia back as Ludwig cheated some more.

"GO!" And they were off. Dog and horse, neck and neck, down the driveway, with Ian shouting encouragement to Ludwig as Medalia Del Oro, Snookie's Preakness contender, left him in the dust. Ludwig would spend the day and most of the evening at the stables with Byron, where he would be over-fed and allowed to chase barn cats to his heart's content.

I picked up Snookie's "rock" invitation and went inside. A formal invitation had been scotch-taped to a fist-sized piece of granite. I had always heard about Snookie's wild Christmas Eve parties, but I had never been invited to one. Lettie had told me that every year Snookie chose a theme for her party. This year Snookie wanted her guests to dress up as their favorite 1930s or 1940s movie star. At the bottom of my invitation Snookie had handwritten in "Bring your sister." Which one? I wondered. I looked at the date and realized the party was in three days. Only Snookie could get away with this. The party "season" in Baltimore was already in full swing. People penned in Christmas party dates a month in advance. Apparently, Snookie took great pleasure in knowing that the people she invited to her party would have to scramble and make up excuses to cancel previous engagements in order to attend her gala. And from what Lettie had told me, they would. Snookie's parties were that good.

As I was rushing out the door for work, the phone rang.

"HELLLLLLLP!"

"Hello, Natalie."

In the background I heard Barbara scream, "No, Mother...put that tomato down...Don't do that...not in my living room...stop it. STOP IT! Those are new draperies, Mother...NO!"

"Getmeouttahere," Natalie whispered into the phone.

"Oh, all right," I said. "Meet me for lunch. Noon. The Diner at Towsontowne.

"Do they serve booze?"

"Absolutely."

"Thank God."

Chapter Twenty-Eight

"Better a diamond with a flaw than a
pebble without."

Confucius

I got to work early only to discover I was still late. I had forgotten I was supposed to be in at eight to attend a meeting on the Big Sale.

"Well, Sara, so glad you've finally decided to grace us with your presence."

"I'm really sorry, Dan. I forgot about the meeting. And about yesterday I—"

"Forget about yesterday," Dan said, picking up a black wing tip. "We saw you on the news. Today, however," he said, pointing the shoe at me, "is another matter. See me in my office after this meeting."

I looked around at the rest of the sales staff who were taking a keen interest in their shoelaces. I sat down next to Jonathon.

"Don't worry," Jonathon whispered. "Sid and Leo were late too. They got here two minutes before you did."

"Do they have to go to the principal's office after school too?"

"Yep, and do does Jim. Seems he forgot to shave this morning." I looked over at Jim. He looked like he'd had one hell of a night.

"It's going to be pretty crowded in that office," I said.

"Just stand next to the filing cabinet."

"Why?"

"When Dan starts throwing shoes around the room, you can duck down behind it."

"You know this routine?"

"Been there many times," Jonathon said.

"Excuse me, Jonathon," Dan said, pointing the wing tip at him. "Am I disturbing you?"

"No, sir."

"In my office...with the rest of them."

It wasn't as bad as I thought it would be. Jonathon and I ducked behind the cabinet when Dan let loose with the first loafer, and the only one who got hit was Sid.

The Big Sale is a big deal at Landstrom. It's always held on the day after Christmas, and every salesperson in the Men's Department has to work the sale. At least this year, I'd know what to expect. I knew I would work from eight to closing without a break. I knew I would be exhausted at the end of it. And I knew I would make lots of money. But before the sale could take place, we had to get the merchandise in order. That meant color-coding endless rows of shoe boxes in the stockroom. When twelve o'clock finally rolled around, I was glad to leave, even if it meant lunch with Natalie.

Natalie was holding court in the back of the Towsontowne Diner when I got there. She had a half-filled glass of white wine in front of her, and two servers were laughing at something she said. I zigzagged my way to the smoking section and listened as Natalie regaled her audience with one of her many flight attendant stories.

"We're serving breakfast in coach on our way to Paris, and I get to the first row and ask this lady if she'd like the omelet or the pancakes…and the lady looks up at me and in this whiny voice says, 'I'm not that hungry…Do you think I could just have a piece of toast?'" The servers start to snicker. Natalie takes a drag off her cigarette and continues. "So…I look around the airplane, and I say to her, 'Lady, this is a 747 not a 7-Eleven!'"

The servers howl and Natalie smiles. I take off my coat and sit down.

"What's with you, kid?" Natalie said finally looking over at me. "Losing your sense of humor?"

"I've heard that story a zillion times."

"Well, excuse me." Nat tucked a stray piece of platinum into her French twist and waved her cigarette in the air. "Why'd you choose this dump?"

"It's not a dump. It's a diner. Besides, it's close to Landstrom."

"It's a dump. They don't sell hard liquor. Natalie took a swig of wine and made a face. "Have you tasted this stuff? Tastes like piss."

"Then don't drink it, Natalie," I said.

Natalie made a face at me and looked at the menu.

"What won't kill me?"

"The food is actually pretty good."

"Sure. How's the lite chicken salad?"

"Light."

"How's the lite turkey platter?"

"Even lighter."

"You're a big help."

Our server arrived to take our order. Natalie smiled and looked at the woman's name tag.

"Judy, I'll have the Caesar salad...but put the dressing on the side... hold the anchovies...and see if you can scare up some fresh parmesan cheese... Oh, and I could do with a refill of pis—uh—chardonnay." Nat taped her wineglass. Judy raised an eyebrow and looked at me.

"Cheeseburger, fries, and a Coke," I said.

"God, how can you eat all that fat and still stay thin?"

"I run."

"Ugh...I'd rather starve." Natalie lit another cigarette. "How's men's shoes? Find anybody you'd like to boink?"

"What?"

"Oh, come on. I know Barbara thinks it's a fall from grace, but as I told her last night, it's the perfect place to meet men. There you are scampering around on the floor, your skirt hiked up to your ass, playing with their toes—"

"I do not play with their toes."

"Well, that's your problem...All you have to do is run your hand up their pants leg a few times, and you'd have a date every night of the week."

"I also wouldn't have a job. And, anyway, I don't want a date every night of the week."

"It's been a year. Time to get back in the saddle again."

"Natalie, I really don't want to talk about this."

"Kid, sometimes you act as repressed as Barbara."

I ignored that comment, reached in my bag for aspirin, and Snookie's invitation fell out. Natalie picked it up.

"Well, well, well...I didn't know you knew Snookie Carmichal."

"She's my landlord. Didn't Barbara tell you?"

"No, she didn't. But then all Barbara wanted to do last night was talk about who saw me do what at Father's funeral."

"Do you know her?" I said, taking the aspirin with Natalie's wine.

"I know of her," she said. "Used to see her when I rode the horses at Granger's Stables." Natalie held up her wineglass as Judy refilled it.

"Well, if you don't know her…then the sister she's telling me to bring must be Barbara."

"Makes sense to me. Snookie's old. She was in Barbara's class at BrownWood."

I didn't point out that Barbara was only seven years older than Natalie. Natalie always aligned herself with me when it came to age.

"That's odd. When I told Barbara I was living in a cottage on Snookie's farm, she had no idea who Snookie was."

"Probably because when Barbara knew her, her name was Agnes McKenzie. She's only Snookie to the racing crowd, and Barbara doesn't keep up with the horsey set."

"Hmmmm…well, guess I'd better ask Barbara if she wants to go—"

"Actually, I'd like to go," Nat said, looking at the invitation. "I've heard her parties are to die for."

"And what if Barbara does want to go?"

"Fat chance of that…Barbara the Martyr?" Natalie thought for a moment. Then she pulled a pen from her purse and scribbled on the invitation. "But just in case."

"What are you doing?"

"Adding an 's' to the 'Bring your sister' line. Now we can all go."

Natalie handed me back the invitation.

"Natalie!"

"Oh, just relax. Snookie won't even know I'm there. I've heard it's usually a cast of thousands."

"Nat, you have no idea how weird Snookie is. Do you know she wears spurs and carries a whip?"

"Ooooh…now I really want to go. Whips and spurs…yee-ha!"

I gave up and put the invitation back in my purse. I asked Nat how Mother was.

"This morning she tore all her clothes off and chased the new aide around the house." Natalie blew a smoke ring in the air. "Needless to say, the aide quit."

"Oh no, not again. What did Barbara do?"

"Got a migraine. Randall called Malqueen. I think that church lady drill sergeant person is coming later today."

"Well, at least somebody will be there. I wish she'd just look at care facilities."

"What on earth for?"

"For Mother."

"Barbara will never agree to that. She's driven by guilt. And I'm not so sure I agree with it either."

"Oh really. And why wouldn't you agree with it? You haven't helped at all."

"You've never been locked up. I have. It's not fun. I wouldn't wish that on anyone...even Mother."

"Natalie, we're not talking about the detox ward at Shepherd Pratt. This is a place where people with Alzheimer's live. Most of the people don't even know where they are. They think it's home."

"Sure, until they try to leave."

Our food arrived and we began to eat. Or at least I began to eat, while Natalie pushed her salad from one side of the plate to the other.

"I guess I'd better tell you."

"What?"

"She kicked him out."

"Who?"

"Barbara kicked Randall out."

"Did you tell her he was the one who called you?"

"No," Natalie said, avoiding my gaze.

"Natalie?"

"Well, she guessed."

"And you didn't deny it?"

"You know how persistent she is. I got tired of listening to her... 'Natalie, why did you do this? Natalie, why did you do that?' Blah, blah, blah..."

"Oh, Natalie. He was only trying to help. Where did he go?"

"He said he was going to his club." Natalie pushed her plate to the side and lit up another cigarette.

"Well," I said. "At least she always forgives him. He'll be back."

"I'm not so sure. She was pretty mad. She even..." Natalie paused.

"She even what?"

"...threw me out too."

I put my burger down and said, "No, you can't."

"I didn't ask you for anything."

"The answer's still no."

"Oh, come on, Sara. Just for a few days. I'll sleep on the sofa. I'll even sleep with that damn ugly dog of yours."

"The dog sleeps with me, and the answer's still...NO!"

Natalie reached for her wallet and counted out $400. She slid it across the table and smiled.

"Don't give me that phony smile," I said. "And what's this?"

"The money I owe you."

"You owe me eight hundred dollars...which you borrowed two years ago and I still don't know what for...and anyway, this," I said, shuffling through the bills, "this is only four."

"Well, it's half the money I owe you." Natalie was still smiling. "And I needed the money to pay off Sherry. It's not a good idea to owe your roommate money."

"But it's OK to owe your sister?"

"You're blood...You have to forgive me. How about it...just for a couple of days?"

"Forget it, Natalie. It won't work. You still can't stay with me.

Natalie put her head in her hands and began to cry.

"Natalie, I know you aren't really crying. Stop it! People are staring."

Nat's fake "boo-hoos" got louder.

"Natalie, stop it!"

She cried louder, and Judy and her fellow servers began giving me dirty looks.

"I said...no."

Natalie abruptly sat up and smiled. "OK, you win."

I bit into my burger as she reached for her wine. I saw her hand shake as she tried to pick up the glass.

"I can't believe I'm doing this," I said as I threw her my house keys. "You need a car to get there."

"I have a Cadillac…thanks to Randall. Where is this godforsaken place anyway?"

"I could take back my offer, you know."

"Sorry. And where is this lovely estate?"

"York Road to Hereford…follow the signs. Take the right in the fork and turn left at the first dirt road."

"Sounds heavenly. Will there be people playing banjos on the front porch?"

"It's Baltimore County, not West Virginia."

"Got any supplies in that log cabin of yours?"

"As in booze? Or food?"

"Both."

I tried to remember what was in the refrigerator. All I could come up with was a jar of pickles and some lemons.

"You don't have anything, do you?"

"I eat out a lot."

"No, you eat at Barbara's a lot. I'll stop at Graul's on my way to your place." Nat stood up.

"Aren't you going to eat your salad?"

"Nah, tastes like old underwear. You eat it."

"Gee, thanks."

Nat struggled into her coat, scooped the key into her purse, and said, "What time do you stop playing with men's feet…I mean, get home?"

"If I stop at Barbara's? About eight."

"Good. Don't eat. I'll whip something up. Abientôt mon petite soeur."

I watched as every head turned in Natalie's direction as she made her way through the diner and out the door.

I took two bites of Nat's salad and decided she was right. It did taste like old underwear. Judy came over and presented me with the check. It was only when I pulled out my wallet to pay that I realized that Natalie must have taken the $400 back when she had scooped up the keys from the table.

I went back to work and labeled more boxes. At six o'clock I left for Barbara's.

The house was dark when I pulled into the driveway. I let myself in through the kitchen door and yelled, "Yoo-hoo! It's me." But the house was quiet and no one answered. There was a faint light flickering from somewhere down the hall. I followed the light and ended up in Barbara's family room. A big man in army fatigues was seated on the sofa. A Bible was open and rested in his lap. The television had been tuned to professional wrestling, but the sound had been muted. I watched as two wrestlers bounced off each other's chests in silence.

Mother was asleep and snoring in Randall's recliner. I stepped into the room and smiled at the man in fatigues. When he saw me, he leaped to his feet and stood at attention. I resisted the urge to say, "At ease," and introduced myself. When he introduced himself, I realized my mistake.

"Nice to meet you, Miss Gorman," he said. "My name's Edwina Snapford. But everybody just calls me Snappy."

He was a she. This was Malqueen's ex-army church lady friend. I asked Snappy where Barbara was.

"Upstairs in the bed. Never saw anybody get a headache like that before. But then there was a whole lotta screaming going on."

I looked over at Mother and said, "How's she been? Any escape attempts?"

"Only one," Snappy said as she stood with her feet twelve inches apart and her hands behind her back. "Tried to sneak past me in the kitchen. But I got twenty-twenty vision. I was a shooting expert in the army. I can still hit a dime at twenty yards. I had my back to her and she thought I couldn't see her... but I was watching her in the glass in the window. I had her before her hand touched the knob on the door." Snappy smiled proudly.

"Keep up the good work," I said. "I think I'll go upstairs and see how Barbara's doing."

I backtracked to the kitchen and pulled out a package of frozen peas. Then I headed upstairs. I knocked once and opened the door. The room was in complete darkness, and it took several seconds for my eyes to adjust. I finally made out a lump in the bed.

"Barbara?" I whispered.

"What?

"I brought another bag of peas."

"Oh...good."

I sat down on the bed, removed the old soggy bag of peas, and put the new bag on her head. "Do you want me to call the doctor?"

"For what? So he can tell me it's stress?"

Barbara had gotten migraines all her life. She had been to all the head docs at Hopkins and tried all the new drugs. Several of the doctors had suggested that perhaps the headaches weren't as bad as Barbara made them out to be. But I could just look at her and see she was in agony. During an attack, her face ballooned to twice its normal size. She couldn't tolerate any light at all, and from time to time she experienced aphasia. Our family doctor had told her to relax and had given her a prescription for Valium. He also promised her the migraines would go away after menopause. Malqueen had said, "Just like a man...gives her pills to knock her out...then tells her in forty years it will go away...got to be something else we can do for her." But there wasn't. And unfortunately, menopause hadn't helped her either.

"Is she gone?"

"Who?"

"Natalie."

"Yes."

"Back to New York?"

"Uh...not exactly."

Barbara sat up and the bag of peas slid off her head. "Where is she?"

"With me."

"How could you?" Barbara sank back down.

I rearranged the bag. "The same reason you let her stay here. Because she's my sister."

"Are you sure?"

"That she's our sister? No. But even if she isn't, we're stuck with her now." I pulled the comforter up over her. "Just sleep. Snappy seems pretty competent. Don't worry about Mother, or Natalie, or me...OK?"

"Did he leave?"

"Randall?"

"Yes, the rat fink."

"Barbara, he only wanted her to see how hard you work. He wanted her to help out...and he has a point. She's done nothing to help us."

"I don't want to talk about it."

I sat there for several minutes saying nothing. Then I told her about Snookie's invitation.

"I did find out some information on Snookie you might be interested in."

"Who?" Barbara mumbled.

"Snookie. My landlord."

"Oh?"

"Guess who she really is?"

There was no answer.

"Agnes McKenzie."

Barbara sat up again. "Agnes McKenzie! That odd little kid? Nobody in class would even talk to her. Agnes McKenzie..." Barbara fell back down in bed.

"Well, she's still odd. But now she's all grown up and the toast of the breeder's circle...by the way, she invited you to her annual Christmas Eve party."

Barbara said, "Me?"

"Yep. It's in two days."

"Is she joking?"

"No. Apparently her parties are so hot that people cancel other engagements just to go to her party."

"How rude."

"Maybe, but I hear they're fun."

"Are you going?"

"I'm not sure. I wanted to see if you'd go."

"Absolutely not! Agnes McKenzie was not my cup of tea. So weird in those thick glasses she wore...looked like she had swimming goggles on...and she always smelled like a horse."

"Well, the glasses are gone, but horses are still her first priority."

Barbara drifted off to sleep. I tiptoed out of her room and went back downstairs.

Mother was snoring loudly, and Snappy was staring at the television set.

"I'm taking off, Snappy."

Snappy still had the open Bible in front of her, but her eyes were glued to the TV. A seven-foot-tall woman with suspicious-looking biceps dressed in a red minidress was pummeling a midget dressed in a Tarzan costume. Snappy sneezed.

"Bless you. I hope you're not coming down with that terrible flu that's going around."

"Not me," Snappy said, pulling out a Kleenex from inside her combat boot. "I get a free flu shot every year from the army. I never even get a cold."

"Well, that's good to know. I'll be home all evening if you need anything. My number's on the refrigerator."

"Don't worry. Everything's fine here." Snappy waved good-bye with the Kleenex just as the midget climbed on the giant's back and pulled back his ears.

"Well, I'll see you later."

But there was no answer. Snappy was bouncing up and down on the sofa as the giant fell facedown on the floor and the midget was officially declared the winner.

I opened the door to my cottage and smelled shallots simmering in wine sauce. One of Natalie's many boyfriends had been the sous chef at the Ritz in Paris, and he had taught Natalie how to cook. Natalie stopped sautéing and poured me a glass of wine. Ludwig had positioned himself against her leg. He wiggled his rear end at me in greeting then looked up at Natalie and started to drool.

"Natalie, have you been feeding Ludwig?"

"Who me?" Natalie looked down at the dog. "I didn't give that damn ugly dog anything." She reached down and wiped his drool away with one of my good linen napkins.

"If you're going to stay here," I said, "stop calling him the 'damn ugly dog.' His name is Ludwig."

"That's the most ridiculous name I've ever heard of for a dog. He looks more like a Spike...or a Fang...especially with those Halloween teeth." Ludie's ears twitched in her direction. "See, he likes Fang."

"No, I just think he likes whatever it is you've been feeding him."

Natalie turned back to her shallots. I went to change.

"By the way," Nat yelled from the kitchen, "you got a call from a guy named Zack."

I turned around and came back out into the kitchen.

"Who?"

"Zack. As in ex-quarterback? He wants to take us to Snookie's party."

"US?"

Well, he wants to take you, but since I'm going as well, I figured he could take both of us."

"Do I have any say in this at all?"

"Of course you do. He's calling back at nine." Natalie added more wine to the shallots, took a swig from the bottle, and stirred furiously. "But if I were you, I'd go."

"I don't need your advice."

"No, what you need is a good—" I stopped her with a look. She put the whisk down. "Sara...Aubrey's ancient history. It wasn't your fault. He's in Mexico for God's sake...Get on with your life."

I didn't say anything. I turned around and went back into my bedroom and changed.

I stalled as long as I could. But I was forced out because the food smelled so good. It was rather ironic that between the three of us, the one who could cook the best was the one who had avoided the kitchen the most. I walked out and caught Natalie feeding Ludwig chicken.

"Natalie...I told you not to feed him."

"But he's hungry, aren't you boy?" Ludie barked.

"He's a big pig. I fed him this morning, and Ian fed him this evening."

"Who's Ian?"

"Snookie's second cousin...He's in charge of the horses."

"Think he'd let me ride one tomorrow?"

"I'm sure he would. He's a great guy."

"How great?"

"Forget it, Natalie. He's an ex-jockey. He's only five feet tall."

"So?"

I shook my head and took a sip of wine. It was very good. Obviously Natalie had spared no expense with my money. Natalie filled two plates with pasta and then poured the sauce on top. I refilled my wineglass and sat down. Ludwig sat next to Natalie.

"Did you see Barbara?"

"Migraine again," I said with a full mouth. "Probably brought on by all the screaming."

"Glad I left. Do you think she's ever made the connection between those migraines and her fights with Randall?"

"Nat, the headaches don't have to be caused by anything...although," I said, looking up at her, "I'm sure your arrival didn't help any either."

We were almost finished when the phone rang. Nat got up to clear the dishes. I answered the phone.

"Sara? This is Zack. We met a few days ago when your mother was on the roof...?"

"I remember. How are you?"

"I got your number from Lightning. I hope you don't mind."

"You know Lightning?"

"We go way back. I'm from Fells Point too. He knows my family."

There was an awkward silence, and then Zack continued. "I guess your sister told you I called earlier? I know it's a last-minute invitation, but Snookie never does send out invitations with any notice. Anyway, would you like to go to her party with me on Christmas Eve...I realize some families celebrate Christmas on Christmas Eve, and I'll understand if you—"

"We don't celebrate then."

"Oh, you don't? That's great."

"However, I have my own invitation to Snookie's party."

"Oh." He sounded disappointed.

Natalie began washing dishes and singing, "Love is a many splendored thing..." in the background.

"Shut up, Natalie."

"Excuse me?"

"Not you. I'm talking to my sister."

Natalie held up a piece of chicken over Ludwig's head. He threw back his head and howled along as she sang.

"Would you two be quiet?"

"Yes, I think the party will be a riot too."

"No, I'm talking to my sister and the dog."

"Ahoooo...Love is a...ahooo...many splendored thing...ahoooo..."

I could barely hear what Zack was saying as Nat and Ludie continued their duet. I motioned for Natalie to cut it out.

"Are we too noisy?" Nat asked innocently.

"YES!" I yelled.

"Great! I'll pick you up at eight," Zack said.

"Wait, I didn't say I'd...Hello?" He had hung up.

I stared at the phone as Ludwig continued to howl. Natalie stopped singing, leaned down, and held Ludwig's snout shut.

"So? Are we going with him or not?"

"I guess so, Natalie. I could barely hear what the man was saying with all that racket you were making." I put the phone down and looked up.

"And just how does he know where I live?"

"I gave him directions the first time he called."

I stomped off to the bedroom as Nat threw Ludie another piece of chicken and said, "Good boy!"

Around midnight, Ludwig, the traitor, crept back into my bed and claimed his pillow. I don't know what time Natalie showed up.

"Get out of my bed."

"Wha?"

"Natalie, you're supposed to sleep on the sofa, not in bed with me. Get out!"

"Oh, all right. That sofa is a medieval torture device," she said, carrying her pillow out to the living room. "What's it made out of anyway...cement?"

I turned over and looked at my alarm clock—only fifteen more minutes before I had to get up and get ready for work. I gave up, got ready, and left for work.

For the first time in months, I actually arrived there when I was supposed to.

I got so busy I didn't have time to think about anything except selling shoes. Christmas was only three days away, and the number of shoppers cruising through the Men's Shoe Department had tripled. When I wasn't on the floor selling shoes, I was supposed to be back in the stockroom sticking labels on boxes, which is exactly what I was doing when Lettie called.

"Call for you," Sid said, pointing to the phone.

"Hello?"

"How about exchanging gifts tonight?" Lettie said.

"Sure. How come so early?" Lettie and I usually exchanged gifts on Christmas Day.

"The 'Beast' is coming in from Philadelphia tomorrow."

"Oh, poor you. How's Oscar holding up?"

"He's immersed in his shrink books trying to find a cure."

"For a meddlesome mother?"

"It's his way of coping. He keeps trying to find a syndrome he can plug her into."

"Will the Wittridge estate pass inspection this time?"

"With four kids, a disappearing father, three dogs, and an obese cat? Are you kidding? So how about joining us for dinner? Beef Wellington with duchess potatoes…baby carrots in brown sugar…pecan pie…?"

"Stop! I'll be there. What time?"

"Is six too early?"

"Make it six thirty."

"See you then."

I got lost in visions of beef Wellington as I continued to stick red, blue, and yellow circles on shoe boxes. Leo, our stock boy, interrupted my food fantasy.

"Get all your shopping done?" Leo asked as he wheeled in a huge rack of new Doc Martins. I groaned when I saw them.

"Haven't even started. Where did they come from?"

"Special Christmas order. When you plan on doing it? Christmas Eve?"

That was exactly when I had planned to do my Christmas shopping. But then I remembered I was having dinner with the Wittridges tonight, and I had Snookie's party on Christmas Eve. I started unloading Doc Martins off the trolley. The boxes dropped out of my hands and onto the floor.

"What the heck is in here? They must weigh fifty pounds."

"Some kinda new boot," Leo said, picking up the boxes. "Looks pretty good too. Be a good seller."

"No wonder teenagers move so slow," I said. "They can't lift their feet."

"So when are you planning to do your Christmas shopping?"

I looked at my watch. I got off work in thirty minutes.

"I might just try to do a little tonight," I said to Leo.

"Good luck. It's mobbed out there."

I called Natalie before I left the store. She answered on the first ring.

"Natalie?"

"Yeah?"

"I won't be home until later this evening. I'm going to Lettie's for dinner. Would you make sure Ludie gets fed?"

"Already done. Tell Red and Baldy hello for me."

I heard a man's voice in the background.

"Is there someone with you?"

"Ian. I've been riding all day, and he dropped off Fang a few minutes ago."

"The dog's name is Lud—"

"Whatever...listen...gotta go. I don't want the sauce to burn."

I heard laughter in the background and then the click of the receiver as she hung up on me. Ian? I thought as I left the department.

I punched out at five and headed upstairs to Young Professionals. The pianist was playing "Jingle Bells," and as I rode up to the third floor, I sang along. Leo was right. It was wall-to-wall shoppers on the third floor. But I hit the floor running, and I had Mother, Barbara, Natalie, and Malqueen done in fifteen minutes. I headed back downstairs to the Children's Department, where I found outfits for Lettie's brood. Then I had everything gift wrapped in Landstrom's trademark red and gold wrapping. I left the store and dashed down the mall to Williams-Sonoma, where I bought Lettie and Oscar an espresso machine. My final stop was the Webbs Chocolate store. Every year I bought four one-pound boxes: one for John Wittridge, one for Malqueen, one for Father, and one for myself.

I took a number and prepared to wait. The displayed number said, "10." I had number "39."

"What number you got?" Jonathon said behind me.

"Thirty-nine...you?"

"Forty-four. If these candies weren't so good, I'd never stand in a line this long. How long you think we'll be here?"

"I've got to get out of here by six..."

"Don't hold your breath," the customer next to me said. "Looks like they're holding another one of those contests." We all sighed.

To make the wait go faster, the ladies behind the counter would ask customers Trivial Pursuit questions. Whoever guessed correctly got a free candy.

"What kind of dance did Captain Hook like to do?" one of the elderly ladies yelled from behind the counter.

I looked around and noted blank stares.

"A tarantella," I yelled.

"Correct," said the lady in pink. "Give that young woman a chocolate butter cream. "Next question..."

"So, looks like somebody finally decided to go Christmas shopping," Jonathon said, eyeing my bags.

"I'm done," I said, chewing on the chocolate. "As soon as I get my candy."

"You got all your gifts in those three piddling bags?" Jonathon said. "Boy, are you ever lucky! My wife buys every toy advertised on television for the boys. Last year she paid a toy scalper a hundred bucks for a Tickle Me Elmo doll. I didn't even know they had toy scalpers!"

"Number fifteen! Who starred in *Duel in the Sun?*"

"And do you know where that doll is now? In the trash. Scared the hell outta the kid, and he tried to flush it down the toilet. Had to pay a plumber three hundred dollars to get the damn thing outta the hopper."

"Jennifer Jones and Gregory Peck!" the man next to me yelled.

"Correct! Number twenty! Name one actor who played The Hunchback!"

"Damn doll ended up costing me four hundred dollars! Every year I go into hock buying presents," Jonathon said. "...not only for my own kids, but also for relatives I either don't know or I don't care to know. And then my wife insists on blowing hundreds of dollars on food to entertain all the misfits and losers in the family."

"Lon Chaney!" shouted a woman in the back.

"That's correct!" the counter lady yelled. "Give her a chocolate. Number twenty-six?"

"Jonathon," I said, "I've met your wife and your boys. She's lovely, and they're adorable."

"That doesn't mean I got to feed her jailbird uncle who shows up wearin' his house arrest bracelet, does it?"

"Number twenty-nine! Who played Captain Queeg in *The Caine Mutiny?*"

"There we were...in the middle of carving the turkey when the cops bang on the door and threaten to drag his ass off to jail 'cause he broke house arrest. My wife ends up inviting them in..."

"Spencer Tracey?" a teenager in the back asked.

"Sorry hon, wrong. Number thirty-one! Anybody else want to guess?"

"Well, I don't think she had much choice, Jonathon."

"But they ate all my pumpkin pie!"

"Bogart?" a woman standing by the counter asked.

"That's right, hon. Have a candy. Number thirty-three?"

"Well," I said, "at least he got to enjoy his dinner and he didn't have to—"

"And then there's her Aunt Betty, who's three hundred pounds, bathes in Eau De Stinko Perfume, and eats a whole ham all by herself."

"Number thirty-five? Who played Spartacus?"

"Boy, now the questions are getting too easy," the man beside me said.

"Well," I said to Jonathon, "why don't you—"

"Or her brother...who shows up just so he can borrow money. But not this year...I already told her I'm not lending that weasel another dime—"

"Jonathon?"

"What?"

"Bah, humbug," I said as the counter lady yelled, "Number thirty-nine?"

I held up my hand and pushed to the front of the counter as the man beside me yelled, "Kirk Douglas." I ordered three one-pound boxes of assorted chocolates, waved good-bye to Jonathon, and headed for the parking garage.

When I got to the VW, I made sure Security wasn't patrolling nearby. The locks on the doors to my fifteen-year-old VW were broken, and the only way I could open them was with a screwdriver. Security tended to question people who resorted to using mechanical devices to open car doors.

I threw my bags on the front seat, got in, and started the car. I pulled out and almost hit a young couple as they ran in front of my Volkswagen. But they didn't even see me because they were laden with so many packages. When they got to a Grand Jeep Cherokee, he dropped all his packages, pushed her against the side of the car, and kissed her. She protested at first, then laughed, dropped her bags too, and kissed him back. I realized I was staring and quickly looked away. But as I drove down the ramp and out of the garage, I looked over on the passenger seat at my three "piddling" shopping bags, and of course, thought of Aubrey.

Mother and Father were very frugal when we were growing up. As Mother liked to remind us, "Those who choose to serve God don't do it for the money." At Christmas, we each got one gift, and it was always something we needed. Our tree was donated by the parish. But the tree was always too big for our house, and every year Father had to saw at least a foot off of the bottom for it to fit in the sitting room. Mother and Father did try to make the tree decorating as festive as possible. Barbara played Christmas carols on our out-of-tune piano. We ate Malqueen's sugar-frosted Santa cookies and drank her extra thick and creamy eggnog as we argued over which angel we wanted to put atop the tree. But we never seemed to have enough ornaments or tinsel to cover the tree properly. Even when I was older and could make my own ornaments, I could never make enough to cover those branches. There was always too much green showing, and the tree always looked like there was something missing.

The first year after Aubrey and I were married, I had come home and discovered a twelve-foot Douglas-fir standing in the middle of our loft.

"What do you think?" Aubrey said, coming up behind me and putting his arms around me.

"I think it's the biggest tree I've ever seen in my life. How'd you get it up here?"

"I kept the doors open on the elevator and prayed."

"You prayed?"

"To the Christmas Tree God." Aubrey winked. "So...do we string white lights or colored lights? Hang tinsel or garland? Put on balls or hand-crafted ornaments?"

I looked into his eyes and saw the excitement of a ten-year-old.

"Yes!"

"Yes, what?"

"All of them," I said, laughing.

"I love you, Sara Gorman," Aubrey said as he lifted me in the air and twirled me around.

"I loved you too," I thought as I pointed the VW in the direction of Lettie's house.

Chapter Twenty-Nine

"Friendship is certainly the finest
balm for the pangs of a disappointed
love."

Jane Austen

While many of the old mansions in Roland Park had fallen into disrepair over the last thirty years, Lettie and Oscar hadn't let that happen to the Wittridge estate. I drove through freshly painted black wrought iron gates and sped up the mile-long drive under Bradford Pear trees that had been pruned to arch gracefully over the driveway. There were some minor changes, but they had more to do with the present occupants and less to do with the upkeep of the estate. Two purple bicycles had been abandoned alongside the stone walkway. A baseball bat and a lacrosse stick had been left on the front porch. And a pale pink tutu was swinging in the breeze from the top limb of a gnarled old oak tree that Lettie and I had often climbed as children. I rang the bell.

Lettie flung open the door and yelled, "Merry Christmas!"

"Merry Christmas to you too," I said, hugging her.

"Come on in. Let me take your bags. Look at all these presents!"

"Well, don't get too excited…There aren't that many," I said, still thinking about Christmas with Aubrey.

Lettie gave me an odd look and then took my coat. Oscar came out of his study.

"Merry Christmas, Sara," he said, kissing me on the cheek.

"Happy Chanukah, Oscar," I said, kissing him back. "Where's the rest of the clan?"

"Upstairs. I believe they're trying to wrap your present. Let's leave them there for the time being…How about a drink?"

"Sounds good to me. I've been putting red, yellow, and green stickers on boxes all day…I'm beginning to see spots before my eyes."

"Still enjoying the shoe-selling business?" Oscar said as he went to mix drinks.

I didn't answer. Oscar had tried to get me into therapy after Aubrey and I had split. I had resisted. To his credit, he didn't push. But every now and then he'd bring up the subject of my employment.

"You better hope she's still selling shoes," Lettie interrupted. "How many did she set aside for you last year? Three? Four?"

Oscar coughed and handed me my drink. I changed the subject.

"The place looks great, Lettie—the tree and all the decorations. The kids must be so excited."

"Oh, they're excited all right. I caught Lindsey trying to break into the guest room where we hide the Christmas presents. And she was using Little Gracie and Darla as the lookouts. The only innocent one in the bunch is the baby, and that's only because he can't walk yet. He'll get recruited as soon as he's mobile. I'm raising a bunch of sneaks!"

At that moment a shriek echoed from upstairs followed by howls and cries.

"Oscar, would you see what they're up to?" Lettie asked.

Oscar didn't hesitate. "Sure," he said. "But if I don't return in ten minutes, send out a posse for me."

We laughed as he picked up a silver tray from the table and used it as a shield as he charged out of the room.

"That's pretty good," I said, waiting until he was out of hearing range. "Is he developing a sense of humor in his old age?"

"I think so. Sorry about the work comment. Sometimes Oscar goes into shrink overload."

"It's OK. He's not the only one who can't understand why I'd rather sell shoes than paint...Although Natalie came up with a different slant on selling shoes the other day. She seems to think it's a good place to meet men."

"Well, actually, she's probably right. When did Natalie get in town?"

I told Lettie the whole story.

"So, you're stuck with her for how long? A week?"

"With Natalie? Who knows."

"How's your mother?"

"When she's not up on the roof, she's fine."

"I'm sorry. I did see that on the news."

"You and the rest of the state."

"What kind of meds do they have her on?" Lettie asked.

I got halfway through Mother's cornucopia of medicine when Lettie's beeper went off.

"Oh, drat. Not now." Lettie pulled the beeper off and looked at the number.

"Sara, I hate to abandon you, but I need to make a call."

"I'm fine. I can entertain myself for a while."

"Actually, you don't have to do that." Lettie got up and pushed a button on the telephone on the side table. A man's voice said, "Hello?"

"Dad? Listen, I've got to abandon Sara for a few minutes. Can you play host for me?"

"Sara? Saralee is here? Great! Send her over. But tell her to be on the lookout when she opens the connecting door."

"Will do." Lettie turned to me.

"Is that all right with you?"

"All right? It'll be my pleasure."

I took my drink and wound my way over to the new wing: an addition John Wittridge had built for himself after Lettie and Oscar had gotten married. Lettie had never wanted to leave her father or her home. From time to time, her father would threaten to move out and into one of those "trendy" retirement communities. But he never did. He enjoyed being close to Lettie and his grandchildren. He actually liked his son-in-law. And he had all the privacy he needed in the new wing. He was eighty-two years old and he teed off at the FairField Country Club at nine o'clock sharp every day except Tuesday and Thursday. On those days he beat everyone else in his age group at tennis. When he wasn't playing golf or tennis, he was squiring rich society matrons to various charity functions. He never remarried after his wife's death, choosing instead to have a series of discreet long-term affairs. Every now and then a gossip tidbit would show up in the society column about a mysterious woman John Wittridge was supposed to be dating ("mysterious" being a euphemism for "married"). Lettie and I didn't talk about that. I didn't really care either. I was impressed that at eight-two he was still cher-chezing la femmes.

When I got to the connecting door, I remembered John Wittridge's warning and slowly cracked the door and peered down the hall. I eased myself in, shut the door again, and began tiptoeing down the corridor. But when I got to the end of the corridor, I was blindsided by three boxers and Puffy.

The noise had alerted Mr. Wittridge. He came out of library and yelled, "Down dogs! And you too, Puffy!" Of course, the only one who obeyed was the cat. Puffy trotted off to the library as the dogs made fools of themselves by leaping up in the air licking my hands and finally falling at my feet. Mr. Wittridge shook his head and yelled, "Dogs! Look! Squirrels! Go get 'em!" The dogs immediately jumped up and ran down the hall to the patio doors.

"Quick, get in here before they get back." I slipped into the library and John Wittridge slid the pocket doors shut.

"Sorry about that. Dumb dogs. The money we've spent trying to train them to behave…Well, I don't have to tell you what boxers are like."

"No, you don't."

"Sit here by the fire."

I looked at the chair by the fire and saw that Puffy had gotten there first.

"I'll sit over here," I said, pointing to a leather chair.

"Well, if you aren't going to sit in that chair then I will," John Wittridge said as he lifted Puffy up and dumped him on the floor. Puffy began washing his face and waited until John Wittridge was comfortable. Then he jumped up on his lap. Mr. Wittridge groaned as the cat rearranged himself several times, finally positioning his huge furry head on Mr. Wittridge's chest and dangling his back feet over one chair arm and his front paws over the other chair arm.

"I hear the Beast is due tomorrow."

"Please," Mr. Wittridge took a sip of bourbon. "I don't want to think about it."

"Can't you just go away and play golf for a few days?"

"Not around Christmas. I'd miss the kids. And it would be awkward for Oscar."

"Too bad."

"Yeah." John Wittridge sighed. "Anyway, I think it's worse for Oscar."

We were silent and I stared up over the fireplace at the picture I had painted of Grace Wittridge when I was fourteen. John followed my gaze.

"Still the best investment I ever made."

"A lot of people would argue with you these days."

"No. I don't think they would. Look at all the wonderful portraits you've painted."

"That certainly was one of my better ones," I said, looking up again. "But then she was a flawless subject."

"No one is without flaws...and Grace would be the first to argue that point with you."

We sat in silence and then I said, "I'm beginning to forget what he looked like."

"Who?" John asked, looking at me. "Aubrey? Or your father?"

"Father."

John Wittridge got up, and Puffy fell on the floor. He landed on all fours and then waddled over to the fire and fell down in front of the flickering flames. John went over and leaned against the fireplace.

"I remember when Lettie and I first came back from Europe. We walked into this house, and I didn't think I could bear it. But then I went back to work and Lettie went back to school. We kept busy and we settled into a comfortable routine." John took another sip of whiskey. "Months passed... and one day I came home and I couldn't remember what she looked like. It sent me into a panic. I dug out all the old albums and looked at the photos, and even though she was right there in front of me, page after page of her in those albums, it wasn't the image I was trying to remember."

I shifted in the chair, and John reached down and scratched Puffy with his foot.

"Then one day a very talented young artist came to dinner," he said, looking over at me, "and presented me with a painting of the very image I was trying to remember."

I smiled at John and said, "You know, I tried to give the portrait to Lettie, but she said she thought you should have it. I remember that day like it was yesterday. I was so nervous. I was afraid you wouldn't like it...or worse, that it would upset you."

"And neither happened, did it?"

"No...Although Lettie and I were a little startled by your reaction."

John Wittridge had held the painting in front of him and laughed. When he saw our shocked reactions, he had reassured us that he was delighted with the picture. He hung the painting over the fireplace in his study that evening. And that's where it had stayed for over twenty years. But he had never explained to me why he had laughed at the painting that day.

John was looking up at his wife now. I remained silent and eventually he began to speak again.

"It was her expression..." He stopped again and looked up. "All the photos showed her society façade. She had a beautiful smile, and it served her well in the circles we traveled. But the Grace I was searching for, the one I could no longer conjure up in my memory, smiled with her eyes. I could look into those eyes and know exactly what she was thinking." John paused again and took a sip of bourbon. "And when I looked at the portrait you painted of her, there were those incredible eyes smiling down on me. It was the Grace I had fallen in love with, and it was the Grace I never wanted for forget."

I looked down and John came over and took my hand. "You must think me a tad touched about all this—"

"No, no, no," I said, looking up. "I think it's terribly romantic."

I watched him stoke the fire, and I thought Grace Wittridge was very lucky to have found a man who loved her so.

"Didn't you paint the bishop a few years ago?" John asked.

"What? Oh, yes, I did. Mother hung it in the formal sitting room... Why?"

"Maybe you should get it out and take a good look at it. It might help."

I looked down into my drink and tried to remember what had become of the painting. I thought I had put it in storage at Malqueen's, along with all my other paintings.

The door slid open, and three children and three dogs burst into the room yelling their hellos.

"As they say in the movies," Lettie said, coming in behind them, "dinner is served."

We ate our beef Wellington, opened our presents, and had a wonderful time. And just like every other year, Lettie and I managed to give each other the same Christmas gift again.

Chapter Thirty

_____ • _____

"To understand yourself is the key
to wisdom."

Confucius

I went through Malqueen's attic and found the portrait of Father.

"What are you going to do with that?" Malqueen asked as I carried it through Mrs. M's and out the front door.

"I think I'll hang it at the cottage."

"Good idea," Malqueen nodded. "That place was looking kinda sparse."

In my effort to create a new life, I hadn't wanted any reminders of my portrait career, and so I hadn't hung any pictures at all. But I told myself that Father's picture was different. John Wittridge's idea had inspired me. After all, Father had nothing to do with Aubrey.

I hung the picture over the fireplace in the living room. I sat down and stared up at the painting. Now all I had to do was look up and I could see his thick white hair, the aristocratic nose, the—I stood up and walked to the other side of the room and looked back at the portrait. It was still there. "How could I have missed that all these years?" I asked myself. Father had Natalie's smile. Or rather, Natalie had inherited Father's smile. Why hadn't I seen that before? It was uncanny. If I covered up the top part of Father's face, I could have been looking at Nat. I was engrossed in the portrait when a voice from behind me said, "What the hell is that?"

I turned to find Natalie staring up at the portrait.

"Father."

"I know that. But what made you dig that up? And why did you have it hang it up there?"

"John Wittridge suggested it. I was starting to forget what he looked like."

"Couldn't you just look at a snapshot?"

"What's with you?"

Natalie looked up at Father and shook her head. "Nothing...It's just larger than life...that's all."

"And that bothers you?"

"I didn't say that. It just startled me."

Natalie held several dresses in her hand. She came over and dumped them on the coffee table in front of me.

"What's this?" I asked.

"Costumes. Ian took me to that consignment shop on York Road, Clothes Rich People Don't Want Anymore, and I found three possibilities for us. This one," she held up a black low-cut slinky number, "is mine. I'm going as Lana Turner and Ian is going as Johnny Stompanato—you know, the gangster she shot..."

"I thought we had to go as movie stars from the thirties and forties. Johnny Stompanato wasn't a movie star. And does this mean you're not going with me?"

"I thought we could all go together...you and Zack and me and Ian. And since Ian is Snookie's cousin, he can go as whomever he likes."

"Since when did you and Ian become an item?"

"We're not an item. We're just friends. I like him. He's a good horseman."

Natalie held up a violet silk dress.

"What is it?" I asked, reaching over and holding the dress out. "It only has one shoulder."

"I think you should go as Susan Hayward. Remember her in that old movie *Bathsheba*? You can be exotic and dramatic and say things like, 'But I don't want to be a night of pleasure...I want to be a queen—'"

"You see me as Susan Hayward in a harem costume?"

"You'll look great. If we curl your hair and—"

"What's the third dress for?"

"Well," Natalie said, holding it up, "I just couldn't make up my mind. Not with me, but with you. At first I saw you in this silky hunter green pantsuit thing as maybe Myrna Loy, but then I saw the violet number and that seemed more like you. So I bought them all and I thought I'd let you decide. Actually, the green number would do for Barbara; she looks more like Myrna Loy than you do. By the way, is she going or is she planning on staying in her room for the next week?"

"She said she didn't want to go. She said Snookie was a weird little kid who wore goggles for glasses and smelled like a horse."

"Times have changed. Snookie is now the hostess with the mostest. Well, what do you think?"

"I think…if I have to go," I said, snatching up the violet dress, "that this is a better color for me."

"OK, Miss Hayward…then I'd better get moving on makeup and accessories. You'll need arm bracelets and a big wide silver belt—"

There was a knock at the door. Natalie and I looked at each other. Ludwig barked at the door and then came over and hid behind me.

"Such a brave dog," I said as I leaned down and patted him. He wagged his rear end and licked my hand.

"Are you expecting someone?" I said as I held Ludie's collar.

"Who me? No."

"Well, here…hold the dog while I answer the door. I handed Ludie off to Nat and opened the door.

"Why am I holding Fang? So he doesn't run off and hide under the bed?"

There was a very tall Episcopal priest standing on my front porch. I didn't recognize him, although he did look familiar. He looked up when I answered the door and then down at a piece of paper in his hand.

"Are you Sara Gorman?"

"Yes, may I help you?"

He looked at me for several seconds as if searching for something in my face and then said, "I'm looking for Natalie Gorman. Do you know her?"

I looked behind me and saw Nat staring at the man on the porch. She still held Ludie with one hand and the green dress in the other, but her face was ashen. I turned to her and said, "Are you—"

"I'm Natalie Gorman," she said, stepping forward.

The two of them stared at each other for several seconds. Finally, the stranger said, "My name is Nicholas Weber. I was born September 30, 1959, in Lancaster, Pennsylvania."

I watched Natalie's face turn even whiter and I said, "Natalie, are you all right?" But she was calm when she said, "Come in. I tried to find you. How did you find me?"

"A computer search," he said, coming into the room. "I almost didn't you know after what happened when I called."

"It was a mistake. I—" Natalie released Ludwig, who began sniffing the stranger's shoes."

"Miss Gorman," he said as he leaned down and patted Ludie on the head. "I don't want to intrude in your life I—"

"You're not intruding. I told you. It was a mistake," Natalie repeated.

"Nat, are you OK?" I asked, looking from the man to Natalie.

"Yes."

Natalie motioned for the tall blond stranger to follow her into the living room. I trailed behind them.

When he walked into the room, he took one look at Father's picture and smiled. And that was when I knew he was Natalie's son.

Chapter Thirty One

—————————— • ——————————

"A picture is a poem without words."
Confucius

I looked at the two of them and saw the resemblance I hadn't seen when I first opened the door. Both had white blond hair, turquoise eyes, and, of course, Father's smile. I watched in silence as Natalie stared at Nicholas and Nicholas stared at Father's portrait. Natalie sat down on the sofa still clutching the green pantsuit. Nicholas continued to stare at the portrait of Father.

I slipped on my coat, hat, and gloves and called Ludwig.

"We're going for a walk," I said to the two of them. "I'll be gone for a couple of hours."

Nicholas turned and looked at me with Natalie's eyes. Natalie still stared at Nicholas but said, "Go...I'll be fine."

I opened the door, and Ludwig bounded outside and into the snow.

We followed our usual path through the woods and past the outbuildings and stables that made up Snookie's four-hundred-acre farm. Ludie ploughed furrows in the snow with his nose and came up snorting in delight. He ran several yards ahead of me, disappeared, and then returned a few minutes later with a look that said, "Why are you so slow? Come on!" I tried not to think for the first mile or so. I just concentrated on the hills, the snow, and the woods. I threw sticks for Ludie to retrieve. He would leap in the air, catch the stick, and then run in the opposite direction.

I reached the highest point of Snookie's farm and sat down on a log. Ludie tore off down the hill in search of a rabbit that had given him a "bet-you-can't-catch-me" look. From here I could look down on Snookie's castle. I watched as four catering trucks slowly drove down the winding road, over the moat, and around to the back of the house. Snookie's party was tomorrow night, and I watched as workers ran back and forth between the trucks and the castle.

I leaned back and looked up at the sky. The local TV stations had been interrupting regular programming all day to warn that snow might be on the way. One weatherman said, "Definitely! Snow!" Another forecaster said, "Put those shovels away." And a third newsman covered all bets and said, "It's too close to call...It all depends on how far south the jet stream dips...Maybe we'll get a blizzard...Maybe we won't."

The clouds overhead were steely gray and heavily layered. Father had taught me about the different types of clouds when I was in third grade. I had listened dutifully and had promptly forgotten all but one. For an eight-year-old in school, the only cloud worth knowing was stratus-nimbus, the snow cloud.

Malqueen never put too much stock in clouds or weathermen. She said, "The only way to tell if it's really going to snow is to sniff the air...Always smells like old frozen ice cream to me."

I watched as the rabbit led Ludwig on a merry chase across the field, up the hill, and back into the woods. I could smell the smoke that was now pouring out of Snookie's many chimneys. It reminded me of the warmth of my fire at home, and I shivered because the air was so frigid it hurt my lungs when I took a deep breath. I didn't have Malqueen's discerning nose, but it was certainly cold enough to snow. And as more trucks snaked down the road to Snookie's castle, I wondered how snow would affect the party.

Ludie and I stayed away as long as we could. I wanted to give Natalie as much time with Nicholas as possible. But I had gotten into a stick-wrestling contest with Ludie and had lost. I now squished when I walked, and Ludwig's entire face was white and frozen. The trip back was much faster than the trip out because we ran all the way home. Ludie beat me to the front door and was waiting on the porch when I got there. I looked around and noted there was no car in the drive. Natalie opened the door, and we both rushed into the warmth of the cottage.

"Take off those wet clothes," Natalie said. "I've made some hot chocolate."

I went and changed. When I came back into the living room, I saw that Natalie had toweled off Ludie, and he was munching on a dog biscuit by the fire. Natalie was seated on the sofa, and she motioned for me to join her. I sat down, and Nat handed me a mug of hot chocolate. There was a plate of chocolate chip cookies on the coffee table in front of me.

"Where did these come from?"

"Ian and I went to Mrs. M's and picked them up."

"You and Ian sure did make the rounds today."

"They're your favorite."

"Yes, they are." I dipped my cookie into my mug.

"Still dunking your cookies?" Natalie said, shaking her head. "Didn't Mother forbid you to do that?"

"She told me I couldn't do a lot of things," I said. "Thank God I ignored most of them."

Natalie looked up at the portrait of Father. Then she looked over *at* me. When I had finished my cookie, I said, "Tell me." And she did.

Chapter Thirty-Two

"We spend our years as a tale that
is told."

Psalms

"I was almost fifteen," Natalie said. "But I looked nineteen and I tried to act twenty-five." Natalie took a sip of cocoa. "Mother and Father didn't know what to do with me. Boys had started to ask me out when I was thirteen. And it wasn't just the boys at school. I could walk down the street and men Father's age would stop their cars and offer me a ride. That's heady stuff for a young girl."

"And dangerous," I added.

"That too. But I thought I knew everything back then. I was just so smart and sophisticated. Even the girls at BrownWood didn't know how to treat me. One minute they were asking me about boys or clothes, and the next minute they were talking about me behind my back. I never really had any close girl-friends when I was growing up. I was different, and they were all afraid of me."

"I know. So was I."

"When I was in ninth grade," Nat continued, "Betty Samms and Martha Griswold asked me to walk home with them. They were both such snobs. But they had never asked me to join them before and I was flattered. We took the long way home, past Hanson's Garage, and all Betty could talk about was the mechanic who worked there. 'He looks just like James Dean,' she told us.

'Does he have a motorcycle?' Martha asked.

'Yes, and he wears leather too.'

"When we got near the garage, Betty dared Martha to go up and talk to him. All we could see were the Cuban heels on his black leather boots as they stuck out from underneath the '57 Chevy he was working on. Martha got all flustered and wouldn't do it. Then Betty looked at me. I didn't even think about what I was doing. I was just showing off for them. I walked right up to the garage, kicked his foot, and said, 'Did anybody ever tell you that you look like James Dean?' He slid out from under the car and looked up at me. Then he said, 'Yeah, all the time. Did anybody ever tell you that you've got legs to put a smile on a man's face?' No one ever had, and I didn't know what to say next. He laughed and rolled back under the car.

"Betty and Martha were standing at the end of the sidewalk with their mouths open. My heart started pounding, so I ran back to Martha and Betty. We giggled all the way home. It was an experience I found both frightening and exhilarating.

"The three of us began walking home from school past the garage every day. He'd watch as we passed. But he never said a word. And of course, we just giggled. Then one day I had to stay after school and clean erasers for Miss Demity because she caught me passing notes to Betty. I left school and took the short way home down Roland Avenue. Suddenly, there he was walking along beside me. He told me he was nineteen and he had a motorcycle. I told him I was seventeen and in the twelfth grade. He believed me.

"He began walking me home after school. Betty and Martha were beside themselves and wanted all the details. But there really wasn't anything to tell them because all we ever did was walk and talk. Then one day I agreed to cut school and go for a ride on his bike. We had talked about going out to Lake Roland to watch the boat races, which back then just meant going somewhere and making out. I hopped on the back of his motorcycle, and halfway to Lake Roland I realized what a dumb idea that was." Nat paused and took a sip of cocoa. "It was December and I wasn't dressed warmly enough for a ride on the back of a motorcycle in the dead of winter. I also knew it wasn't going to be any warmer at the lake. Well, I was dumb on more than one count. We got to the lake, and he took me to one of those lean-to-looking shelters that are set up in case it rains on your picnic. One thing led to another, and despite my protests...the deed was done." Natalie stopped again and took another sip.

"Nat, you were only fourteen...You were a kid."

"He didn't know I was only fourteen. Yes, he should have stopped when I asked him to. But I didn't know that at fourteen. It's taken me almost twenty years of therapy to understand what happened that day. And you know what? I'm not sure it matters anymore. It just happened."

We both stared into the fire. Ludie got up and put his head in Natalie's lap. She scratched him behind the ears. She took a deep breath and said, "And, of course, I got pregnant."

I looked at her and thought how frightening that must have been back then. Abortion, never an easy choice, wasn't legal in the fifties. We heard rumors in school about a friend, who knew someone's sister, who knew another friend who had gone to New York and gotten an illegal abortion. But we never had any firsthand knowledge of anybody who had been brave enough to do this. To be that young, pregnant, and single would have been terrifying.

"I was five months pregnant when Mother confronted me," Nat continued. "I don't know how she found out, but I remember I was relieved. At least now I had somebody to tell me what to do. When I finally got the story out, she just stood there and stared at me. Then she slapped me so hard across the face I hit my head on the bookcase."

I sat up. Mother had never hit any of us. All she had ever had to do to me was frown and it set my knees to shaking.

"I guess I must have felt I deserved it at the time because I don't remember being shocked by it." Mother said, 'How could you do this to your Father? He's being groomed for bishop. This could ruin him.' I told her I was sorry. I told her I didn't know what to do. I told her I'd never do it again." Natalie stopped scratching Ludwig and looked up at Father's portrait. "I begged her not to tell him. I said I could go out to Montana and live with one of her sisters. Then we could put the baby up for adoption and I could come home. She told me to go to my room and she'd discuss it with me later. I waited all that night, and finally the next morning she came in and told me to pack my bags. When I asked her if I was going to Montana, she had just looked at me and shook her head. 'Where are you sending me?' I asked over and over again. Finally, she told me I was going to the Cynthia Freedman Home for UnWed Mothers in Pennsylvania. That's when I knew she had told Father."

I looked at Nat and saw tears rolling down her face. She quickly wiped them away and said, "I was scared to death before. Now I was humiliated. Looking back, I know how irrational that sounds. Of course she had to tell him. He was my father. But I knew he would never forgive me for what I had done."

"Natalie," I broke in, "he was a priest. Of course he forgave you."

"Oh, maybe he forgave me as a priest. But he never forgave me as a father.

I'll never forget that ride to the Home. I sat in the front seat with Father, and he didn't speak to me for four hours. He listened to a stupid football game the entire time. When we got there, he took my bags and walked me into the reception area. He shook hands with Mrs. Gorsuch, the lady who ran the Home, and then he just left. I stood there and watched him get in the car and drive away. He didn't even say good-bye." Nat paused again and looked down at Ludwig. Before I got pregnant, Father used to joke with me and laugh at my smart remarks. Afterward, he didn't act the same anymore. Most of the time, he acted like I wasn't even there."

I started to protest this, but I stopped because I couldn't remember Father ever joking with Natalie either. I was the one he joked with all the time.

"Who cooked up the exchange student story?" I asked. "Father or Mother?"

"Mother. She sent me tapes from the library so I could practice. She also sent me travel books on Paris." Nat looked at me. "Actually, they did help."

"Why didn't Mother go with you?"

"I don't know. But at least she did write."

We sat in silence and watched the wood spit out a red splinter from the fire. Ludie jumped and snuggled closer to Natalie.

"Do you remember what I told you when you asked me why I didn't encourage Barbara to have Mother put in a care facility?"

"You said it was no fun being locked up."

"You thought I was talking about being locked up at Pratt. But I wasn't. I was thinking about that Home for UnWed Mothers. They used to lock us in at nine o'clock every night. I would sit in a chair by the window reading my French books and hear the key turn in the lock. What did they think we were going to do? Run out and party when most of us were so huge we couldn't even bend over? I look back and the whole experience seems surreal. Especially in this day and age…when young single women have babies all the time, and nobody bats an eye." Natalie continued to stroke Ludie who had fallen asleep with his head in her lap. "I was terrified of giving birth. Nobody explained anything to me. What I knew I heard from the other girls, although we didn't really talk to each other that much. We didn't want to talk about how we got pregnant because we were embarrassed. We couldn't talk about our husbands because we didn't have any. And we couldn't talk about our babies because we knew we couldn't keep them. Imagine how strange that is, Sara…feeling life inside you and not being able to acknowledge it. Our lives were on hold. And our futures couldn't begin until after we had given away our children."

I had to look away from Natalie's face at that point. I focused on the window that overlooked the pasture. Medalia Del Oro, Snookie's Preakness contender, hung his head over the fence and shook his mane. When he turned sideways, I saw tiny white flakes against his ebony coat.

"I knew I delivered a boy," Natalie said. "They let me hold him for a few minutes before I had to give him up. I remember he was bald, and it looked like he had no eyebrows. And I thought of Mother telling Frances Lymington that she thought I was an albino when the nurse had handed me to her. I knew he would look like me, but just as soon as I thought that, someone took him out of my arms." Natalie looked into the fire. "I stayed at the Home for another whole week before Father came and got me. The car pulled up, he got out and put my bag in the trunk, and then he told me to get in the car. I watched him talk to Miss Gorsuch, and when I saw him hand her a check, I took out my French book and began to read. Halfway home, Father said, "Natalie, we told everyone that you went to Paris on an exchange program. Your Mother has the details. I hope you studied your French." I said, 'Qui.' And that was the last time we ever talked about it."

"Ever?" I asked.

"Ever."

"What about Mother?"

"She tried. I remember she asked me how I felt when I got back. I told her I felt fine. She filled me in on what had happened while I was away. She told me what I was supposed to tell everyone. She wanted to make sure I had my story straight before I went back to school. I didn't want to go back. I was sure everyone knew. But when I got to school, no one suspected. Even my French teacher thought I had been to France."

"That's kind of hard to believe," I said.

"Not if you knew Miss Bozzell. I didn't realize how bad her French was until I did live in Paris. They would have laughed her out of the city with her accent."

"Did Mother ever bring up the subject again?"

"One time," Natalie said, taking a deep breath. "I was about to graduate from high school, and she came into my room with my cap and gown. She seemed nervous. She hung the robe over the door and stood there fidgeting with the pleats. Then she stood back and said, 'What was it, Natalie? Was it a boy or a girl?' It took me a few minutes before I realized what she was talking about. I said, 'You mean the baby?' And she said, 'Yes, the baby.' I watched her nervously twist her wedding ring around her finger. Then I said, 'It was a boy. Didn't they tell you that?' She closed her eyes and looked like she was going to be sick and said, 'No…he didn't tell me anything.' Then she walked out of the room." Natalie looked out the window and said, "Oh, it's snowing."

"For some time."

We watched the tiny flakes fall, then Natalie continued. "After I got hired with TWA and really did live in Paris, I thought I could start over, build a new life, fall in love, have other children. But even though I loved Paris and met some wonderful people, none of that happened. When I was forced to move back to New York, I told myself that now I could begin again. Now I could forget…Now I could start over. But not too long after I moved to New York, I began seeing him."

"Seeing who?"

"My son."

"You saw him in New York? How did you find him?"

"I didn't. It wasn't like that. I would see little boys on the airplane, and I would think that's how old he is now. I wondered what he looked like. I wondered if he was happy. The more I thought about him, the more I worried. And the more I worried, the more I drank. One day I even called the Freedman Home and tried to find out where he was. Of course, they wouldn't tell me."

"But there were ways of finding children back then, weren't there?" I asked this having no idea if there was or not.

"Not really. A closed adoption, which is what Father had requested, is pretty much that. Closed…no information…end of story."

I got up and threw another log on the fire. The temperature had dropped again. I pulled an afghan from a chair and draped it over Natalie's shoulders.

"Then one day, I got a phone call. I had just come in from a trip, and I was trying to get in the shower to get that airplane smell off of me. I picked up the phone and said, 'Hello.' But there was no answer. I said, 'Who is this? For God's sake, talk or hang up.' Finally, this boy's voice said, 'Hello? Is this Natalie?' His voice must have been changing because he squeaked on every other word. And I said, 'Yes, what do you want? You don't sound old enough to vote.' I waited and finally he blurted out, 'My name is Nicholas...and I think you're my mother.' I stood in the hallway of my apartment, and I suddenly forgot where I was. The walls began to close in on me, and I couldn't breathe. I held the phone to my heart and heard a voice that sounded like it was far, far away. Finally, I realized that I was holding the receiver to my chest and not my ear. I lifted the phone and I heard him ask, 'Are you my mother?' I said, 'No,' and hung up the phone." Natalie pulled the afghan up to her chin and stared at the snow. "I realized I had made a terrible mistake as soon as I had put down the receiver. But when I jerked the phone back up to my ear, he was gone. I took the pills that night. You know the rest."

"Couldn't you trace the call?" I asked.

"I did. All I got was the number of a phone booth along the Pennsylvania Turnpike."

I got under the covers with Natalie. The snow was now falling fast and furiously.

"But Nat, how did he find you? He was a kid. Kids back then didn't have the resources to find their adoptive parents."

"I never knew until today." Natalie moved Ludwig's head and got up. She walked over to her purse and pulled out a piece of paper. Then she sat back down on the sofa alongside me.

"Nicholas told me he had received a letter when he was fifteen. It was unsigned and all it said was 'Your mother's name is Natalie and she lives in New York. Here's her phone number. I think she'd like to hear from you.' Nicholas always knew he was adopted; his parents had never kept that a secret. But like most kids, he was curious about who his real parents were. He didn't want to hurt his adoptive parents, and he never told them about the letter. Nicholas dialed the number in the note and got me. And, of course, I hung up on him. He just figured I never wanted to see him."

"But Nat, who told him where you were? Who knew that he was your son?"

Natalie passed the note over to me and I stared at it. I looked up in disbelief because the handwriting was unmistakable.

"Mother?"

Natalie shook her head yes and began to cry.

When it got dark, and Natalie had cried herself out, I got up and poured two glasses of wine. I fixed Campbell's chicken noodle soup, and we ate in silence. When we had finished, she told me about Nicholas.

"He grew up in Harrisburg, Pennsylvania. His parents are Marion and Ed, who were both teachers...They're retired now. He has a sister who's also adopted. He had only nice things to say about his family. I could tell he loves them very much. He went to Penn State on a scholarship and after that seminary school. He said he always knew he wanted to be a minister. He was raised Methodist—"

"A Methodist!"

"But when he got to college," Nat said, ignoring my outburst, "he started attending the Episcopal church on campus, and the parish priest became a close friend. He decided he liked the Episcopal doctrine better than the Methodist doctrine—"

"I should hope so..."

"So he became an Episcopal priest." Natalie paused. "Rather ironic, isn't it?"

"Not if you consider his genes."

"He told his parents before he started his search for me because he didn't want to hurt them. He's married, Sara, and his wife's expecting. It was his wife who urged him to find me."

I looked at Natalie and smiled. "You? A grandmother?"

"Unbelievable, isn't it?"

"When will you see him again?"

"I don't know. I told him exactly what I just told you. I also told him I'd respect whatever decision he makes about me...I don't want to upset his life either."

"What do you really think?" I asked.

"I think he's dumbfounded that his grandfather was the bishop of Maryland. And I think because of that, he'll come back to see me...eventually."

Chapter Thirty-Three

•

"If music be the food of love, play on."

Shakespeare

We woke up to a foot of newly fallen snow. I let Ludwig out; he dove off the front porch and disappeared into a snow drift three feet high. He sat down and howled because he couldn't figure out how to get out. I got a shovel and rescued him.

"You know," Natalie said from the kitchen, "I worry about that dog."

While I was digging, I again thought about Snookie's party. How could people possibly attend a gala in a blizzard?

Natalie and I were in the kitchen having coffee when we heard the sleigh bells. I opened the door just as Ian drove up in a horse-drawn sleigh.

"What is it?" Natalie asked.

"This, you've got to see."

Natalie stood behind me and laughed. "Hey, Ian! Is that our mode of transportation for the evening?"

"Aye. Snookie's got four of 'em. We'll be transporting the partyers from York Road up to the castle in these."

"But how will people get from their houses to York Road?" I asked.

"Snookie's got a deal with the county road commissioner. The roads will be clear from Hunt Valley to Snookie's."

"She must have shelled out a bundle for that," Natalie said.

"Oh, she dinna have to. The road commissioner and Snookie go way back...She 'plies him with Glenlivet."

I turned around to Natalie and said, "And you wonder why I'm afraid of her?" Natalie just said, "Hmmmm."

I began getting nervous around five.

"You sure are jumpy," Nat said.

"I haven't been on a date in years. How am I supposed to act?"

"Don't act. Just be yourself. Besides, the place will be packed. If you hate him, you can hide for hours."

"Just what I want to do. Get all dressed up so I can hide for hours."

"Don't worry. I'll be there...We'll have fun."

We were almost dressed when we heard a knock at the door.

"God...they're early. You'll have to get it," Natalie said. "I'm still in my underwear."

I went out and opened the door and found Mother and Barbara standing on the front porch. Barbara looked confused. Mother looked beyond me and said, "Horse?"

"Why are you dressed like a harem girl?" Barbara asked.

"Snookie's party?"

"You're going to Agnes's party? In this snow?"

"Well, I don't normally parade around my house dressed like Bathsheba."

Barbara and Mother came in and took off their coats.

"What are you doing out here anyway? And where is your car?"

"Snappy got the flu. Just keeled over on the sofa and couldn't get up. I dropped her off at the emergency room on my way over here."

"Is she going to be OK?"

"I think so. The nurse in the emergency room said she was dehydrated."

"Is she conscious?" I asked.

"Very much so. She's furious that she has the flu. Kept saying, 'I can't have the flu! The army gave me a flu shot. I can't have the flu. I want a second opinion!' They gave her a shot and knocked her out. I'll call later and find out how she did. Our electricity went out and we got cold. I thought maybe you could help with Mother."

Mother had discovered Ludwig's dog biscuits. She had one hanging out of her mouth while Ludie drooled in front of her.

"But how did you get here?"

"The roads in the city aren't that bad yet. It's worse out here. I got out of Guilford and to the hospital fine. It got hairy from there to York Road. But York Road is absolutely clear. It looks like it never snowed. You have great plow service out here. Then when I got to the entrance to the farm I got stuck.

But this nice Scottish fellow came by in a sleigh and offered us a ride to your cottage." Barbara looked around and said, "Where is she?"

"Natalie?"

"Who else?"

As if on cue, Natalie strolled out of the bedroom. Barbara looked her up and down and then said, "My, my…aren't we all dolled up…Who are you supposed to be?"

"Lana Turner. What are you doing here?"

"The power's out. It got cold."

"Don't you have a fireplace?"

"I don't have any wood. Randall always orders it and he's—"

"Been banished," Natalie finished for her. Natalie noticed Mother for the first time. She hesitated and then walked over and tried to take the box of dog biscuits away from her. Mother fought her, but Nat whispered something in her ear. Mother smiled and released her hold on the biscuits. Natalie went into the kitchen, got some cookies, and led Mother over to the sofa.

Barbara watched all this in amazement. Several times she opened her mouth and tried to say something but couldn't. Finally, she managed to get out, "How'd you do that?"

"Do what?" Natalie said as she turned and walked back into the kitchen.

There was another knock at the door.

"Sara, will you get that? It's probably our dates."

"Dates?" Barbara asked, looking at me. "You have dates?"

I shrugged and opened the door. Zack stood on the porch, and Ian stood beside him. Ian was in a white suit, black shirt, and a white fedora. Zack was dressed like a sheriff, complete with boots, hat, and a six-shooter.

"Well, if it isn't Johnny Stompanato and his *High Noon* pal Gary Cooper."

"And if I'm not mistaken," Zack said, "it looks like Bathsheba…Or should I call you Miss Hayward this evening."

"I think you've all lost your minds," Barbara said.

"Come in," I motioned to Zack and Ian. "This is my sister Barbara, who I think you met at the old rectory…my mother, who you met on the roof, Ludwig my dog, and, of course, the lovely Lana Turner." Natalie waltzed out for her introduction. Zack said hello, and Ian's eyes popped out. Natalie went over and kissed him hello. Ian turned bright red and looked down. I noted that Ian must have had lifts put in his shoes because even in heels Natalie was now only a head taller.

"You people are really going to a costume party at that weirdo Agnes's house in the middle of a snowstorm? No one will show up!"

"Barbara," I said. "Ian is Snookie's cousin. And may I remind you that you got here in the middle of a snowstorm."

Barbara mumbled an apology to Ian. But Ian just laughed and said, "Aye, she's a wee touched, our Snookie." Then he looked at Barbara and said, "Why don't you come to the party too, lass?"

Barbara shook her head and said, "No, no, I couldn't. I don't have anything to—"

"Oh, yes you do," Natalie said, disappearing into the bedroom and returning with the green silk pantsuit. I bought this for you just in case you changed your mind. Myrna Loy...in *Whipsaw*." Natalie held the suit out in front of her.

"You think I look like Myrna Loy?" Barbara was visibly flattered.

We all shook our heads yes.

"Well, I don't know," Barbara said, looking down at her Eddie Bauer boots. "I don't have any shoes to match that outfit with me...It is a lovely green, isn't it?" Barbara felt the fabric.

"I have shoes you can wear," I said. "Why don't you come with us? You were invited."

Barbara was now smiling, but then she looked over at Mother and her face fell. "I can't. I have Mother." She handed Natalie back the suit.

"Bring Mum with you," Ian said.

"Oh, I couldn't possibly...I mean, I would be afraid that she would do something embarrassing."

"Obviously you've never been to a party at Snookie's!" Ian said, laughing.

"Barbara," Natalie said, "who cares what she does? Most of the people there will be blotto anyway...Come on...We'll take turns watching her."

"You'll watch her?" Barbara raised an eyebrow.

"Yes, I'll watch her. Now here, put this on and get dressed." Natalie handed Barbara the pantsuit.

After Barbara was gone, Ian said, "There's a wee problem. Snookie doesn't mind if you crash her parties...but if you crash, you'd best be in costume."

We all turned to look at Mother. She was still on the sofa, but she turned around to look at us and smiled.

"I need help on this one," Natalie said, scratching her head.

Zack and I looked at each other and said, "Margaret Hamilton—The Wicked Witch."

Ian smiled at Natalie and Natalie said, "Perfect. Although, where are we going to get that costume?"

"We'll make one," I said. "She can wear my old graduation robe with a belt."

"You kept your old graduation robe?" Zack said.

"Didn't you?" I turned to Natalie. "The broom is in the hall closet. The hat is packed in a box under the bed."

"You just happen to have a witch's hat?" Zack said.

"I painted Drucilla Whitman."

"The witch?" They all said in unison.

"It's a long story. But when the portrait was finished, she made me an honorary member of the coven and gave me a hat and a pentagram necklace."

They all gave me a strange look.

"She's not nearly as strange as everybody thinks she is," I said defensively.

I went to get the hat and the necklace, and while I was in the bedroom, I fished around for the shoes that would match Barbara's pantsuit. I handed off the witch accoutrements to Natalie and helped Barbara transform herself into Myrna Loy. When she reentered the room, everybody nodded their heads in approval. But then Barbara saw Mother.

"You must be joking."

"About what?" Natalie said.

"She can't go like that. She'll be the laughing stock of the party."

Once again Ian intervened. "On the contrary, lass...she'll probably win first prize."

Mother certainly did look the part. Natalie had even found an old stuffed monkey and had tied it to Mother's broom.

"Come on," Natalie said. "We're already late. Let's stop quibbling about costumes and go to the party."

We all donned coats and started for the door. Mother had a firm grip on Ludwig, and when I tried to pry him away, Ian said, "Let the fine lad come. He can loll by the fire with the Danes."

And so the six of us and the dog climbed into the sleigh and rode off into the falling snow to Snookie's Christmas Eve party.

Chapter Thirty-Four

•

"Ill met by moonlight…"
Shakespeare

The party was in full swing when we pulled up to the front entrance. Snookie's lads were still making trips back and forth to York Road to pick up guests. Ian pulled the sleigh into a spot next to the door. We got out and hurried inside. We were stopped by Snookie's butler, Horst, dressed as Peter Lorre, and a midget, costumed as Shirley Temple. Peter looked the part. Shirley was a man with a full day's growth of beard.

"Invitations please," Peter said, holding out his hand.

I handed him my invitation, the one that Natalie had added an "s" to and smiled. He looked at the invite and then said, "And your sisters are?"

I pointed to Barbara, Natalie, and Mother and held my breath.

"Who's the ugly dog with?" Shirley Temple asked.

We all pointed to Mother.

"That's the ugliest Toto I've ever seen," Shirley said while Peter Lorre stamped our wrists. Shirley Temple handed me the invitation back.

We filed through the door, and as Mother passed, I heard Peter say to Shirley, "Great witch costume." We were in.

I watched Barbara and Natalie as we followed the other guests to the grand ballroom. Barbara never closed her mouth. Natalie barely looked at anything. She, Ian, and Mother had locked arms and were walking in front of us.

"Where did she get the money for this place?" Barbara whispered to me.

"Third husband was a charm. Dropped dead at forty."

"He must have been worth millions."

"I heard billions," Zack said.

"Where is Agnes—I mean, Snookie? Shouldn't she be greeting her guests?"

"Snookie doesn't work that way," Zack said. "She circulates after the party gets going."

"Do you know who she decided to go as?" I asked Zack.

"No, but I wouldn't be surprised if it was Gloria Swanson as Norma Desmond."

The band was playing "Dancing In the Dark" as we rounded the corner and entered the grand ballroom.

"Oh my God," Barbara whispered.

"My sentiments exactly," I said.

"Nice decorations," Zack added.

"Nice?" Barbara said. "This is exquisite."

Snookie had transformed the grand ballroom into what appeared to be a duplicate of a scene from the movie *The Great Ziegfeld*. The ballroom had become an elegant thirties nightclub. There was a grand staircase in one corner and a stage where the band played in the other corner. Showgirls, dressed in little more than feathers and a headdress, paraded up and down the staircase. Partygoers danced on a polished teak floor. Beautiful mermaids swam in tanks of water mounted into the walls beside movie screens that showed old films from the thirties and forties. We passed by several Clark Gables and even more Joan Crawfords. I saw another Susan Hayward, although she wasn't dressed as Bathsheba. We sat down at a table covered in fine linen and set with Stieff silver and Wedgewood china. Barbara fondled the tablecloth, and Ian and Natalie took off for the dance floor. Zack, Barbara, Mother, and I watched Fred and Ginger float by.

"No wonder people cancel other party engagements," Barbara said. "Are those walls marble?"

"I think so," I said, turning around. "And when was the last time you saw a ten-foot *David* peeing champagne?" I said, pointing to the center of the room where guests were filling their champagne glasses.

Zack got up and offered to get us some. I watched as Nat and Ian glided around the dance floor. It was funny, but when they danced, I didn't notice the height difference. Zack placed three glasses of champagne down. The fourth he set down in front of Mother and said, "Mrs. Gorman, it's special brew. Don't chug it. It's strong stuff." I watched as Mother did indeed chug the clear liquid.

"That's not champagne, is it?" I whispered.

"No...water."

Mother held her glass down and Ludie took a drink. So far, the only thing that had spooked Ludwig were Snookie's two Great Danes who wandered around the party as if they were the hosts. Ludie had taken one look at the dogs and had disappeared under the table. I looked at Barbara and thought how pretty she looked, but when I leaned over to tell her that, I was interrupted.

"May I have this dance?"

We all turned at the low, sexy voice and found ourselves staring at a very debonair Errol Flynn. He was focused on Barbara, who became quite flustered.

"Uh, oh my. I just couldn't...I mean—"

But Errol didn't listen. He swooped her up and off they went around the ballroom floor. I never realized my sister was such a good dancer. Errol was the epitome of grace, and they put everyone else on the dance floor to shame. Natalie and Ian saw them pass by, and Natalie looked over at Barbara and smiled. When they passed our table, Natalie winked at me. I turned to Zack.

"I'm sorry, seems I got stuck babysitting tonight. Please feel free to ask someone else to dance. You won't hurt my feelings."

"Actually, I don't dance all that well."

I remembered the limp, but I didn't ask him about it. I kept my eye on Barbara and Errol. As I watched them round the bend again, my eye caught another couple who looked familiar.

"Zack, is that Malqueen and Lightning?"

"I believe it is. That's odd. He never goes to dances. Malqueen must really be special."

"She is. I didn't know Lightning knew Snookie," I said.

"He knows her from the track...I believe they used to own a racehorse together."

"Lightning and Snookie?" I said.

"She may be odd, but she does know horses, and she's a good businesswoman."

"But he never said a word to me...He even moved me out here."

"Well, maybe he was still a little put out about you moving."

I watched Lightning twirl Malqueen around and back into his arms. I stood up and waved. They danced over to our table.

"Well, if it isn't Ernest Borgnine and Josephine Baker," I said.

Malqueen sat down and adjusted her headdress.

"I've a feelin' I'll be coming down with a headache from this thing before the night's over," she said.

Mother reached up and touched Malqueen's headdress. Malqueen turned her head, and Mother said, "Is that you, Malqueen?"

"Yessam."

"What's for dinner?"

"Roasted pork and beef on a spit...fresh asparagus, baby carrots in brown sugar, fresh snap beans, rice and potatoes, and fruit...Lawd, you should see the fruit...strawberries the size of this ruby in my tiara...and desserts you wouldn't believe. I even saw individual Grand Marnier soufflés," Malqueen said. "And, honey, tonight that's no lie...'cause I already checked it out."

Mother giggled and reached up for the ruby from her headdress. Malqueen gently moved her hand away.

"Why didn't you tell me you were coming?" I asked her.

"Didn't know until the last minute," Malqueen said, looking at Lightning. "A certain man I know don't like to dance, and he forgot to tell me about it until it was almost too late to go. Lucky for him I already had a costume."

Lightning looked at the ceiling. Malqueen looked at Mother and said, "What happened?" I explained about Snappy.

"I hope Barbara don't hold that against her," Malqueen said. "She's a good woman...So where is Barbara?"

I pointed to the dance floor. Malqueen sat up and said, "Does she know who she's—"

"No, not yet," I said as Natalie and Ian rejoined our group.

Well, if it isn't Josephine Baker and Mr. Borgnine," Natalie said, kissing Lightning on the cheek.

"And who're you supposed to be in that let-it-all-hang-out-butt-huggin' dress?"

"Lana Turner," Natalie said, taking a bow, "on a date with her friend Johnny Stompanato." Ian bowed and kissed Malqueen's hand. Malqueen looked Ian up and down and said, "He ain't bad lookin' for a short fellow."

Natalie and Ian laughed, and Ian spun her back out onto the dance floor.

"Why don't you and Zachary go on and dance. Lightning and I will watch over Miz Gorman." Mother's head had fallen down to her chin, and I heard a faint snore. I peeked under the table and saw that Ludwig had followed suit. I looked over at Zack.

"Well, if you don't mind dancing with a cripple," he said, getting up. "Just go easy on me."

Lightning sighed and said, "Now, if only they'd play a polka." We laughed and slipped onto the dance floor.

Zack wasn't a great dancer, but then I wasn't a great dancer either. We talked as we shuffled our feet around the floor, and before we knew it, the song was over. We stayed on the floor and talked and shuffled through three more songs. When we finally returned to the table, Nat and Ian were back. Mother was still sleep.

"Did Barbara ever come back to the table?" I asked.

Everybody shook their heads no.

"Is she still dancing?"

They all nodded yes. I leaned over to Natalie. "We've got to tell her when she comes back."

"I know," Natalie said. "But it does seem a shame. She's having such a good time...Look at her."

I did. I had never seen such joy on my sister's face. She and Errol were just a symphony together.

"Did you know she could dance like that?" I asked Natalie.

"No...but why should that surprise you. She always did everything else better than we did."

"Maybe we should tell her now," I said.

"Oh, come on. Let her have some fun."

"When she finds out, she's not going to be very happy."

"She may never find out. He may always be just Errol Flynn to her."

"Natalie, if she knows that we knew all this time, she'll kill us."

"Just let it ride. We'll tell her when the band breaks."

But when the band took a break, Barbara disappeared.

"Let's eat," Malqueen announced when the band left.

"But Barbara—"

"She'll find us. I can't wait to sink my teeth into that roasted pig," Malqueen said.

"You were serious about the roasted pig?"

"You didn't see the food room?"

I looked at Natalie who shrugged. "No, what food room? I thought the food was in this room."

"This room just has champagne and hors d'oeuvres. The room next door has a huge fire going with a cow and a pig being barbecued."

Malqueen wasn't kidding. The room was actually another hall with a fireplace that was almost as tall as the ceiling. A spit turned two sides of beef and a whole pig inside the fireplace while two servants smeared sauce over the meat. Long banquet tables had been set along the walls. Harried servants, dressed in crisp white uniforms, carried food to the tables while the guests helped themselves. We weren't disappointed. Everything was delicious. Barbara finally found us in the banquet hall.

"There you are. I was wondering where you had all gone."

"Coulda fooled me," Natalie said between bites. "Looked like you only had eyes for Errol."

"Isn't he divine?" Barbara blushed. "Not much of a talker, but what a dancer."

I opened my mouth and said, "Barbara I think you ought to—"

Natalie hit me in the side.

"Ought to know what?" Barbara said.

"That we don't want you to worry about Mother," Natalie broke in. "She'll be fine with us. Go and enjoy yourself."

"That's really sweet of you, Natalie. Are you sure?"

"Barbara," I started and was interrupted by Errol's arrival and Barbara's squeal of delight as he swept her away again.

Malqueen shook her head. "You best tell her."

"I just tried," I said. "But someone stopped me." I glared at Natalie.

"We'll tell her. Just let her enjoy herself for a few more minutes."

A few minutes turned out to be the rest of the night. Somewhere between the banquet hall and the grand ballroom, we lost Mother.

One minute she was behind me, and the next minute she was gone. Zack held one of my hands as we made our way through the crowd, and

Mother held the other. I felt Mother's hand let go when I was bumped by two men dressed as Jack Lemmon and Tony Curtis from *Some Like It Hot*. I quickly turned around, but she had disappeared.

Zack and I began an all-out search. The crowd had grown since we had arrived, and I hadn't realized just how packed the party had become. When Zack and I came up empty-handed, I sent him to look for Natalie, and I went to the front door. Peter Lorre and Shirley were still there.

"Excuse me," I said. "But did either of you see the Wicked Witch of the West go by?"

Peter looked up from his invitations and said, "Yes, as a matter of fact…about five minutes ago. She left."

"What do you mean she left?" I said, feeling faint.

"I mean, she walked out the front door."

"Are you sure it was the same Wicked Witch who came with me? I did see several other witches on the dance floor."

"Lady," Peter Lorre said, "I just told you. The Wicked Witch of the West, the one who came with you, left the party about five minutes ago."

"How can you be so sure?"

"Because she was with that ugly dog."

I screamed and ran to get Zack.

Natalie, Ian, Zack, and I searched the grounds outside the castle. We even enlisted the help of two security guards. But we didn't find Mother. Finally Natalie said, "OK…stop…We've got to think like she thinks—"

"Oh, don't be ridiculous," I said. "She's not thinking anymore. She has Alzheimer's. We should just call the police."

Natalie paced back and forth and then came to an abrupt stop.

"Ian," she said, "does Snookie keep any horses nearby?"

"There's a small stable close to the house. Snookie keeps her favorites in there."

Natalie grabbed my arm. "Ian, take us to the stables."

The stables were on the other side of the castle. I thought it unlikely that Mother could have found her way there in the dark. But once we were away from the castle, Ian pointed to the ground and said, "Look." There were footprints, along with paw prints, in the newly fallen snow. When we got there, the stable door was open. Ian ran inside and groaned.

"What is it? " I asked, fearing Mother had been kicked to death by a horse.

"There's a horse missin'," Ian said. "And it's Medalia Del Oro."

"The Preakness horse?" Zack said.

"Aye. Come on. Perhaps we can catch her in the sleigh."

"No," Natalie said. "Sara and Zack can take the sleigh. "We'll do better on horseback." Ian nodded and began to saddle up two horses.

"Natalie, how can she ride? She can barely talk anymore."

"One of the books you sent me," Natalie said, looking around the stable, "said to expect the unexpected when it comes to Alzheimer's. Mother was an excellent horsewoman. Hopefully, it's one of the things she still remembers how to do."

"You read those books I sent you?"

"Of course I did."

"But I never thought you cared—"

"Sara, she's my mother too...Ian? Are you almost ready?"

"I can't believe this," I said. "What will I tell Barbara?"

"It's not Barbara I'd be worrying about, lass," Ian said as he threw a saddle on a brown mare. "It's Snookie."

"Don't worry," Natalie said. "We'll find her before you have to tell anybody." Natalie finally spotted what she was looking for. She grabbed a pair of jeans hanging on a hook and put them on under her dress. She slid the dress off and pulled on an old flannel shirt someone had left in the stall. She tossed her gown aside and was ready to ride by the time Ian led the horses out. Zack and I stood back and watched as they mounted and then turned the horses in the direction of the pastures. Ian had a high-powered flashlight, and he kept it aimed at the ground as they followed the trail left in the snow. We watched the yellow light bounce as they broke into a full gallop once they hit the fields.

"I hope they find her," I said but not really believing that they would.

"Come on," Zack said. "Let's go to the cottage. You never know. She might just decide to go there." We walked to the sleigh and Zack helped me up. Then he picked up the reins and tentatively said, "Giddyap." The horse turned its head around and looked at him. "Giddyap," he said again. This time the horse didn't even turn around. He just lifted his tail and ignored us.

"Have you ever done this before?" I asked.

"Well, no," he confessed. "Horses really aren't my thing."

"We're a great pair. They terrify me."

Zack tried again and still the horse wouldn't budge. Since this was getting us nowhere, I told him to move over. I thought about how frightened I had always been of horses. And then I thought of Mother out in the snow bouncing around on a skittish racehorse. I decided that Mother on the racehorse frightened me more than the horse attached to the sleigh. I lifted the reins as high as I could, slapped the horse on the rump, and yelled, "Yeee-ahhh." The horse took off, throwing us back into the seat. It wasn't until we were over the moat and halfway up the hill that we managed to sit up. I slowed the horse down by pulling slightly on the reins and saying, "Whoa, baby…now whoa." Zack sat up and held onto the sides of the sleigh as I guided the horse through the snow and down the road. After a few minutes, he said, "Good job. Where did you learn to do that?"

"My sister," I said as I sat up straight and negotiated the turn down my driveway. I pulled up in front of the dark cottage and jumped down. I started to go up the steps but turned around and walked back to the horse. I hesitated and then reached up and patted his head. "Good boy," I told him. He nodded at me and shook his mane. "Now stay," I said, wagging a finger at him.

We walked into the house to find Mother and Ludwig asleep on the sofa.

"Thank God," I said as I got Mother out of wet clothes and covered them both with a blanket. "Now pray they find Medalia."

Chapter Thirty-Five

—————————————— • ——————————————

"I can't go back to yesterday because
I was a different person then."
Lewis Caroll

Two hours later Zack and Natalie showed up at the cottage. Nat's lips were blue, and Ian's wiry black eyebrows were frozen. I pushed them into the bedroom and told them to dry off and change. When they reemerged, I asked if they had found the horse.

"Well?"

"He's back in the stable," Ian said. "We found him dancing around in the fields not far from here."

"The hard part," Natalie said, "was convincing him to come with us. Thank God Ian was there. I couldn't have done that by myself."

"Oh, I dinna know," Ian said. "You're as fine a horsewoman as I've ever seen." Natalie actually blushed.

I found four mugs while Natalie made hot brandy punch. The four of us sat in front of the fire Zack had made and drank our toddies. We talked as the lights began to blink on and off. When they finally went out for good, I got up and lit some candles. The brandy and the fire kept us warm. Ian was halfway through the story of how Snookie had gotten rid of her second husband when the front door flew open and a very wet and angry Barbara stood in the doorway.

"You left me!" she yelled.

I got up and tried to pull her into the house and shut the door. I got the door closed, but she pushed me away.

"You knew!" she said, coming into the living room and pointing a finger at Natalie. Ian and Zack stood up. Natalie remained seated and said, "Knew what?"

"That Errol was a woman."

I covered my eyes. Natalie stood up and said, "Barbara, go change out of those clothes while Sara and I say good night to Ian and Zack. You can see right through that outfit." Barbara looked down at her clingy wet pantsuit and realized that you could indeed see right through it. She ran for the bedroom. I started to apologize, but Ian stopped me.

"Lass, it's best we be getting back anyway. I have the horses to return, and I should help the other lads transport the people back to their cars." He turned to Natalie, smiled, and said, "I'll be callin' ye."

While Natalie kissed Ian good-bye, I walked onto the porch with Zack. He didn't attempt to kiss me, but instead he said, "I think you missed your calling."

"Oh?"

"You should have been a stagecoach driver."

"I'll consider that the highest compliment...especially since it came from Marshall Will Kane."

Zack bowed and tipped his hat. Natalie and I watched as Ian tied the two horses to the sleigh, took the reins, and then drove off down the drive.

"I like Zack," Natalie said.

"I like Ian," I replied.

I closed the door and prepared for World War III.

When Barbara came out, Natalie handed her a hot brandy. She guzzled it down in one swallow. Natalie poured her another one.

"I can't believe you let me make a fool of myself, "Barbara said, downing the second brandy and holding out her glass for a third. "Everybody at that party saw me dancing with a woman! Did you know the mayor was there? And the governor? I even saw Senator Kulminski! And what was I doing? Waltzing around the dance floor with a woman dressed like a man...acting like I was having the time of my life!"

"You were having the time of your life," Natalie said.

"I was not."

"Was too."

"I was not having a good time with a woman."

"Barbara, you looked like heaven dancing around that ballroom. Who cares if you were dancing with a woman? Half the people there were cross-dressers anyway!"

"What do you mean half of them were cross-dressers?" Barbara was now genuinely confused. I took a candle and went into the kitchen for more brandy. I couldn't believe how naïve my sister was.

"Barbara, did you get a good look at Shirley Temple?" I yelled from the other room.

"The one at the front door?"

"Yes. That was a man."

"What?"

"You didn't notice the beard?"

"I just assumed...Well...some women do have facial hair..."

"Not a full five o'clock shadow," Natalie said. "...unless they're in the circus. And how about the band?"

"What about the band?"

"They were all women dressed like men."

I turned to look at Nat. I hadn't even noticed that.

"No."

"Yes."

"Did you look at the mermaids in the tanks?" Nat asked.

"Yes."

"All men."

"It's not possible." Barbara shook her head.

"Yes it is. And the showgirls too."

Barbara sat down with a stunned look on her face. She drank her brandy, and Natalie refilled her glass again. Barbara normally didn't drink all that much, and I noticed she was having a hard time sitting up.

"But why didn't you tell me?" she whined.

"We tried," I said, coming back into the living room with more brandy. "But you kept dancing away...and you looked so good on the dance floor...It just seemed a shame."

We were quiet for a few minutes. Finally, Natalie asked, "When did you find out?"

"On the ride home," Barbara said into her brandy. "He...I mean, she... or whatever it was...offered to drive me home when I couldn't find you. I thought you had left me, but that man at the front door...was he a man?...told me you had gone looking for Mother. How could you let her get away?" Barbara looked over at the sofa where Mother was now sleeping. "Anyway, Errol...that woman...that thing...offered to drive me home in the sleigh." Barbara took another big gulp of brandy. "It had stopped snowing and the moon came out just as we got in the sleigh. It was so romantic...We were singing 'Putting on your Top Hat' as we flew down the road...And the moon was dead ahead of us above the road...It looked like we could have driven right through it. Then, all the sudden, he pulled the sleigh over and stopped, and I just thought..."

Natalie and I looked at each other, and I had to look away. I was on the verge of laughing and Nat knew it.

"Anyway, he was so nice that I thought it wouldn't hurt to kiss him good night. I had had such a lovely evening...I just wanted to forget that rat fink husband of mine...and Mother...and well...one quick kiss, I told myself. What could that hurt? What was wrong with that?" Barbara polished off the brandy, and Natalie filled her glass again.

"Well," Barbara said, starting to slur her words, "one kiss turned into two, then three, and before I knew it, we were under those nice thick warm animal skins...and one thing led to another." Barbara took another gulp of brandy. "But then," she said, trying to sit up, "...in the middle of it all, I discovered that HE was missing an important piece of equipment!" Barbara fell back down and rolled over on the floor.

I started to laugh. Natalie put her hands over her mouth but couldn't stop herself from laughing either. Pretty soon we were howling and we couldn't stop. And of course that infuriated Barbara.

"You're laughing at me! I knew it! You planned this all along. You just wanted to humiliate me, didn't you Natalie? You've always been jealous...from the very beginning. I was smarter than you, and I married into a good family and had two fine sons. You're just jealous—"

"Barbara," Natalie said, trying to stop laughing. "Trust me. I'm not jealous."

"Yes...you...are. You've always wanted what I had. Admit it."

"No, Barbara. I don't want what you have."

"Yes, you do. You just won't admit it. You're a failure, Natalie. You've never done anything with your life. You've always been jealous of what I've had."

"Of a husband who can't keep his zipper up?" Natalie had stopped laughing. "Of two boys who couldn't wait to go to college because their mother was driving them crazy? And who go skiing instead of going home for the holidays? Of a house that was bought and paid for by Frances Lymington? I think not."

"How dare you! I do not drive my sons crazy. And they didn't go skiing last Christmas."

"Barbara, I was in Denver last Christmas. I met up with them. We went skiing together."

I hadn't known any of this. I looked from Natalie to Barbara.

"You're a liar! Liar! Liar! Liar!"

"No, I'm telling the truth, and you know it."

"I know that you're a worthless piece of shit—a shit so jealous that you'd make up any story to make me look bad. How dare you say those lies!"

"No, Barbara. How dare you. I'm tired of your sanctimonious attitude. I don't care about your life...Your life is pathetic. Trust me. I've never wanted it."

Barbara turned purple. "And what kind of life did you want, Natalie? Pregnant at fourteen? A drunk all your life? Is that the kind of life you always dreamed about?"

There was silence in the room. I looked at Natalie. She was very still.

"How did you know?" she said to Barbara.

"I knew when you starting throwing up. It runs in the family."

"And you didn't say anything?"

"I wanted to be sure. I waited until I saw you in the bathroom one day."

"So then you told Mother?"

"Of course I told Mother."

Natalie sat down and shook her head.

"Did it ever occur to you, Barbara, that you could have helped me?"

"Do what? You were pregnant!"

"I was also only fourteen. You were twenty-one. You could have talked to me. You could have helped me."

"I did what I thought was best. Mother had to handle it—"

"I'm not saying she shouldn't have handled it. I'm asking you why you didn't tell me you knew. Don't you know how frightened I was? I had no one to talk to."

"You should have thought about that before you let him stick it in you. Besides, Mother had to handle it. Father was going to be bishop. You could have ruined his chances for—"

"Barbara," I said.

"What?"

"Shut up."

I got up and went over to Natalie.

"Nat?" I said. "She's drunk. She doesn't mean any of this."

"I'm not drunk," Barbara said, drinking the last of the brandy.

"No," Natalie sighed. "I'm sure she does. But you know what? I don't care anymore. It's ancient history. I'm just glad he found me. And whatever happens next, so be it."

"Found who?" Barbara snapped.

"Her son."

"Son?" Barbara repeated.

"She had a son, Barbara. I'm surprised you didn't know that since you and Mother were so buddy-buddy. He even came to see her yesterday. He's tall, blond, and he looks just like Natalie. "And," I said smiling at her, "he's an Episcopal priest."

"That's a lie!" Barbara said.

"No, it's the truth. And Barbara? Believe this too. I'm a little tired of your we-are-better-than-other-people attitude. We're not. We're just like everybody else. We bleed red...not blue."

"Don't you talk to me like that, you little ingrate!" Barbara stood up. "I've put up with your bohemian lifestyle long enough for God's sake...taking Wittridge money to go to art school...sleeping around with those unkempt-looking weirdos. Then when you finally do make something of your life, you turn around and give it all up so that you can sell shoes in a department store? Do you know how embarrassing that was for me? And that fiasco with Frances. Lord, that took months to mend. How could you be so selfish? You know how hard I—"

"That's your problem, Barbara."

"My problem? No, I think it's your problem. You're the one with the husband who sleeps with other men!"

"What?" I stood up.

"Barbara," Natalie said. "That's enough."

"No," I said. "How did you know about Aubrey?" I had never told anyone about Aubrey and Tom Bennett.

Barbara realized what she had done. She looked at Natalie and sat back down on the chair.

"Tell me."

Barbara sagged in her chair and looked at the floor.

"Who told you?" I said quietly.

Barbara looked at Natalie again. This time Natalie shook her head no.

"And how could you both know?" I said. Neither of them would look at me.

I thought back to that day. I remembered walking up to the house, seeing Aubrey's coat on the hook, and then walking up the steps and into the bedroom. How could anyone know? I hadn't told a soul. Father and Mother had been the only people who knew I had even been to Tom's that day... been to Tom's that day...been to Tom's that day. And why was I at Tom's that day? Why? Why? I was there delivering a document for Father...for Father... Mother was sick. But Father didn't look sick. Mother didn't want me to go. Father did. Father never did get the flu. Father called me...Father called me. Why did he want me there at a specific time? Why? I looked up at the portrait and whispered, "Father."

I knew it was true as soon as I said it, and the look on Barbara's face confirmed it. Natalie still wouldn't look at me.

"Why?"

Barbara put her head down and started to cry.

"Natalie?"

Natalie looked over at Barbara and shook her head. Then she looked up at Father's picture and sighed. "Father found out about Tom and Aubrey a month before you did. He said he had always heard rumors about Tom's sexual orientation...After all, Tom never married...But Father never did object to homosexuality in a priest...He had the same 'no-tell policy' as the military has now…As long as the priest did his job, Father didn't care what he did with his private time. But when Father found out that Tom and Aubrey were lovers, and I'm still not clear on how he found that out, he was so horrified he wanted the marriage to end immediately. Mother tried to reason with him. She told him that the right thing to do would be to tell you and let you make up your own mind. She said Aubrey was your husband and it was your life. But Father wouldn't listen."

"So he set me up?"

"Mother tried to stop him. But Father said the only way you'd leave Aubrey immediately was to catch him in the act."

"He set me up?"

Barbara looked up. "It wasn't like that. He just wanted to shock you into seeing what Aubrey was really like."

"He had no right to do that."

"Sara," Barbara said. "He was your father—"

"No," Natalie said. "He didn't have any right to do what he did."

My head pounded. I looked up at Father's portrait, yanked it off the wall, and threw it on the floor. Natalie and Barbara did nothing. But when I put my foot through it and began stuffing it into the fire, Natalie jumped up and tried to pull it out of my hands.

"Give me that painting," I screamed.

Natalie hung on. "No, you don't," she said. "What he did was cruel and selfish and terribly unfair…but he did love you, Sara. He did love you." I stopped and looked at her. Black mascara ran down her face.

"Of all of us," she said, taking the picture out of my hands and putting it aside, "he loved you best. He always loved you best. We all knew that. Even Mother."

"That's…not…love," I said. "It's some kind of sick obsession. What kind of father sets up his own daughter? To send me over there knowing that I'd walk into a room where my husband was in bed with another man…what kind of father would do that?"

"A father who made a terrible mistake," Nat said. "But a father who did love you."

"How can you defend him after what he did to you?"

"I'm not defending him. I'm still trying to understand him. And I may not ever understand why he did what he did to me. But I am certain that he thought he was protecting you. He honestly believed it was the right thing to do."

"Why didn't you just tell me the truth, Natalie? You of all people..."

"I didn't want to be the one to break your heart."

"So you let me walk in on that scene? God, you're as bad as Father."

"Yes, I guess I am. I guess we all were. But then none of us really believed he'd go through with it...not even Mother."

I looked up and said, "Mother? Mother was just an adjunct to Father."

"No, she wasn't. She tried to talk him out of it. When he wouldn't budge, she called me in New York and asked me to talk to you. When I balked, she told Barbara and asked Barbara to talk to you. But we didn't. We were both convinced that he would come to his senses and change his mind."

I thought back to that day in the library when Mother was so sick. She had tried to get me to stay there. It was Father who had pushed me out the door.

"She could have told me herself."

"Maybe. But would you have believed her?"

"I don't know. But she should have tried."

"She did the best she could. As soon as you were out the door she was on the phone to Tom Bennet. But no one answered, and she didn't know if they had left the rectory or if they just weren't answering the telephone. So she called Barbara and told her to go over and stop you before you got to Tom's house." I looked over at Barbara who had fallen off the chair and was now passed out on the floor.

"I never saw Barbara."

"She was too late. She arrived as you were leaving. She followed you to Lettie's," Natalie said. "Mother called me in New York and told me what had happened. I couldn't believe Father had gone through with his plan. Mother was hysterical on the phone. She kept saying, 'She'll never get over this...She's so sensitive...I'm just afraid of what this will do.'"

"And what was Father doing all this time? Gloating?"

"Father went after Tom Bennet," Natalie said. "And then he went after Aubrey."

I looked up at her and said, "How?"

"The papers Father gave you were legitimate plans. But they weren't what Tom thought they were. The design that Tom thought Father was helping him with was a copy of a design the new bishop already had. When the new bishop saw it, he realized that something fishy was going on and he called Tom in to explain the design. Tom called Father for help, but Father made sure he was unavailable. Tom didn't do well in his interview with the new bishop. He lost St. David's and had to transfer out of state."

"And Aubrey?"

"Father visited Aubrey in the hospital the day after he had been beaten by the loan sharks. I don't know what he said. I just know Aubrey left town."

"Aubrey left town because his life was in jeopardy."

"Maybe," Natalie said. "All I know is that Aubrey left immediately after Father saw him." Natalie nodded over to Mother on the sofa. "In the meantime, Mother called Lettie every day. She was worried about you, especially when you got sick. She sent Barbara over to Mrs. M's. She knew you would listen to Malqueen."

"Mother enlisted the aid of Malqueen?"

Natalie had been holding me by the wrist all this time. She released me and said, "Yes, she did, although Malqueen never knew how Father was involved. And after it was all over, Mother swore Barbara and me to secrecy. She never wanted you to know what Father had done. She knew how much you loved him."

I looked into the fire. My stomach was twisting and turning in knots. I couldn't make up my mind if I wanted to throw up or kill somebody.

"I'm going to put Barbara to bed," Nat said. "She's such a sad drunk, I can almost forgive her."

I didn't answer. I heard Natalie rouse Barbara and half walk and half drag her into the bedroom.

I didn't know how long I looked into the fire, but when I looked up, Mother was staring at me. She was sitting on the sofa with Ludwig's beside her. The golden light from the fire flickered across her face, and I saw a peace there that I had never seen before. She looked puzzled and said, "Horse?" I went over and sat down next to her. She turned to face me, and I saw that her face was remarkably unlined for a woman of eighty-three. Where were the crow's feet of old age? I thought as I touched the corner of her eye. And what had happened to the lines in her forehead that had always made her look like she was scowling?

Alzheimer's was an amazing wrinkle remover. Too bad her brain disappeared with the lines. She looked young and innocent in the firelight. She said "horse" again and looked at me. I didn't know what she meant, but I pointed to the window and said, "Yes, there's a horse." Her entire face lit up, and I saw my mother at twenty-two, much like Father must have seen her when he met her for the first time. There was kindness in her eyes with just a hint of mischief. She looked at my face and then down at my hand. I realized that I was drawing her face in the dust on the coffee table. I stopped and looked back up at her. She smiled. I calmly walked over to the hall closet and dragged out a canvas and my paints—items I had buried behind boxes, and shoes, and winter coats. Mother never moved. She just sat there with Ludie sprawled beside her and smiled at me.From time to time she'd say "horse?" and look toward the window. I'd reply "yes," and she would smile again. At some point, Natalie came back into the room, saw what I was doing, and went back into the bedroom and closed the door. I painted through the night.

I finished at the first gray light of morning. It was still snowing and Mother had fallen asleep again. I covered her up. Then I sat down at the kitchen table, put my head down, and fell asleep.

This time I dreamed Father and I were in his old study at the rectory. He was talking about a baseball game, and I was cutting out paper dolls. Mother came into the room and sat down next to me and helped me put the dresses on the dolls I had just cut out. We laughed as we worked. Father's voice kept getting louder and louder. He was trying to get my attention, but I wasn't listening. I was too busy looking up into my mother's face as she smiled down at me.

"Sara?" I felt someone shaking my shoulder. "Sara?"

I sat up. I was in the kitchen and Natalie was standing over me.

"You were asleep. Are you all right?"

I got up and stretched. "I'm not sure. My neck feels like it's on backward, and my back is killing me." I looked up and saw Barbara, with a bag of frozen peas on her head, standing in front of the portrait of Mother.

"Natalie?"

"What?" Natalie turned around and looked over at Barbara.

"Just come here."

Natalie walked over to where Barbara stood and looked down at the painting.

They both looked up at me at the same time.

"Merry Christmas," I said, getting up and walking over to the closet.

"Sara," Barbara gushed, "she looks exactly the way I remember her—"

"No," Nat broke in. "Look at the eyes. The eyes remind me of somebody else…the eyes…" Natalie turned to Barbara. "The eyes look like Sara's." They both looked up at me.

"Do they?" I said as I put on my coat, boots, and hat.

"Are you going somewhere?" Barbara asked, still staring at the portrait.

I walked over to the sofa and helped Mother get into her coat. She held her feet in the air as I worked her boots on. She only fought me when I tried to get her mittens on. Ludie stood anxiously by the front door.

"Where are you going?" Barbara repeated.

"I promised Mother I'd take her to see a horse," I said as I opened the door and led Mother outside.

"But, Sara, it's still snowing. You'll both get soaked."

"No we won't. We're only going to the back fence to see Medalia…a short distance…from here to there."

Epilogue

———————————— • ————————————

"Fortune, good night.
Smile once more.
Turn thy wheel!"

Shakespeare

"I'm getting down," Barbara said. "Randall will be here any minute."

"Tennis again?" Natalie asked.

"No. We've enrolled in a class on opera at Hopkins."

"I hope it's not Wagner," Natalie said.

"Why?"

"He's like meat loaf...I forget how heavy it is...I wolf it down and then I get indigestion."

"I don't know what it is. I let Randall pick this time."

"I think I'll get down too, "Natalie said. "Ian said he'd be here as soon as he finished feeding the horses."

I looked at my watch. "Me too," I said. "Zack said three."

We all climbed down the ladder that the fully recovered Reverend Dobb had set up for us.

"Next year I get to choose where we celebrate her birthday," Barbara said as we stood by the curb.

"I thought it was my turn," Natalie said.

"Nope, mine."

"But when we drew straws..."

We had drawn straws and I had won the right to choose where we would celebrate Mother's birthday this year. I had chosen the roof because one of my favorite memories of Mother was of her up there dancing.

A car horn honked, and a bright red Ferrari pulled up. Randall was at the wheel, and he smiled at us as Barbara ran around and got in the other side.

"Behave yourself," I yelled.

"Never!" he yelled back as he shot away from the curb and sped down the street.

"Hard to believe they've been married thirty-five years," Natalie said.

Barbara and Randall had patched things up once again. But there were changes. Barbara told Randall he could come back on one condition: she wanted to have fun. They now played tennis, skied, danced, and even went scuba diving in the Caribbean. Barbara dropped out of the Ladies Luncheon Prayer Meeting, and Randall stopped wearing his toupee.

"Hard to believe you've been married for six months," I said, pushing her off the curb. Natalie laughed. She and Ian had gotten married in the spring. Natalie had transferred to Baltimore and now flew out of BWI airport. She and Ian lived in my old cottage on Snookie's farm. Snookie was ecstatic to have Natalie join the family. At their wedding Snookie had toasted the bride and groom, telling everyone that "Not only was she gaining a breathtakingly beautiful cousin-in-law, but also one who could exercise her horses." Snookie had made this announcement as she stared wistfully at Barbara. Everyone, save Barbara, knew that the "cousin-in-law who could exercise her horse" was, of course, Natalie, and the "breathtakingly beautiful cousin-in-law" was Barbara. We had never told Barbara that Errol, the woman she had played "touchy-feely" with in the sleigh that night, had been Snookie. Natalie wanted to save that tidbit for another fight. We had forgiven Barbara her drunken outbursts, but we hadn't forgotten them.

Natalie was still working out her relationship with her son. Nicholas did come see her again, and this time he brought his wife and their new bald, blue-eyed daughter. Natalie was a complete failure as a grandmother. She had no mothering skills at all. But Ian did. He cooed and sang and charmed all of us with his antics. Natalie learned from him, and pretty soon Natalie was showing her granddaughter how to feed sugar cubes to Medalia Del Oro, now the winner of the Triple Crown.

A beat-up Toyota truck pulled up to the curb, and Ian grinned and said, "Hello, lass...need a ride?"

"No, he should be here any minute. I'll see you tomorrow."

Natalie and Ian waved as the truck backfired, jerked, and then slowly moved on up the street.

I turned around and stared at the old rectory. We never did put Mother in a care facility. She's still with Barbara and Randall. Snappy is her primary caregiver and Snappy's two sisters, Bootie and Donda, take turns watching

Mother at night. She's bedridden and doesn't recognize us anymore, not even Barbara. The only one she occasionally remembers is Malqueen.

"Is that you, Malqueen?" she'll ask. And Malqueen always says, "Yessam. Wants to know what's for dinner?" But Mother has forgotten that part of their banter. Most days she just stares at a spot above the television with unseeing eyes.

Zack and Lightning have decided to go into business together. They opened a microbrewery on Broadway, a site Lightning had been holding onto for years and the perfect location to attract the tourists. When I had asked them what they knew about making beer, Malqueen had rolled her eyes and said, "They don't know nothing...They just drink too much of it."

Malqueen still runs Mrs. M's, and Lightning still owns the Blue Parrot, and they also got married this spring. I went to visit them right after they got married and ended up taking the elevator up to my old loft. The sun almost blinded me when I came out of the cage, and it reminded me of the first time I had seen the loft, when I was an art student almost twenty-five years ago. I walked around the apartment and looked in every corner and closet. But I didn't find any ghosts. All I saw was the light...and so I moved back in.

I left Landstrom right after the Big Sale and began to paint again. But business was very slow. I had been out of the portrait-painting business for several years, and unfortunately clients have short memories. Zack hired me to design a label for the brewery's signature beer. It took me a few days, but I did finally come up with an idea. I took a picture of Ludwig with his back to the camera and his head turned around looking over his shoulder. Then I had a friend turn it into a poster. At the top I wrote: Life can get ugly. And on the bottom: Drink Ugly Dog Beer. Zack loved it and his line of Ugly Dog Beer was born. The Ugly Dog Poster, as it became known, made me famous on college campuses all over the country. My phone started ringing again. I'm now not only painting portraits, I'm designing as well.

Zack and I are still dating, but we're both in no hurry to make any kind of commitment. I have issues to deal with before I settle down again. Besides, I like my life now. I have family and friends I care a great deal about, and I have my life back as a painter. I also have Ludwig, who initially missed the farm, but is finally adjusting to the loft and city life. We go on runs together along the waterfront, and he's become quite popular in the business district. The regulars at the Blue Parrot spoil him almost as much as the lads did on Snookie's farm. The parrot calls him "SWEETIE PIE!"

Lettie is pregnant again. This will be number five. She's not at all upset about it even though she confessed to me "it wasn't planned." We had lunch the other day, and she was more concerned that one of the girls let Gretchen, her female boxer, out by mistake while she was in heat. It seems Gretchen found love with a rather mangy-looking Afghan.

"A hairy boxer? That's not a pretty picture."

"Pretty scary, huh?" Lettie said as she played with her salad. "How am I going to find a home for those puppies?"

"Beats me. Good luck."

I saw Lettie smile and look at me out of the corner of her eye.

"Oh, no...not me," I said. "No way."

"Did I ask you?"

"No, but you looked like you were about to."

I kept eating and suddenly Lettie said, "Oh, look! There's Oscar."

I made the mistake of looking up. A woman at the next table said, "What on earth is it?" And her dining partner said, "Probably escaped from one of those laboratories where they experiment on animals."

Oscar stood in the window in front of me holding up a white hairy puppy with a boxer's face. The puppy looked at me, wagged its droopy tail, and drooled. And I found myself with another damn ugly dog.

Made in the USA
Lexington, KY
01 December 2013